THE GER
REPUBLI

German History in Focus

Series Editors
Lisa Pine, Institute of Historical Research, University of London, UK
Peter C. Caldwell, Rice University, USA

Editorial Advisory Board
Benjamin Marschke, Humboldt State University, USA
Monica Black, University of Tennessee, Knoxville, USA
Matthew Jefferies, University of Manchester, UK
Neil Gregor, University of Southampton, UK
Christina Morina, Bielefeld University, Germany
Joachim Whaley, University of Cambridge, UK
Bridget Heal, University of St. Andrews, UK

Published Titles
Under the Swastika in Nazi Germany, Kristin Semmens
The Empire's Reformations: Politics and Religion in Germany, 1495–1648, David M. Luebke
West Germany: A Society in Motion, 1949–89, Julia Sneeringer
The German Democratic Republic: The Rise and Fall of a Cold War State, Ned Richardson-Little

Upcoming Titles
Germany in the Long Eighteenth Century: Princely States and Global Entanglements, 1648–1815, Thomas Biskup
The Weimar Republic: A Democracy, Christopher Dillon
Late Medieval Germany: The Making of the Holy Roman Empire, 1250–1495, Duncan Hardy
Germany in the Mid-19th Century: A Nation of Mobility, 1815–71, Jasper Heinzen
A New and Different Germany: The Federal Republic in the Post-Unification Era, Sarah Elise Wiliarty

THE GERMAN DEMOCRATIC REPUBLIC

THE RISE AND FALL OF A COLD WAR STATE

Ned Richardson-Little

BLOOMSBURY ACADEMIC
LONDON • NEW YORK • OXFORD • NEW DELHI • SYDNEY

BLOOMSBURY ACADEMIC

Bloomsbury Publishing Plc, 50 Bedford Square, London, WC1B 3DP, UK
Bloomsbury Publishing Inc, 1359 Broadway, New York, NY 10018, USA
Bloomsbury Publishing Ireland, 29 Earlsfort Terrace, Dublin 2, D02 AY28, Ireland

BLOOMSBURY, BLOOMSBURY ACADEMIC and the Diana logo are trademarks of
Bloomsbury Publishing Plc

First published in Great Britain 2025

Copyright © Ned Richardson-Little, 2025

Ned Richardson-Little has asserted his right under the Copyright,
Designs and Patents Act, 1988, to be identified as Author of this work.

For legal purposes the Acknowledgments on pp. x–xi constitute
an extension of this copyright page.

Series design by Toby Way
Cover image: Karl Marx Monument, Chemnitz, Saxony, Germany
© iStock photo

All rights reserved. No part of this publication may be: i) reproduced or transmitted in any form, electronic or mechanical, including photocopying, recording or by means of any information storage or retrieval system without prior permission in writing from the publishers; or ii) used or reproduced in any way for the training, development or operation of artificial intelligence (AI) technologies, including generative AI technologies. The rights holders expressly reserve this publication from the text and data mining exception as per Article 4(3) of the Digital Single Market Directive (EU) 2019/790.

Bloomsbury Publishing Plc does not have any control over, or responsibility for, any third-party websites referred to or in this book. All internet addresses given in this book were correct at the time of going to press. The author and publisher regret any inconvenience caused if addresses have changed or sites have ceased to exist, but can accept no responsibility for any such changes.

A catalogue record for this book is available from the British Library.

A catalog record for this book is available from the Library of Congress.

ISBN:	HB:	978-1-3503-4152-4
	PB:	978-1-3503-4151-7
	ePDF:	978-1-3503-4153-1
	eBook:	978-1-3503-4154-8

Series: German History in Focus

Typeset by Integra Software Services Pvt. Ltd.
Printed and bound in Great Britain

For product safety related questions contact productsafety@bloomsbury.com.

To find out more about our authors and books visit www.bloomsbury.com and sign
up for our newsletters.

To Lilo,
Whose first word was *hallo*
And whose hundredth was *Fernsehturm*
and
To my pandemic bubble,
When the world shrank, you maintained its expanse

CONTENTS

List of Figures	viii
Acknowledgments	x
List of Abbreviations	xii
Glossaries	xiv
Introduction: Below the Surface of the Berlin Republic	**1**
1 From the Third Reich to the Berlin Wall	9
2 Socialist Society and Its Discontents	53
3 East Germany and the World	101
4 Stagnation, Collapse, and Reunification	143
Conclusion: A Cold War Germany	**197**
Epilogue: The GDR after the End of the GDR	**203**
Notes	214
Further Reading	250
Index	258

FIGURES

I.1	The head of a statue of Vladimir Lenin lies on display at the exhibition "Uncovered. Berlin and Its Monuments"	2
1.1	Map of the Occupation Zones and the Division of Germany, as well as the Polish Occupation Zone	12
1.2	Poster featuring the logo of the SED immortalizing the handshake of founders Otto Grotewohl (SPD) and Wilhelm Pieck (KPD) and the slogan "The Future Belongs to Us"	20
1.3	Protestors throw stones at a Soviet tank in East Berlin during the Uprising of June 17, 1953	35
1.4	The hastily constructed initial cinder-block and barbed-wire version of the Berlin Wall	47
2.1	"Hero of Labor" Otto Trinks receiving a bouquet of flowers for fulfilling his annual mining quota by October 20, 1952	61
2.2	Caroline Lange working on a Textima large format knitting machine to produce fabric for casual wear and undergarments	63
2.3	Three girls who have just completed their Jugendweihe in Berlin-Friedrichshain	83
3.1	Ariel view of the still visible death strip at the former border between two Germanies, Rhön Mountains	104
3.2	Karl Marx monument in present-day Chemnitz	107
3.3	GDR cosmonaut Sigmund Jähn (right) with Soviet cosmonaut Valery Bykovsky (left) at their landing site near Zhezkazgan, USSR	112
3.4	Free German Youth mass rally at the Leipzig Staatsoper	118
3.5	Dean Reed performing on GDR television	122
3.6	Mozambican worker-trainees at VEB Fischfang Rostock	125

Figures

3.7	The Interhotel "Merkur" in Leipzig, designed by the Kajima Corporation of Japan	141
4.1	More than 500,000 East Germans take part in the demonstration at Alexanderplatz in East Berlin on November 4, 1989	179
4.2	Nearly 500,000 East Germans take part in the demonstration during a rainstorm in Leipzig on November 6, 1989	179
4.3	Graffiti in Jena mocks demands from nationalists for the return of territory from Poland	184
4.4	View from inside the Stasi headquarters in Leipzig shortly before it was stormed by protestors on December 4, 1989	186
4.5	Bündnis 90 campaign sticker from the March 1990 elections found in Berlin-Buch in 2017	190
E.1	The demolition of the Palace of the Republic in 2006	209
E.2	The Berlin TV Tower made to look like a magenta football as part of a Deutsche Telekom sponsorship in connection with the FIFA World Cup in Summer 2006	210
E.3	The Sandmännchen on set at the Babelsberg film studios in Potsdam	211

ACKNOWLEDGMENTS

Convention dictates that the acknowledgments of any book be written last, once the manuscript is finished, polished, and submitted. In this case, they have been a constant companion in the writing process. This book was an opportunity to rally together a historiography and a generous group of scholars on the GDR and the two Germanies. My thanks to Paul Betts, Stephen Brown, Kerstin Brückweh, Peter Caldwell, Celia Donert, Jennifer Evans, Tiffany Florvil, Sebastian Gehrig, Jens Gieseke, Konrad Jarausch, Mario Keßler, Damian Mac Con Uladh, Patrice Poutrus, Eli Rubin, Zoé Samudzi, Daniel Siemens, Annette Weintke, and Lora Wildenthal, who have all influenced, challenged, and furthered my thinking and writing about the GDR in various ways over the last fifteen years (all errors and omissions remain my own).

This book would not exist without Peter Caldwell and Lisa Pine, who entrusted me with this project and provided invaluable guidance (and much patience!). Thank you also to Rhodri Mogford and Gabriella Cox at Bloomsbury for expertly shepherding the book through the production process, the anonymous reviewers for their keen critiques, and Sascha Harnisch and Elise Schmidt for their careful work on the literature survey. The production of this book was generously supported by the Leibniz Centre for Contemporary History (ZZF) in Potsdam. My gratitude to Isabella Löhr, Frank Bösch, Jens Gieseke, Katja Stopka, and Annette Schumann at the ZZF, and Iris Schröder at the University of Erfurt. In addition, this book could not have been completed without the support and resources of the ZZF library and its librarians—thank you!

I am also incredibly grateful to Andrea Speltz, Benjamin Gögge-Feiersinger, Cristian Cercel, Isabel Enzenbach, Jakub Szumski, Jane Freeland, Jennifer Lynn, Julia Sittmann, Julie Ault, Lisa Haegele, Luisa

Acknowledgments

Feiersinger, Nikolai Okunew, Richard Millington, Sophie Lange, Tara Dominguez Twarecki, Thomas Escritt, Tiffany Florvil, Zach Sporn, and the ZZF Ostzone group, for reading individual chapters and providing not only incisive (and surprisingly unique!) feedback but also invaluable encouragement from desks across the world—and, memorably, from at least one Montenegrin long-distance bus.

To Liane, Simone, Kjell, Ines, Manuela, Christine, Kerstin, Ole, Michel, and all the Erzieher*innen at Lilo's KiTa. Ohne Ihr liebevolles Engagement hätte ich—buchstäblich—kein einziges Wort schreiben können. Die Gewissheit, dass Lilo gut aufgehoben und glücklich in Ihrer Obhut ist, ist ein enormes Geschenk.

Working with words all day, it becomes a force of habit to see everything in chapters. To that end, this book is dedicated to the people, near and far, with whom I was lucky enough to navigate the confluence of a very global pandemic and the very small world of early parenthood—all the while writing this book: (in order of appearance) Kathleen Perry, Julia Sittmann, Ellen Sittmann, Andrea Speltz, Gregory Bouchard, Ryan Bouma, Tara Dominguez Twarecki, Jen Lynn, Joseph Bryan, Benjamin Gögge-Feiersinger, Carolyn Taratko, Lisa Haegele, Kate Horning, Raluca Grosescu, Maria Kosboth, Bogdan Iacob, Luisa Feiersinger, Sophie Lange, Jakub Szumski, Zach Sporn, and Lilo Sittmann, who arrived to the sound of a masks-required outdoor rave in Volkspark Friedrichshain, the quintessential twenty-first-century East Berlinerin.

ABBREVIATIONS

BEK	Bund der Evangelischen Kirchen, League of Evangelical Churches of the GDR
CMEA	Council for Mutual Economic Assistance
DDR	Deutsche Demokratische Republik, German Democratic Republic
DEFA	Deutsche Film-Aktiengesellschaft, GDR state film studio
DM	Deutsche Mark (Federal Republic of Germany)
FRG	Federal Republic of Germany
GDR	German Democratic Republic
IM	inoffizielle(r) Mitarbeiter(in), unofficial collaborator
KgU	Kampfgruppe gegen Unmenschlichkeit, Action Group against Inhumanity
KoKo	Kommerzielle Koordinierung, GDR Commercial Coordination office
KVP	Kasernierte Volkspolizei, Barracked People's Police
LPG	Landwirtschaftliche Produktionsgenossenschaft, Agricultural Production Cooperative
MTS	Maschinen-Traktoren-Stationen, Machine Tractor Stations
ND	*Neues Deutschland*, New Germany (SED Party Newspaper)
NVA	Nationale Volksarmee, National People's Army
PRC	People's Republic of China

Abbreviations

SED	Sozialistische Einheitspartei Deutschland, Socialist Unity Party
SMAD	Soviet Military Administration in Germany
Stasi	Ministerium für **Sta**at**ssi**cherheit, Ministry for State Security
VEB	Volkseigene Betriebe, People's Owned Industries
ZKG	Zentrale Koordinierungsgruppe zur Bekämpfung von Flucht und Übersiedlung, Central Coordination Group for Flight and Emigration

Non-German Political Parties and Revolutionary Movements

ANC	African National Congress (South Africa)
FLN	Front de libération nationale, National Liberation Front (Algeria)
FRELIMO	Frente de Libertação de Moçambique, Mozambique Liberation Front
ICP	Iraqi Communist Party
PFLP	People's Front for the Liberation of Palestine
PLO	Palestinian Liberation Organization
Solidarność	Solidarity, independent trade union (Poland)
SWAPO	South West African People's Organization (Namibia)
ZAPU	Zimbabwe African People's Union

GLOSSARIES

Glossary of German Political Parties, Mass Organizations, and Dissident Groups

AfD	Alternative für Deutschland, Alternative for Germany. Far-right populist party founded in 2013 in the Federal Republic.
Allianz für Deutschland	Alliance for Germany. A coalition of a dozen Christian, liberal, and bourgeois-conservative opposition groups (including DA and the DSU led by the GDR CDU). It was absorbed into the West German CDU during reunification.
Bündnis 90	Alliance 1990. A left-leaning coalition of East German dissident and activist groups including New Forum, Democracy Now, and the Initiative for Peace and Human Rights. Formed for the March 1990 GDR elections and later merged with the West German Green Party.
CDU	Christlich Demokratische Union, Christian Democratic Union. Post-Second World War center-right party of the Federal Republic as well as the name of a GDR bloc party aimed at Christian voters. The CDU of the GDR was absorbed into the West German CDU during reunification.
CSU	Christlich-Soziale Union, Christian Social Union (Bavaria). Post-Second World War center-right party of the Federal Republic and sister party of the CDU (West).
DA	Demokratischer Aufbruch, Democratic Awakening. Conservative-leaning church-oriented party founded in 1989 in the GDR and absorbed into the CDU during reunification.
DBD	Demokratische Bauernpartei Deutschlands, Democratic Farmers' Party. GDR bloc party aimed at rural voters and farmers. Absorbed into the CDU during reunification.

Glossaries

DFD	Demokratischer Frauenbund Deutschlands, Democratic Women's League. GDR mass organization for women. Dissolved shortly before reunification.
DJ	Demokratie Jetzt, Democracy Now. Dissident civic rights organization that emerged largely from Church activist circles and founded in September 1989. Part of Bündnis 90 coalition and eventually absorbed into the Green Party.
Domowina	Home (in Sorbian). Sorbian cultural association founded in 1912 and made into a mass organization in the GDR. Continues to exist as an independent NGO.
DSU	Deutsche Soziale Union, German Social Union. Conservative-populist party founded in 1989 in the GDR and supported by the CSU. Absorbed into the CDU during reunification, since the CSU cannot operate outside Bavaria.
FDGB	Freier Deutscher Gewerkschaftsbund, German Trade Union Federation. Umbrella trade union organization in the GDR and the largest of the mass organizations. Did not survive German reunification as an organization.
FDJ	Freie Deutsche Jugend, Free German Youth. East German youth mass organization. Survived reunification as a very small fringe organization.
FDP	Freie Demokratische Partei, Free Democratic Party. Post-Second World War liberal party in the Federal Republic often serving as the junior partner in federal coalition governments. Absorbed LDPD and NDPD after reunification.
IFM	Initiative Frieden und Menschenrechte, Initiative for Peace and Human Rights. The first East German human rights group organized independently of the church at the end of 1985. Became part of the Bündnis 90 coalition in 1990.
KPD	Kommunistische Partei Deutschlands, Communist Party of Germany. Far-left party allied to the Soviet Union during the Weimar Republic and merged with the Social Democrats to form the SED in 1946.
LDPD	Liberal-Demokratische Partei Deutschlands, Liberal Democratic Party of (East) Germany. GDR bloc party aimed at small business owners and liberals in general. Absorbed into the FDP during reunification.

Glossaries

NDPD	National-Demokratische Partei Deutschlands, National-Democratic Party of Germany. GDR bloc party of the middle classes and former Nazis. Absorbed into FDP during reunification.
PDS	Partei des Demokratischen Sozialismus, Party of Democratic Socialism. Successor party to the SED in the GDR and then in reunified Germany. Briefly the SED-PDS in 1989. Since transformed into Die Linke (the Left).
PEGIDA	Patriotische Europäer gegen die Islamisierung des Abendlandes, Patriotic Europeans against the Islamization of the West. Anti-immigration protest movement originating in Dresden, founded 2014; largely disbanded during the Covid-19 pandemic.
RAF	Rote Armee Fraktion, Red Army Faction. Far-left West German urban guerilla and anti-imperialist terrorist organization founded in 1970 and active until 1998.
SED	Sozialistische Einheitspartei Deutschland, Socialist Unity Party. Far-left Soviet-aligned party created through the merger of the SPD and the KPD in 1946. Ruled the GDR from 1949 to 1990. Transformed into the PDS in 1989.
SPD	Sozialdemokratische Partei Deutschlands, Social Democratic Party. Center-left party founded in 1875. In the Soviet Zone, it was merged with the KPD to form the SED. Led several governments in the postwar Federal Republic.
VdgB	Vereinigung der gegenseitigen Bauernhilfe, Peasants' Mutual Aid Association. GDR mass organization for peasants, farmers, and eventually gardeners. Did not survive German reunification.

Glossaries

Glossary of GDR Terms and Institutions

Abgrenzung (demarcation) — Policy pursued under Erich Honecker to keep the GDR culturally and politically separated from the West.

Altbau (old build) — Pre-Second World War housing stock that made up a large proportion of buildings in the GDR.

antifaschistischer Schutzwall (anti-fascist defense rampart) — SED term for the Berlin Wall.

Feindlich-negativ (hostile-negative) — Stasi terminology for the oppositional or deviant disposition of a GDR citizen.

Freikörperkultur (FKK, free body culture) — Nudist culture that became mainstream in East Germany.

Friedensstaat (peaceful state) — SED claim that the GDR represented the forces of peace in contrast to the war-mongering West.

Held(in) der Arbeit (Hero/Heroine of Labor) — Designation for workers who significantly overfulfilled their quotas as assigned by the centralized economic plan.

Jugendwerkhof (youth work camp) — Extreme version of a Spezialheim for youth deemed difficult or deviant. Closed camps such as Torgau held young people under guard and subjected them to relentless work projects and forced physical training.

Kampfgruppen der Arbeiterklasse (Combat Groups of the Working Class) — The SED's volunteer militia force.

Nationaler Verteidigungsrat (National Defense Council) — The body responsible for national security affairs in the GDR.

Plattenbauten (prefabricated housing) — Mass-constructed multi-unit high-rise buildings that were central to the SED's housing program.

Glossaries

Politisch-ideologische Diversion/PiD (political ideological diversion)	Stasi terminology for all forms of advocacy for the liberalization of socialism.
Politische Untergrundtätigkeit/ PUT (political underground activity)	Stasi terminology for unwanted political organizing.
Republikflucht (desertion of the Republic)	SED terminology for the crime of emigrating from East Germany without official permission.
Selbstschussanlagen (automatic firing devices)	Automatic shrapnel-firing devices used along the GDR's border with the FRG. Removed from service in the late 1970s due to international reaction over their use.
Staatsrat der DDR (Council of State of the GDR)	Executive body of the East German state, led by Walther Ulbricht and then Erich Honecker as most senior members of the SED.
Todesstreifen (death strips)	The open spaces created near the German-German border and the border around West Berlin that were designed to create clear firing opportunities for guards to shoot those trying to cross.
Untersuchungshaft (investigative detention)	Used by Stasi to detain GDR citizens without charges or trial as part of investigations.
Vertrauensmann (confidence man)	Designated supervisor in multi-unit buildings tasked with keeping tabs on tenants and maintaining a "housebook" to document all visitors to the building.
Volksaussprache (mass consultation)	Process of controlled mass engagement over major legal reform in the GDR. Used prior to the referendum on a new constitution in 1968.
Volkskammer (People's Chamber)	The East German parliament, which had representatives from a range of bloc parties and mass organizations that made up the National Front led by the SED, but was almost entirely decorative and had no power.

Glossaries

Volkspolizei (People's Police) — East German police force under the command of the Ministry of the Interior.

Zentraler Runder Tisch (Central Round Table) — Ad hoc institution created in December 1989 composed of the SED and the mass parties as well as dissident and church groups to negotiate the process of transition prior to first open election in 1990.

Zersetzung (decomposition) — Stasi tactic of psychological pressure used to disrupt and impede dissident activity in contrast to direct forms of suppression.

INTRODUCTION: BELOW THE SURFACE OF THE BERLIN REPUBLIC

In 2015, a 3.5-ton granite head was excavated from a forest in the suburbs of reunified Berlin. It had once been attached to a 19-meter-tall monument to the Soviet revolutionary Vladimir Lenin. Sculpted by Soviet artist Nikolai Tomsky, the statue was installed in East Berlin to honor the centenary of Lenin's birth in 1970, and demolished after the collapse of East Germany, dismembered into 129 individual pieces, and then unceremoniously buried in Berlin-Köpenick. When a museum asked for Lenin's head for an exhibition of the many fallen statues representing past regimes in German history, the request was initially denied by officials, in part to ostensibly protect a community of endangered sand lizards. Only after several years in court was permission finally granted to track down the symbolic grave of the communist icon and dig up his red granite representation. Like East Germany itself, the monument remained politically contentious and just below the surface of the Berlin Republic.[1]

Since its dissolution in 1990, the German Democratic Republic (GDR) has lived on as a representative for the worst aspects of state socialism. The Ministry for State Security—the Stasi—has become international short-hand for mass surveillance and the destruction of personal privacy. Around the world, the Berlin Wall is invoked as the ultimate form of an inhuman and lethal border regime, whether it be to criticize the Spanish enclave of Ceuta in Morocco, the Israeli boundary walls to the Palestinian territories, the fortifications on the Mexico-US border, or Europe's outer-border enforcement agency Frontex. Along with the crimes of the Nazis, life in the GDR is a key point of reference in postunification Germany as a negative example of a past dictatorship that must never be allowed to be repeated in the "Berlin Republic." At the same time, there is a different version of

The German Democratic Republic

the GDR that has lived on in the form of kitsch: the GDR's coat of arms (a hammer and a compass) emblazoned on furry hats sold to tourists alongside "Hero of Labor" pins and Free German Youth neckerchiefs. This GDR is also remembered as a land of plastic consumer goods, polyester outfits, and bygone food brands accompanied by ironic portraits of Socialist Unity Party leaders Walter Ulbricht or Erich Honecker.

Figure I.1 The head of a statue of Vladimir Lenin lies on display at the exhibition "Uncovered. Berlin and Its Monuments" at the Spandau citadel on April 29, 2016. Sean Gallup/Getty Images.

This book is neither a demonology of the GDR nor does it aim to rehabilitate East Germany as it existed under the de facto one-party rule of the Socialist Unity Party (SED). Instead, it explores how the GDR was created, how it functioned, and how it ultimately collapsed, in order to provide a more expansive and nuanced understanding of how East Germany worked and how its people experienced life within it than the one provided by the gray stereotypes of Cold War anticommunism, the rosy nostalgia of SED propaganda, or the bright images of GDR consumer goods uncritically reposted on social media. East Germany was a complex country that should not simply be reduced to a one-dimensional metaphor to be deployed for use in present-day political debates.

The opening of the East German state archives after reunification produced a wealth of new scholarship. Numerous academic monographs have documented the victims of the Berlin Wall and the East German border regime, and explored the persecution of those who challenged the power of the SED or sought to emigrate to the West. New research challenged the Cold War vision of the GDR as a monolithic totalitarian state dominated by an all-powerful party and surveillance apparatus.[2] Instead of just looking at the dictatorial structures of the East German state, historians also began to look at the participation of the population in state and social institutions, the limits of state power, and the experiences of those who lived in the GDR.[3] Through an emphasis on the history of everyday life (*Alltagsgeschichte*), historians investigated the spaces between compliance and resistance to see how East Germans continued to express themselves through nonconformity and self-will (*Eigen-Sinn*).[4] The perspective thus shifted from describing systems of domination to analyzing the tension between the overarching power of Party and state institutions and the continued agency of the individuals who lived in the GDR. Rather than seeing histories of dictatorship and everyday life as competing and at cross-purposes, however, most historians in recent years have aimed at employing an "analysis of the intermeshing of domination practices and social behavior."[5] They have thus begun to move beyond the focus on the dichotomy of state and society by examining a wide range of topics including gender and sexuality,

East Germany's place in global history, material cultures generated in the GDR, and how Eastern Germany was transformed as a result of reunification.[6] Conversely, there are still some historians who reject any perspective that does not focus on state power and coercion as the defining features of the East German dictatorship.[7]

Although academic debates surrounding the history of the GDR have become less heated, the history of the GDR still has the power to provoke vociferous public debate. The publication of Katja Hoyer's popular history of the GDR, *Beyond the Wall*, demonstrated this in 2023. The book proved to be a bestseller both in English and German, and gained praise from some reviewers for moving beyond Cold War stereotypes and casting fresh light on everyday life in the GDR.[8] But it was met with widespread scorn and derision in the German media as an apologia for the SED, privileging the experiences and memories of those who comfortably served the state over those who did not conform and suffered the consequences.[9] One review by a historian in *Der Spiegel* ran with the headline: "One-sided, grotesquely abbreviated, factual errors—this GDR book is an annoyance [Ärgernis]."[10] The discourse around the book split sharply between those who perceived it as challenging an undifferentiated view of East Germany as an unrelenting totalitarian nightmare and those who saw it as reinforcing a widespread nostalgia for the GDR that erased the suffering of dissenters, non-conformists and wall victims. Despite their diametrically opposing conclusions, these takes all nonetheless coalesce around their authors' conviction that some kind of "dominant narrative" exists that deserves to be reinforced or dismantled and is thus central to the praise and criticism of the book. In short, the history of the GDR is still a work in progress even if scholarly debates have become less contentious over time.

This book aims to be an accessible gateway to the mass of scholarly work that has emerged since the fall of the Wall and particularly in the past twenty years. Drawing from this academic literature, three main themes run through the text: first, the GDR was a de facto one-party dictatorship that was part of the Soviet sphere of influence, but its history cannot be understood by looking only at the top levels of

Introduction

power. The leaders of the SED did not act alone, and their actions were shaped by the collective demands of the East German people. Second, there was no single experience of life in the GDR. Although many sought to leave East Germany and were willing to risk their lives to do so, the state socialist system also inspired everything from apathy to fierce loyalty from a minority who saw it as a vehicle to realizing an egalitarian society in the ruins of the genocidal destruction of Nazism. Third, East German history requires a transnational and global perspective. The GDR was a product of Cold War dynamics generated between the two German states, within Eastern Europe, and on the global stage. Political, economic, and social life in East Germany was entangled with international affairs from cross-border cultural trends, global commodities trading, and transnational solidarity movements.

The book has been arranged semi-chronologically: the first chapter examines the creation of the GDR from the Soviet Zone of Occupation after 1945 and the establishment of SED rule up to the construction of the Berlin Wall in 1961; the second chapter looks at how society was structured and how that influenced the experiences of everyday life in the first decades of the GDR's existence. The third chapter focuses on the international history of East Germany in terms of its interconnections with West Germany, the Eastern Bloc, and the Global South from the 1950s to the end of the 1970s. The fourth and final chapter explores the structural problems that emerged in the 1970s and led up to the crisis of 1989 and traces how the fall of the Berlin Wall led to reunification within a year. A short conclusion covers some of the major signposts in the history of the transition to the Berlin Republic.

This volume was written for a broad audience and not just academic specialists: for those studying history, interested in the Cold War, or just wanting to know more about East Germany after a trip to Berlin, Leipzig or Dresden, this book is intended for you. It was purposefully conceived as a short volume and cannot cover every topic in depth. In addition to their job as direct citations, the endnotes (and the list of further reading) point the way to important scholarly works, significant primary sources, and recent specialist publications—

primarily in English, but also in German—that are an ideal starting point for a deeper engagement with the subject. Ultimately, the purpose here is to uncover the GDR as living history—recent enough to affect the daily lives of people living in Germany today and yet distant enough to already be shrouded in myth. In short, the history of East Germany is a much more interesting story than the simplified versions deployed solely to damn or praise its memory.

A Note on Tools in This Book

In the beginning of this book, there is a list of abbreviations, a guide to the many German political parties, mass organizations, and dissident groups mentioned in the book and a glossary of GDR terms.

There are also text boxes throughout the book containing biographies that were chosen because they reveal something particular about the GDR or the two Germanies. This collection is not meant to be exhaustive, nor to reflect a definitive list of "most important people" in the GDR; many were chosen because their story did not fit in the main narrative of the book. Although it was not a criterion as the list was being drawn up (only a fact revealed upon its completion), it is worthy of note that no one on this list died (or will one day die) in the country in which they were born, indicating the extreme upheaval of the twentieth century in this corner of Europe. In order of appearance:

Hilde Benjamin, GDR Minister of Justice
Born 1902, Bernburg, German Empire
Died 1989, East Berlin, GDR

Victor Klemperer, scholar and diarist
Born 1881, Landsberg an der Warthe, German Empire (today Gorzów Wielkopolski, Poland)
Died 1960, Dresden, GDR

The Wolf Family

—Friedrich Wolf, doctor, DEFA founder, GDR ambassador to Poland
Born 1888, Nieuwied, German Empire
Died 1953, Lehnitz, GDR

—Markus Wolf, member of the Ulbricht group, head of Stasi foreign intelligence
Born 1923, Hechingen, Weimar Republic
Died 2006, Berlin, FRG

—Konrad Wolf, Red Army soldier, filmmaker
Born 1925, Hechingen, Weimar Republic
Died 1982, East Berlin, GDR

Dean Reed, singer and actor
Born 1938, Denver, Colorado, United States of America
Died 1986, Zeuthen, GDR

Willy Brandt, Mayor of West Berlin, Chancellor of West Germany
Born 1913, Lübeck, German Empire
Died 1992, Unkel, FRG

Margot Honecker, GDR Minister of Education
Born 1927, Halle, Weimar Republic
Died 2016, Santiago de Chile, Chile

Ulrike Poppe, dissident
Born 1953, Rostock, GDR

The Informants
—Ibrahim Böhme, dissident
Born 1944, Bad Dürrenberg, Nazi Germany
Died 1999, Neustrelitz, FRG

The German Democratic Republic

—**Wolfgang Schnur, lawyer, politician**
Born 1944, Stettin, Nazi Germany (today Szczecin, Poland)
Died 2016, Vienna, Austria

—**Lothar de Maizière, last Prime Minister of the GDR**
Born 1940, Nordhausen, Nazi Germany

CHAPTER 1
FROM THE THIRD REICH TO THE BERLIN WALL

The history of East Germany begins with the unconditional surrender of the Nazi regime on May 8, 1945. But the end of the Third Reich did not guarantee the division of Germany, nor the creation of a socialist German state four years later. In fact, the postwar power struggle in Germany created a wide range of possibilities, and few of the actors on the ground were in a position to single-handedly implement a political agenda on their own. Soviet plans in Germany were constrained by their wider geopolitical goals for a stable sphere of influence in Eastern Europe and their desire for flexibility in their diplomatic maneuvering with the West as wartime cooperation deteriorated into the Cold War. Ultimately, the split of Germany into two states aligned to opposing camps in the Cold War was part of a larger process of dividing Europe (and the world) into competing blocs aligned either to the United States or to the Soviet Union. The emergence of a border between the two German states thus represented the dividing line in Europe—but it was one of many sites of Cold War conflict on the global stage.

While the Soviet occupiers played a decisive role in shaping the creation of the German Democratic Republic (GDR), so too did the German communists of the Socialist Unity Party (Sozialistische Einheitspartei Deutschland, SED), the product of a forced merger of the Communist Party and the Social Democrats. Although led primarily by communists returning from years of exile in the Soviet Union, the leaders of the SED clashed with their Soviet sponsors over both how quickly socialism should be implemented and the drastic program of restitution imposed on the Soviet Zone of Occupation. The Soviets and their local allies initially signaled that they sought to overcome the legacy of the Third Reich and establish a democratic system for all antifascist Germans, be they socialist or bourgeois. Yet any hopes that postwar Germany could evolve into a socialist state democratically, or at least without heavy-handed coercion, were soon dashed when it became clear that the SED would never triumph at the ballot box. Once any democratic paths to power through cooperation with non-socialist parties appeared impossible, SED leaders moved to assert one-party control. Yet, as the SED created a Soviet-style state, the rhetoric of a democratic coalition of antifascists remained, as did the façade of parliamentary rule. Although the construction of a dictatorship under the leadership of the SED came about incrementally, it was firmly in place even before the formal creation of the GDR on October 7, 1949.

The establishment of the GDR did not, however, secure its permanence as a socialist state—or as a country. The economic condition of East Germany was precarious from the beginning, in part due to extensive looting by the Soviet occupation forces. Even after any organized resistance had been crushed by a Soviet intervention, East Germans continued to vote with their feet through mass emigration, fleeing the SED's burgeoning socialist revolution. In 1961, the construction of the Berlin Wall sealed the last opening in the GDR's border, ending the population drain that threatened the stability of the state, but also confirming that East Germany could not exist without suppressing freedom of movement. Support for the SED remained limited to a minority of active followers and collaborators in the population; the GDR would always be defined by both the occupation of Soviet troops (who did not leave until 1994, after German reunification) and the existence of the Berlin Wall—a visible symbol of its failure to create a viable state without confining its population within its borders.

The Soviet Occupation: Denazification, Expropriation, and Stalinization

When German forces unconditionally surrendered on May 8, 1945, the Nazi state ceased to exist. By August 1945, the leaders of the United

States, the United Kingdom, France, and the Soviet Union had met in Potsdam, just outside of Berlin, to determine what would become of the defeated Third Reich. As Soviet leader Joseph Stalin told his fellow leaders: "This is a country that has no government and no fixed borders, because the borders have not yet been decided by our troops."[1] The USSR occupied Central and Eastern Prussia, Silesia, Mecklenburg, and most of Saxony, but the aim of the Potsdam Conference was to create a formal system of occupation. Despite growing tensions between the wartime allies, all four leaders agreed on the main goals of their joint-occupation of Germany—denazification, demilitarization, democratization, and decartelization—and set the borders of the zones each Allied state was to govern. This occupation system was mirrored in Austria, which had been split off from Germany, undoing the Nazi annexation of 1938. Via the Potsdam negotiations, what would become the GDR grew beyond the territory first occupied by the Red Army, as US forces pulled back from Thuringia and Saxony to accommodate the Soviet Occupation Zone's further expansion in exchange for an occupation sector in Berlin (a city American forces had not reached in the initial invasion). The city of Berlin, deep in the heart of the Soviet Zone, was divided into four occupied sectors to be run by the four occupying powers, recreating the division of Nazi Germany on a smaller scale.

This preliminary division of Germany took place as the whole of Eastern Europe was also being remade. With Stalin unwilling to return eastern Poland (which the Soviet Union had gained through its joint invasion with the Nazis in 1939), the restored Polish state was effectively moved several hundred kilometers westwards. To compensate Poland for the territory lost to the Soviets, German territory east of the Oder-Neisse river line, including the cities of Stettin (Szczecin) in Pomerania and Breslau (Wrocław) in Silesia, was transferred from the Soviet Zone of Occupation and directly annexed to Poland. East Prussia, including its capital Königsberg, was annexed to the USSR, which transformed it into Kaliningrad (it remains a discontiguous territory of post-Soviet Russia today).[2] At Potsdam, the Soviets presented these border revisions as established fact, to the dismay of the Western Allies; the status of the German-Polish border would remain politically contentious until reunification in 1990. This redrawing of borders was also intertwined with a mass population transfer across Eastern Europe as Germans fled or were expelled. The German minority in the Sudetenland—the group whose protection was the pretext for the Nazi annexation of much of Czechoslovakia in 1938—was forced out of the country by the new government in Prague, and the Germans in the newly annexed territories of Western Poland were pushed out to allow for the settlement of Poles displaced from further East.[3]

On the ground in Eastern Germany, the Soviet Military Administration in Germany (SMAD) took control as the governing authority. In theory, an Allied Control Council—comprised of all four

Figure 1.1 Map of the Occupation Zones and the Division of Germany, as well as the Polish Occupation Zone, likely produced in 1950. World History Archive/Alamy Stock Foto.

occupying powers—governed Germany, but the Soviets allowed little outside influence on how they operated in their Zone. Already in June 1945, only weeks after the Nazi surrender and before the occupation had been formalized by the Potsdam Agreement, SMAD had authorized the creation of a collection of antifascist political parties that would form a Democratic Front led by the revived Communist Party of Germany (KPD) as the basis for a post-Nazi political order.[4] At the KPD's core were three groups of exiled German communists who had been brought in by the Red Army to begin political work on the ground in the Soviet Zone. One group led by Anton Ackermann was sent to Saxony, a second led by Gustav Sobottka was set to Mecklenburg on the Baltic coast, but the most important third group was based in Berlin and led by Walter Ulbricht: a veteran KPD member, Ulbricht fled Germany in 1933 after the rise of the Nazis, served as a political commissar in the Spanish Civil War, and then lived in exile in the Soviet Union from 1937 until the end of the war.[5] Ulbricht would become the first leader of the GDR, and his rise owed a great deal to the support of SMAD's influential propaganda chief, Colonel Sergei Ti'ulpanov.[6] Both shared the belief that the Zone of Occupation should be rapidly Sovietized, even if Stalin himself did not think that Germany, so soon after a fascist dictatorship, was historically prepared for the transition to socialism. While the line from Moscow called for caution and ideological flexibility, Ulbricht and Ti'ulpanov pushed for radical measures toward the goal of socialist revolution.[7]

In keeping with Stalin's belief that Germany was not yet ready for a socialist revolution, the KPD's founding proclamation stressed that it sought cooperation with bourgeois democratic parties: "With the destruction of Hitlerism, it is also necessary to complete the cause of the democratization of Germany, the cause of the bourgeois democratic transformation that was begun in 1848, to completely eliminate all remnants of feudalism and destroy the old reactionary Prussian militarism with all its economic and political offshoots."[8] Remedial corrections to Germany's historical evolution were needed to both enact a bourgeois liberal democracy on the path to eventual socialism and prevent a repeated descent into fascism. As Stalin instructed Ulbricht and other exiled German communists sent back to the occupied Zone, the Soviets sought "the hegemony of the working classes and its revolutionary party," but these were to be secured through a "parliamentary democratic republic."[9] As such, the KPD was under clear instructions to cooperate with the other antifascist parties that were allowed to operate in the Soviet Zone: the Sozialdemokratische Partei Deutschlands (Social Democratic Party, SPD), the Christlich Demokratische Union (Christian Democratic Union, CDU), and the Liberal-Demokratische Partei Deutschlands (Liberal Democratic Party of (East) Germany, LDPD). Seeking to integrate the population, most of whom were recently loyal to the Nazis, into the nascent political system, each party targeted a specific demographic that was generally not inclined toward communism. The SPD aimed to attract noncommunist workers, the CDU sought to organize the Christian middle-class, and the LDPD looked to build a base among professionals and small-business owners. In the early years, these parties had some room to maneuver politically and were able to voice concerns to Soviet authorities, but this window for dissent was rapidly closing.

While antifascist forces were officially welcomed to take part in the new Germany, the Soviets also initiated a program of comprehensive denazification through targeted action and structural reforms. High-level Nazis, military elites and business leaders were delivered to the International Military Tribunal at Nuremberg. Contrary to some in the West who wanted the Nazi elite summarily executed, the Soviets saw trials and legal proceedings as an educational facet of denazification and an opportunity to present their version of the war as the definitive narrative. This was a chance to create an international version of the Moscow show trials at the height of the Great Terror in the 1930s. The collaboration between the Allies, however, resulted in war crimes trials that preserved aspects of the Soviet vision, including prosecuting the crime of "war of aggression," while also incorporating certain Allied demands, including prosecuting crimes against humanity and allowing the accused to mount a legal defense of their actions.[10]

In addition to the Nuremberg trials, the Soviet secret police, the NKVD (the precursor to the KGB) converted several former concentration camps into "special camps" to house thousands of Nazis, Soviet prisoners of war (who were presumed traitors), and a wide range of Germans deemed to be politically unreliable (or merely picked up in mass security sweeps). Around 154,000 Germans were held in camps across the Soviet Zone. Conditions were grim and at least 44,000 Germans died from starvation or disease. Several hundred more were shot after trial.[11] Occupation officials initially held public trials in part to satisfy the Soviet population's demands for justice for the crimes of the Third Reich; in the first two years alone, 65,138 Germans were prosecuted for "membership in a criminal organization," resulting in 17,175 convictions. During the occupation years, the trials held in East and West were generally similarly fair in terms of legal procedure and the tendency toward execution of the guilty.[12] As Cold War tensions increased, the trials in the Soviet Zone became secret, and then in 1950, after the establishment of the GDR, those who remained in the Soviet camps were transferred to East German custody for possible further prosecution. While Soviet denazification produced greater numbers of unintended deaths via poor nutrition and hygiene in the camps, their general methods were not terribly dissimilar from the mass extrajudicial detention system of the Western Allies.[13]

Although the USSR and later the SED trumpeted the total success of Soviet denazification, the actual results were more ambiguous. On the one hand, Soviet orders to purge all Nazis did have a major impact, as the vast majority of the old social elite of the Nazi era still in the Zone—including the aristocracy, major industrialists, and high-level Nazi bureaucrats and judges—were removed from power. Denazification had also already begun spontaneously in many communities—even in areas not under formal occupation—by antifascist committees seeking retribution against the local Nazis in their midst.[14] On the other hand, initial efforts to crack down on the wider net of former Nazis were also undermined at the local level by those who sought more selective leniency for friends, relatives, and neighbors whom they deemed to be only "minor" Nazis.[15] In addition, political and economic necessity also resulted in a tendency toward reintegration over exclusion, especially after the founding of the GDR. An "underlying arrangement of mutual silence and control" created the perpetual possibility for blackmail of former Nazis, which allowed for the social and political reintegration of ex-Nazis and even war criminals under the implicit condition that they were always under threat of losing everything if their wartime behavior were exposed.[16] Former Nazis were thus brought back into key economic positions, especially when mass emigration to the West exacerbated shortages of qualified personnel without a tainted past in many fields. In spite of SED claims to have fully purged the GDR (in contrast to the West which was still riddled with Nazis), around 44,000 ex-Nazis gained positions in the East German bureaucracy, and some were even able to rise to positions of power, including serving as government ministers. By 1952, restrictions on the political rights of former Nazis and former Wehrmacht officers were lifted. Over the course of the GDR's existence, several former Nazis became high-ranking SED members, including Hans Bentzien (Minister of Culture, 1961–5), Werner Schmieder (Minister of Finance, 1980–1), Bruno Lietz (Minister of Agriculture, 1982–9), and Gerhard Beil (Minister of Foreign Trade, 1986–90). In the final years of the GDR, the SED's Central Committee, the party's highest decision-making body, had 13 ex-Nazis among its 165 members.[17]

Although certain segments of the Soviet occupation bureaucracy had planned for a long and transformative stay in Germany, those tasked with economic reparations worked as quickly as possible, anticipating that the window of opportunity to enact reparations was closing fast. The pillaging of Nazi technology and industry began immediately after the war ended, but was later formalized as Allied policy at the Potsdam Conference. These actions eliminated more than two-thirds of the Zone's production capacity in sectors from motors, iron, machine tools, railway engines, optics to textiles.[18] Transportation infrastructure was also hit hard, with railcars seized to ship goods to the Soviet Union and even railway lines pulled up and added to the reparations tally. In addition to Red Army troops engaging in the individual looting of valuables, Soviet teams surveyed the conquered territory, creating a target list of more than 17,000 "industrial objects" of which around a quarter were marked as reparations. Key technologies and even whole factories were dismantled and sent East by train to the USSR.[19] In October 1946, the Soviet reparations project expanded beyond material goods. Operation Osoaviakhim was launched to transport key scientists and technical specialists, sometimes with their families, to the Soviet Union, where they stayed for years before being returned to the GDR, as a form of reparations. Thousands were rounded up in the night.[20] One priority, as it was for the American Operation Paperclip, was to collect Nazi engineers who had worked on the V2 rocket program, in order to force them to participate in the development of Soviet missiles and eventually the space program.

In the countryside, Soviet authorities also worked quickly to break up the large farming estates that had dominated Germany east of the Elbe River. The Soviets identified the Junkers—the aristocratic class who owned much of this land—as a key group that needed to be eliminated from power through expropriation. Land reform had been a long-standing communist priority, but it also held widespread appeal among Social Democrats, Christian Democrats, and liberals who resented the reactionary aristocracy. The first wave of uncompensated expropriations began in September 1945 under the slogan "the land of the Junkers into the hands of the farmers." SMAD limited farms to 100 hectares, resulting in the seizure of 3.3 million hectares. One-third was placed under direct state control, while the rest was redistributed to refugees from the East, many of whom had no experience in agriculture.

The Socialist Unity Party and the Mythology of Antifascism

The Kommunistische Partei Deutschlands (KPD, Communist Party of Germany) that was revived in occupied Germany was deeply marked by its history. Officially founded on January 1, 1919, the KPD emerged from a faction of the Social Democrats that had refused to continue voting to fund the costs of the ongoing World War. When the German Empire collapsed at the close of the First World War in 1918, the SPD came to power in the new Weimar Republic, and one of its first acts was to deploy far-right militias, the Freikorps, to put down a communist uprising, a decision that led to the assassination of KPD leaders Rosa Luxemburg and Karl Liebknecht on January 15, 1919. This violent beginning to the first German democracy produced a lasting split on the left.[21] Over the course of the Weimar Republic, communists viewed Social Democrats as the puppets of bourgeois capitalism and willing collaborators with the reactionary forces of militarism and clericalism. The SPD, for their part, viewed the communists as extremist pawns of the newly formed Soviet Union who threatened Germany's fragile democracy.

From 1925 onward, the KPD—now under the leadership of Ernst Thälmann—aligned itself with Moscow and, following Stalin's strategy, refused to cooperate with Social Democrats, whom they deemed "social fascists." A mass political party with more than 300,000 members, the KPD was able to consistently draw more than 10 percent of the vote in Weimar elections. In the last free national election in 1932, they garnered nearly six million votes—third, behind the Nazis with nearly twelve million votes and the SPD with seven million. After taking power in 1933, the Nazis quickly banned the KPD; its members faced imprisonment, torture, and murder. Alongside tens of thousands of communists, Thälmann was arrested and executed at the Buchenwald concentration camp. Those active communists who were not arrested went underground or fled into exile—many to the Soviet Union (like Walter Ulbricht), others to various European capitals, and some to the Americas.[22]

The Nazi rise to power and the destruction of the KPD—the largest mass Communist Party on the continent—forced Stalin to reconsider his strategy in Europe. Communist parties were now directed to form a "popular front" with Social Democrats and bourgeois parties in an attempt to stem the rising tide of fascism. Although some in the KPD illicitly took part in active resistance in Germany, the core of the party leadership decamped to Moscow, where they also faced persecution from their Soviet hosts. Caught in the purges of the Terror, 178 were killed under suspicion of being agents of Stalin's nemesis in exile, Leon Trotsky. After the German invasion of the Soviet Union in 1941, the KPD was tasked with organizing prisoners of war and exiles into the National Committee for a Free Germany, which was to act as a kind of popular front government in reserve that could be deployed once the conflict was over. As a result, the exiles who survived their time in the USSR were all well-seasoned in the dangerous in-fighting of communist party politics and had developed strong alliances with key Soviet political figures.[23]

While the Soviet occupiers initially saw the KPD as destined to become the leading political force in postwar Germany via democratic means, they soon began to have their doubts about the path forward. In elections held in November 1945, communist parties in other parts of occupied Europe failed to attract mass support: in Hungary, less than 17 percent of the vote; in Austria, a mere 5 percent. Both Walter Ulbricht and Joseph Stalin feared that these results would be replicated in the Soviet Zone of Occupation and sought to forestall disaster. They subsequently proposed a merger of the KPD and the SPD to create a unified party of the left as an extension of the popular front and wartime cooperation in exile. While there were many in both parties who believed in the hope of a unified left, there was also intense opposition to the merger. Whereas SPD members feared it would suffocate internal party democracy and make them into Stalinist foot soldiers for their Soviet occupiers, members of the KPD feared the Social Democrats would dilute their political program and turn the party toward gradualist reform. Ultimately the Soviet occupiers forced a merger of the two parties through a combination of coercion from above and negotiations from below. Social democratic dissenters were pressured to agree to the merger: prominent SPD leaders who cooperated were offered the possibility of leading a united political party that could remake Germany with the backing of the USSR, while those who vocally opposed the merger faced threats and even imprisonment. This combination of carrots and sticks ultimately led to the creation of the SED in April 1946. The iconic handshake between KPD chairman Wilhelm Pieck and SPD leader Otto Grotewohl was adopted as the symbol of the new Socialist *Unity* Party. While both men were formally co-chairs of the new party, it was Walter Ulbricht who was ultimately in control—in large part due to his deep connections to key figures in the Soviet Occupation Authority.

Figure 1.2 Poster featuring the logo of the SED immortalizing the handshake of founders Otto Grotewohl (SPD) and Wilhelm Pieck (KPD) and the slogan "The Future Belongs to Us," May 1946. Verlag Einheit, Karl Huth, Berlin.

The Socialist Unity Party espoused a vision of antifascism as the founding mythology of the Party and the GDR as a whole.[24] The SED stood for socialism, but, more broadly, it stood for the victory of the forces that had opposed Nazism—and those who joined with them could now, retroactively, also become part of that victory. This ideological offer stood to generate a wider coalition of supporters, united by their desire to associate themselves with the triumph over the Third Reich. Antifascism appealed to those who had always opposed Nazism, but it also provided a new cause for those whose belief in Hitler had been shattered by defeat. This mythology developed further over the course of the GDR, absorbing an array of events, like the Spanish Civil War, and martyrs like Ernst Thälmann, who was installed as the symbolic patron of the East German youth movement (and was memorialized in an enormous bronze monument in East Berlin that continues to cause controversy today).[25] Former concentration camps were made into memorial sites celebrating resistance to Nazism and the heroic struggle, primarily by the KPD and its Soviet allies, against the tyranny of the Third Reich.[26] The Holocaust of European Jews and Nazi racial persecution writ large were not erased, but rather subsumed as elements of fascist terror, institutionalizing a coequality of all victims, but primarily communist resistors.[27]

The flip side to the heroic SED's antifascist mythology was the villainy of the Federal Republic of Germany (FRG). If the GDR embodied victory over the Third Reich, West Germany represented the rump of Nazi rule and the enduring home of war criminals, collaborators, and culpable bystanders. The continued public role of former Nazis in the judiciary, the military, and political life was used by the SED to frame the state's democracy as a sham and a mere cover for its revanchist and neo-fascist ambitions. While the turn to antifascism allowed those who had once supported the Nazis to integrate into the GDR, anti-Nazis who now supported the West were understood to be turning away from their previous antifascism. Their past actions were now dismissed as hollow in the face of their current collaboration and their role in perpetuating a bourgeois system that would itself again inevitably crumble into open fascism due to the contradictions inherent to the capitalist order.

The creation of the SED and the vilification of democratic forces in the West did not, at first, alter the KPD's earlier stance promoting a democratic transition in the Soviet Zone. While figures like Walter Ulbricht supported rapid Sovietization, there were others, like Anton

Ackermann, who called for a "German path to socialism." Ackermann had been sent to Saxony to lead one of the three groups of German communists who had returned to set up the party in the Soviet Zone in 1945. Citing Vladimir Lenin that "all peoples will arrive at socialism, that is inevitable, but they will not all get there in exactly the same way," Ackermann argued that Germany would not require a violent revolution and could realize socialism via peaceful and democratic means.[28] Stalin backed this approach, expecting to demonstrate that the SED had widespread democratic support in the Soviet Zone. Elections were planned for October 1946 to test the theory that a unified party of the left could achieve what communists had failed to do on their own elsewhere in occupied Europe: win a (relatively) open and competitive election against bourgeois parties. SMAD oversaw the planning of regional elections across the Soviet Zone with the support of the occupying Red Army, so conditions were ideal for the SED to gain a majority. The city of Berlin, however, complicated this plan. Because the merger of the Communists and Social Democrats had only taken place in the Soviet Zone, the SPD was still independent in the rest of Berlin, under four-power occupation. This meant the SED was going to have to run against the Social Democrats in open elections in a city the Soviets did not fully control.

The SED ran a cautious campaign, vowing to follow in the footsteps of the German liberal nationalists who failed to seize power in the 1848 Revolution rather than emulating the Bolsheviks who seized power in Russia in 1917 to create the Soviet Union. By contrast, the Social Democrats ran a scorched earth campaign denouncing the SED as Soviet lackeys and linking them to the hardships inflicted by the occupying Red Army, including ceaseless looting, industrial reparations, and the mass rape of German women—with an estimated two million victims.[29] SPD leader Kurt Schumacher attacked the SED as the moral equivalent of the Nazis and warned that their election would trample on the human rights of Germans and lead to a new dictatorship. Despite the vitriol of the election, SED leaders were convinced until election day that voters would choose socialist unity over socialist division. In reality, the SED suffered a terrible defeat: narrow victory had been achieved in regional elections across the

Soviet Zone beyond Berlin, but the SPD had won across the ruined capital city, including in the Soviet Sector. In most of Berlin, the SED trailed behind even the Christian Democrats, landing in third place. Despite a party merger that was designed to forestall such an electoral humiliation akin to what had already happened to the communists in Hungary and Austria, the SED had hit the same wall of democratic failure.

While blame for the disaster was vociferously debated within the SED, the experiment with a peaceful transition to socialism through broad democratic appeal was over in the GDR. Under Ulbricht's leadership, the SED maintained a public stance of cooperation with bourgeois forces, but internally it shifted from a mass party to a Leninist "party of the new type," guided by the principle of democratic centralism with power concentrated in the hands of a select leadership.[30] The number of bloc parties was expanded to further dilute their overall influence. The Demokratische Bauernpartei Deutschlands (Democratic Farmers' Party, DBD) was formed to split rural voters off from the CDU and the LDPD, and the National-Demokratische Partei Deutschlands (National-Democratic Party of Germany, NDPD) was created to provide a political home for middle-class former Nazis who found the communitarian nature of the GDR more appealing than the liberalism of the West. After the workers of Berlin failed to rally under their banner, the SED looked increasingly to the countryside and small towns for their audience. The Vereinigung der gegenseitigen Bauernhilfe (VdgB, Peasants Mutual Aid Association) was formed to provide greater financial support to farmers, many of whom owed their land to Soviet expropriations. This was not a matter of securing electoral support, but dividing and suppressing opposition. As Ulbricht told one colleague, "it has to look democratic, but we must have everything firmly in our hands."[31]

Creating the German Democratic Republic

There was no single decision that led to the division of Germany, but a sequence of events set in motion by many actors over time that accumulated to result in the creation of two German states from the ruins of the Third Reich. In 1947, the probability of a united Germany began to decisively fade as elites in East and West began to see division as the only means of realizing their political goals: for Moscow and the SED, the possibility of a demilitarized neutral Germany with a strong Soviet influence no longer seemed possible. The previous year's election losses had already demonstrated that the SED could not secure power via democratic means outside of spaces directly occupied by the Red Army. Conversely, the United States, the United Kingdom, France, and their local allies increasingly saw the potential in a separate West Germany as a bulwark against the solidifying bloc of socialist states in Eastern Europe, and believed that any plans for a unified Germany would leave the door open to Sovietization by stealth. On January 1, 1947, the United States and the United Kingdom effectively merged their two Zones of Occupation to facilitate a currency reform and introduce the Deutsche Mark. Although Stalin had not been intent on dividing Germany at the end of the war, the economic integration of the Western Zones of Occupation prompted the Soviets to secure their zone as a socialist holdout against the rest.[32] This included refusing American Marshall Plan economic aid to the Soviet Zone to forestall any integration into the market-oriented Bretton Woods international monetary management system.

Across Europe, the emerging Cold War between the United States and the Soviet Union hardened the ideological division of the continent, and the superpowers increasingly intervened in the internal affairs of states in their respective spheres of influence. In Greece, the United States and the United Kingdom worked with royalist forces to crush a local communist insurgency. When the USSR tried to pressure neutral Turkey into allowing it equal control over the straits between the Black Sea and the Mediterranean, Turkey chose to align itself with the United States instead. In Czechoslovakia, although the Communist Party had been democratically elected as the junior partner in a coalition government with nationalists and Social Democrats, it launched a coup, backed by the Soviets, to seize total control in 1948. Fearing similar results in Italy in elections that same year, the United States successfully backed the local Italian Christian

Democrats who won a near-absolute electoral majority, with help from covert funding operations by the CIA, preventing a popular front of the Socialist and Communist parties from coming to power. Across Eastern Europe, the Soviets ensured that local allies were firmly in control: mirroring events in Germany, the Soviets orchestrated a "soft coup" in Hungary, via the forced merger of the Communists and Social Democrats, following the model of the SED. By the end of the 1940s, almost all of Eastern and Central Europe was run by allied communist parties implementing political and economic programs emulating those of the USSR. The only exceptions were Yugoslavia and Austria. Antifascist partisans led by Josip Broz Tito—and not the Soviet Red Army—had liberated Yugoslavia, so it was free to chart a socialist path independent of the USSR. While both the West and East jockeyed for influence in occupied Austria, both sides eventually agreed to allow it to regain independence as a neutral, unified, and sovereign state in 1955.

With so much power in the hands of the Soviets in their zone of occupied Germany, there was no need to abolish other political parties, and the SED was able to work steadily to bully the bloc parties and internal dissenters into submission. In 1947, Soviet occupation authorities forced the popular Eastern CDU leader Jakob Kaiser to resign and then emigrate to the West.[33] Within the SED itself, those who objected to the party evolving from a mass organization into a Leninist party devoted to revolution were dealt with similarly. Some faced open suppression, but many more simply chose to emigrate to the West. Erich Gniffke, an SPD member who had been prominent in the newly founded SED, fled to West Germany in 1948 on the grounds that the party was on a course toward totalitarianism.[34] In a pattern that would continue in the coming decades, it was easier for political opponents of the SED to emigrate to the West than fight for change from within.

By 1948, the fiction of Allied cooperation over the occupation of Germany was unraveling quickly. At the London Conference to discuss Germany's debt, the emerging East-West split was clear. The United Kingdom, the United States, and France invited the Benelux countries to participate, but not the Soviet Union—in retaliation for the communist

The German Democratic Republic

coup in Czechoslovakia. By March, the Soviet representative to the Allied Control Council walked out of a contentious meeting, and no one from the USSR returned to replace him until decades later. On the ground in Berlin, unified civil administration similarly broke down: when Western Allies dismissed the chief of police, the Soviets backed him; Berlin suddenly had two separate police forces, one operating in the Western Sectors and another in the Soviet Sector.[35] This acrimony was only exacerbated by the blockade of West Berlin initiated by the Soviets in retaliation for the introduction of the Deutsche Mark in the Western Zones. On June 24, 1948, the Soviet military closed down all access to West Berlin from the Western Zones aside from three air corridors that had been legally guaranteed in an earlier agreement. As a result, the Allies had to airlift in practically all civilian supplies needed to keep the city going and to prevent its de facto annexation into the Soviet Zone. For nearly a year, hundreds of daily of cargo flights to the Western sectors of Berlin provided enough food and fuel to sustain the city. The persistence of the airlift made the Soviets relent and lift the blockade on May 11, 1949.

Over the course of 1949, the division of Germany into West and East was formalized. On May 23—less than two weeks after the end of the Berlin blockade—the three Western Zones of Occupation merged to form the FRG; on October 7, the USSR proclaimed the Soviet Zone of Occupation to be the German Democratic Republic. Berlin remained under four-power occupation, awkwardly situated in the center of the GDR. From the beginning, the Federal Republic claimed to be the only legitimate German state, the legal successor to Nazi Germany, and the representative of all Germans regardless of their location. Making the sleepy Rhineland town of Bonn its capital, the leaders of the FRG sought to make it clear that they saw the division of Germany as temporary. The Basic Law of the Federal Republic—adopted in place of a permanent constitution—contained explicit provisions for a reunification not only with the GDR but also with the Eastern territories annexed to Poland and the Soviet Union.[36] In the FRG, the GDR was treated as an artificial Soviet creation, with some West German media outlets referring to it as the "so-called GDR" or simply "the Zone" well into the 1980s.

The GDR's founding constitution also rejected the division of Germany and declared that there was only one German nationality. In its early years, however, the GDR remained symbolically ill-defined against its West German counterpart: East and West Germany shared an identical black, red, gold tricolor flag; the GDR's hammer and compass in front of a wreath of rye crest was only added in 1959. East Germany had its own money, but here too it was a slow evolution toward a national currency—only in 1968 was East German money provided with a specific national label, becoming the *Mark of the German Democratic Republic*. From its founding, the GDR had its own national anthem, "Risen from the Ruins," but even it spoke of "Germany, united Fatherland." East Berlin—the Soviet Sector—was the capital of the country, but since Berlin as a whole was technically under four-power occupation, the annexation of East Berlin into the GDR proper took place only slowly over a number of years. Citizens of East Berlin were only issued with GDR identification documents beginning in 1953, and the SED only introduced a citizenship law in 1967.[37] It took the building of the Berlin Wall in 1961 for East Berlin to become one of the districts of East Germany, designated as "Berlin, Capital of the GDR."

The constitution and the political structures of the GDR formally resembled those of a parliamentary democratic state, but political life was completely dominated by the SED as the party of workers and farmers, ruling according to the scientific principles of Marxism-Leninism. East Germany had a national legislature, the Volkskammer (People's Chamber), with representatives from multiple political parties and mass organizations who were elected every four to five years. From 1949 to 1952, the Volkskammer had an upper house to represent the five East German provinces (Länder), but this was abolished along with the provincial boundaries; the map of the GDR was redrawn into fourteen districts (Bezirke). On paper, the Volkskammer selected a prime minister, who led a Council of Ministers that acted as the executive body of the government that implemented legislation. In practice, all of this was elaborate political theater. True power was in the hands of the Politburo of the Central Committee of the Socialist Unity Party led by Walter Ulbricht as General Secretary. Replicating the Soviet model, the Central Committee was formally selected by the SED membership, but they were given pre-filled lists of candidates to approve, not to choose from. In theory, the SED ran according to the Leninist principle of democratic centralism in which there was internal party debate, but a united front to the outside once a decision had been made. In practice, however, dissenting voices within the party were systematically suppressed over the course of the 1950s and political power centralized at the top of the party through the position of the General Secretary of the SED. As the chorus in the SED anthem said, "the Party, the Party is always right!"

Marxism-Leninism

The official ideology of the Soviet Union, the German Democratic Republic, and other states in Eastern Europe and beyond during the Cold War, Marxism-Leninism originated in the writings of German philosophers, historians, and revolutionary socialists Karl Marx (1818–83) and Friedrich Engels (1820–95). In the *Communist Manifesto* (1848), they outlined a theory of historical materialism based on the idea that "the history of all hitherto existing society is the history of class struggles." The driver of history is the evolution of the means of production in a society, and classes are formed in relation to the ownership of those means of production. In modern times, the capital-owning bourgeoisie had displaced the formerly dominant land-owning aristocracy to dominate the means of production, while all groups below them were becoming part of an undifferentiated working class—the proletariat—that labored for those who owned capital. Marx and Engels argued that competition among capitalists for profit would result in the steady immiseration of the proletarian class who were being squeezed for ever-greater productivity for less pay by the bourgeoisie. This dynamic would eventually create a systemic crisis when there were no longer enough people with money to purchase what was being produced by the new industrialized economy. They theorized that this would inevitably lead to a sequence of revolutions that would conclude with the triumph of the proletariat, which would take control of the means of production and usher in an era of utopian communism organized under the principle "from each according to their ability, to each according to their need."

This theory was modified by Bolshevik leader Vladimir Lenin, who argued that instead of waiting for the inevitable forces of history to bring about revolution, it was the responsibility of a small revolutionary vanguard to bring about change. This was put into practice with the Bolshevik seizure of power in Russia in October 1917. Marxism-Leninism became the mix of these two ideas: a historical-materialist view of the rise of capitalism and the inevitability of communism, alongside the need for the guiding hand of the revolutionary vanguard party to make it happen in practice. In the GDR, the SED claimed the position of this revolutionary vanguard party and asserted its right to rule on the basis of the objective scientific correctness of Marxism-Leninism. The subject of Marxism-Leninism was compulsory in schools and universities. Ongoing political developments were overseen by the Institute for Marxism-Leninism in East Berlin, led from 1957 to 1989 by the so-called chief ideologue of the SED, Kurt Hager.

In 1950, the two chairmen of the SED, Wilhelm Pieck (ex-KPD) and Otto Grotewohl (ex-SPD), became president and prime minister, respectively, but neither had the political power to match their new titles. The Volkskammer itself did little more than generate speeches and provide light editing of the legislation that came from the Politburo before giving it a "democratic" stamp of approval. The legislature was organized around the National Front—the SED-led coalition with the other bloc parties including the Christian Democrats, National Democrats, Liberal Democrats, and Democratic

Farmers. Already largely docile before the founding of the GDR, those who still sought to use these parties to organize any opposition to the SED were quickly suppressed. Arno Esch, who served on the executive of the LDPD, was arrested by the Soviet NKVD in 1949 for "counterrevolutionary activities" and executed in Lubyanka prison in Moscow.[38] The following year, his LDPD colleague Günter Stempel was sentenced to twenty-five years in a Soviet penal colony for voting against a new election law (he was released in 1956, and subsequently emigrated to West Berlin).[39] Before 1989, there was only one free vote in the Volkskammer: in 1972, the Christian Democrats were (alone) allowed to vote against the liberalization of abortion.[40] After a few early incidents, all other votes were unanimous as a signal of the unity of the people and their representatives under the leadership of the SED.

While Article 3 of the constitution declared that "all state power originates with the people," this was reflected only in ritualized votes engineered to create an image of total unanimity. Elections for the Volkskammer, as well for more minor offices, were not competitive, and East Germans were given ballots pre-printed with a slate from the National Front. Citizens could vote against the list, but this required them to publicly deposit the ballot in a separate urn, exposing them to political and social repercussions ranging from losing their jobs and benefits to being placed under active surveillance by the Ministry for State Security (Ministerium für **Sta**ats**si**cherheit—the Stasi). Instead of democratic legitimacy, elections and other forms of voting acted as a means of mass mobilization and the ritualization of popular consent for SED rule.[41] At times, it was also about providing the endorsement for specific revolutionary reforms. In 1946, the Soviet Occupation Authority held a referendum in Saxony on the expropriation without compensation of war criminals and active Nazis (as well as major landholders and industries) with 77.6 percent voting in favor. In 1954, in the GDR, there was a vote asking the citizenry if they favored a general European peace treaty (the SED's preferred option) over the establishment of a Western European military alliance. Results improved to more than 99 percent in favor of peace. Between 1950 and 1990, every Volkskammer election in the GDR resulted in a vote of more than 99 percent for the National Front.

This unity of opinion was reflected in the media landscape of the GDR, where the SED put a priority on controlling public discourse.[42] Western media could not be distributed in the GDR, but Western publications were still smuggled in, and East Germans widely enjoyed Western public television and the West Berlin radio station RIAS (Rundfunk im amerikanischen Sektor, Radio in the American sector, only inherited by the German state-owned international broadcaster Deutsche Welle in 1992)—aside from two pockets around Dresden and the island of Rügen, nicknamed the Valley of the Clueless (*Tal der Ahnungslosen*), where the geography blocked the signal.[43] In response, the SED developed its own television broadcasting and counter-programming on the channel DFF (Deutscher Fernsehfunk).[44] But the most important media for the dissemination of the party line was the national daily newspaper *Neues Deutschland* (*ND*), the official organ of the Central Committee of the Socialist Unity Party. Every day, *ND* ran a mix of speeches from party leaders, policy announcements, profiles on the achievements of socialism in the GDR, and coverage of the ill-intentioned politics of the Federal Republic, the social ills of the capitalist world, and the successes of post-colonial states and socialist movements abroad (as well as a smattering of classified ads and advertisements for East German products).

Beyond the SED's main organ, there were hundreds of publications replicating the controlled plurality of the GDR's political system: Each of the bloc parties had their own daily newspaper, as did the Free German Trade Union and other mass organizations and professional groups, which presented essentially the same information as *ND* but spun at their particular demographic; the Freie Deutsche Jugend (Free German Youth, FDJ) produced the daily *Junge Welt* to provide a youth-oriented version of the SED's organ. Each city had its own newspaper that contained *ND*-content mixed with coverage of local events and cultural offerings.[45] There were also multiple illustrated news and culture magazines like the *Neue Berliner Illustrierte*, which focused on current events, *Eulenspiegel*, which featured humorous satire, *Sinn und Form* (Sense and Form), which provided high-brow literary and cultural criticism as well as fiction and poetry, *Das Magazin*, which had an eclectic mix of culture, poetry and erotica, and several publications aimed at women, including the illustrated magazines *Für Dich*, the high fashion magazine *Sybille*, and crafting and sewing magazines such as *Praktische Mode, Guter Rat,* and *Die Handarbeit* (Practical Fashion, Good Advice, and Handmade). There were also publications aimed at foreign audiences: the *GDR Review* was a glossy monthly magazine published in German, English, French, Swedish, and Spanish that aimed to "help win new friends for the GDR" around the world.[46] Since the British left was seen as a potential ally of the East German cause, there was also a twice monthly newsletter, the *Democratic German Report*, produced by the English journalist John Peet who had defected to the GDR in 1950.[47] All of these publications spoke to separate populations in different ways, but none contradicted the main party line demanded by the SED.

The 1953 Uprising and the Rise of the Stasi

The establishment of the two German states in 1949 did not settle the problem of German division. Both sides agreed, in theory, that Germany should be reunited; in parallel, the permanent division of Germany was also rejected in international forums like the United Nations. But in this era, the splitting of countries along ideological, ethnic, and religious grounds was hardly unprecedented. The partitions of India and Mandate Palestine, leading to the creation of a Muslim-majority Pakistan and a Jewish-majority Israel, had taken place shortly before the creation of the two German states. Similarly, the retreat of the nationalists to Taiwan had prompted the declaration of the People's Republic of China only a few days before the GDR's founding. On the Korean peninsula, war between the North and South had settled into a stalemate by 1951, setting the stage for a division that has lasted until today. Both the West and the Soviet Union preferred division to facing a reunited Germany as a member of their rival's Cold War coalition. In 1952, Stalin sent a series of notes to the Western Allies with various proposals for German reunification as a neutral state, primarily as a last-ditch propaganda effort to undermine the Federal Republic's integration into Western defense alliances rather than a genuine attempt to reunite the two states. From their perspective, the Western Allies understood the notes as a ploy to Sovietize West Germany under the cover of neutrality, and thus rejected Stalin's proposals.[48] Although German unity was ostensibly a priority for all involved, the superpowers and the elites of both Germanies were driven by strong political motivations to avoid it.

With the rejection of the Stalin Notes, the SED leadership was able to move past public hesitancy toward the Sovietization of East Germany. With the green light from Moscow, Ulbricht announced the start of the "construction of socialism" during the SED's Second Party Congress at the end of 1952. Church youth groups were banned, the education system was made more explicitly ideological, and the art world was instructed to adhere to the norms of "socialist realism."[49] On the economic front, the SED now committed to nationalizing all major industries and accelerating the pace of reconstruction via the development of heavy industry and agricultural collectivization. For East Germans, this was essentially an austerity program based on the promise of a future utopia: Reparations to the Soviet Union continued unabated while the state poured money into the development of industrial production at the expense of consumer goods. At the same time, East Germans were expected to work even more during the standard six-day work week, while rationing for basics increased. In the countryside, the pace of collectivization quickened with a new wave of land expropriation, and show trials were conducted against obstinate farmers on charges of sabotage. In tandem with these economic reforms, there was also a turn toward re-militarization. The Kasernierte Volkspolizei (KVP, Barracked People's Police) was founded as a paramilitary force under command of the SED whose members were recruited with a mind toward ideological conformity. The FDJ was tasked with propagandizing and training young people toward armed service, much to the deep dismay of many in the organization who were distrustful of compulsory military service so soon after the end of the Third Reich.[50]

Although the SED had charged ahead with the rapid construction of socialism despite widespread public dissatisfaction and resistance, this overconfidence was soon met by the largest public unrest seen in East Germany until its collapse in 1989. The "June 17, 1953" Uprising had many causes: the first signal of violent discontent came two years earlier, when uranium miners in Thuringia attacked police when their protests over working conditions went unheard.[51] As the continuous raising of production norms in heavy industry and construction escalated tensions in the cities, the beginnings of agricultural collectivization at the end of 1952 created dissent in the countryside. The ongoing strain of reparations to the Soviet Union further exacerbated resentment at both the occupiers and the SED as their agents.[52] In spring 1953, there was a growing sense of revolt in small towns across the GDR, and by early June, dozens of incidents of low-level violence directed at SED officials in the countryside were recorded.[53]

In both Germanies, the death of Joseph Stalin in March 1953 had generated hopes that changing conditions in the Soviet Union could encourage reunification or at least the end of SED rule in the GDR. At the same time, the Soviets feared for the stability of the GDR and warned Ulbricht that his zeal for Sovietization had put East Germany on a path to possible collapse.[54] On June 9, the SED sought to head off the growing unrest by announcing a "New Course," which reduced worker norms and increased the provision of basic consumer goods. But it was too little, too late. In East Berlin, construction workers at the site of the massive Stalinallee building complex walked off the job, sparking a nationwide uprising the following day: June 17, 1953. Widespread economic grievances quickly transformed into a general political demand to remove the SED from power. Strikes took place at 600 workplaces, and around one million people took part in demonstrations from big cities to country villages.[55] Western radio broadcasts about the initial strike actions in East Berlin actively encouraged East Germans to rise up. Across the whole of the GDR, demonstrations called for the end of SED rule and free elections; protestors attacked SED members and occupied state buildings.[56]

The weakness of the SED was quickly exposed when the Volkspolizei (People's Police) and the KVP failed to contain the crowds, and FDJ members barely mobilized against the protest (and in many cases actively took part).[57] The Soviet occupation forces were quickly called

Figure 1.3 Protestors throw stones at a Soviet tank in East Berlin during the Uprising of June 17, 1953. Archives Snark.

in to crush the demonstrations, and tanks based in the GDR were deployed to put down the uprising. While estimates of the death toll from 1953 vary wildly, at least fifty-five people have been confirmed by historical research to have died due to the uprising: at least thirty-four protestors (or passers-by) were killed by gunfire from Volkspolizei or Soviet troops, with five more summarily executed by the occupation forces, and four people dying due to inhumane prison conditions. At least five members of the SED security forces were also killed in the uprising.[58] On June 24, the Stasi declared the uprising to be over, but in more remote communities, order was not fully restored until late July. A political purge followed: the SED's own Minister of Justice Max Fechner was imprisoned and expelled from the party after publicly stating that rebels would be prosecuted, but striking workers were only exercising their constitutional rights. He was replaced by Hilde Benjamin—a hardliner from the judiciary with extensive experience running high-profile show trials.⁵⁹ Benjamin subsequently oversaw the crackdown on those who had participated in the uprising, including a series of show trials to punish those accused of being ringleaders or murdering state officials. More than 6,000 people were arrested, and by the end of the following year, 1,526 people had been found guilty of charges relating to the uprising, with two receiving the death penalty.⁶⁰

Hilde Benjamin

Born 1902, Bernburg (Saale), German Empire
Died 1989, East Berlin, GDR

Hilde Benjamin was one of the first women in Germany to study law, the first woman to hold the position of Minister of Justice in any German state, and notorious for overseeing numerous show trials in the GDR.

In 1926, Helene Marie Hildegard Lange married Georg Benjamin, an eminent doctor, communist, and brother of the philosopher Walter. Joining him in the KPD in 1928, Benjamin taught at a Marxist worker's school in addition to her day job as a lawyer. After the Nazi takeover in 1933, her husband, who was Jewish, was arrested and eventually murdered in the Mauthausen concentration camp. Benjamin herself was barred from practicing law due to her marriage to a Jew; her son faced legal discrimination as a so-called "mixed race" child. She survived the Second World War by working in the garment industry. In 1946, she joined the SED and became a representative of the Volkskammer upon its creation in 1949.

In the GDR, Benjamin played a key role in establishing the judicial system as a political instrument, presiding over many show trials and taking after the Soviet Great Terror prosecutor Andrei Vyshinsky. As vice-president of the High Court, she presided over show trials against Jehovah's Witnesses, managers accused of economic sabotage, and the trial of two members of the CIA-backed KgU on trial for plotting to bomb a train. These trials were crucial to bringing the economy of the GDR under full control of the SED, disciplining members of the bloc parties who had sought to defend private industry, and demonstrating the SED's willingness to use the death penalty against enemies of the state. Benjamin's performance in carrying out the theatrical elements of the show trial, including questioning defendants, earned her infamy in West Germany, where the media nicknamed her "Bloody Hilde" and compared her to the Nazi judge Roland Freisler, who had presided over many political trials in the Third Reich.

In 1953, in the wake of the June 17 Uprising, she was appointed Minister of Justice, recruited by Walter Ulbricht to crack down on dissent; she again presided over a series of show trials. She was also instrumental in the modernization of family law, eliminating penalties for illegitimate children and introducing gender equality into the laws on marriage and divorce. In 1967, she was dismissed from her role by Ulbricht, who saw her hardline reputation as a liability for international diplomacy. Although politically marginalized, she continued to serve on the SED's Central Committee until her death in early 1989.

The SED understood the uprising as a counterrevolutionary plot, orchestrated by enemy elements in the West, and not as a spontaneous revolt by its own population. Since the founding of the GDR, SED elites had harbored an apocalyptic fear of "Day X" when the imperialists in the FRG would try to extinguish the GDR through internal subversion and mass invasion. Although the West did not invade in 1953, the role of Western radio (and covert CIA psychological warfare programs) in encouraging the protests was taken as proof that the uprising was a coordinated operation to destroy the GDR from within. Many in the GDR believed that the United States could possibly step in to openly aid a rebellion (based on the confrontational rhetoric of the Eisenhower administration), but to the consternation of some in the leadership of the uprising, the United States failed to intervene directly.[61] The playwright Bertolt Brecht, who had migrated to the GDR as a committed socialist, satirized the official incapacity to cope with dissent in his poem "The Solution" (which was not published at the time), wherein he asked, would it not "Be simpler for the government / To dissolve the people / And elect another?" Conversely, others welcomed the suppression of the uprising, which they feared was a possible resurgence of fascism only eight years after the end of the war; the diarist Victor Klemperer, who had been persecuted as a Jew and narrowly avoided deportation under the Nazis, believed that "to me, the Soviet tanks are doves of peace."[62] While June 17 was commemorated as the Day of Unity in West Germany, the events of 1953 became a taboo subject in East Germany, only discussed publicly as part of the SED's official narrative of a counterrevolution that had been successfully put down.[63]

Victor Klemperer

Born 1881, Landsberg an der Warthe, German Empire (today Gorzów Wielkopolski, Poland)
Died 1960, Dresden, GDR

A scholar of language and literature, Victor Klemperer is today remembered for his 1947 classic *LTI—Lingua Tertii Imperii* (The Language of the Third Reich) on the manipulation of language by the Nazis and for his voluminous diaries, published posthumously, on his experiences in Germany from 1933 to 1959.

Born to an upwardly mobile Jewish family, Klemperer converted to Christianity in 1912. He volunteered for service during the First World War and fought in an artillery unit on the Western Front. In 1920, he was made professor at the Technical University of Dresden. After the Nazi takeover in 1933, his status as a veteran initially spared him from losing his university post, but he was eventually forced into early retirement. Saved from deportation because of his marriage to an "Aryan" woman,

> Klemperer and his wife were nonetheless persecuted and eventually forced out of their home into special housing for Jews. As deportation orders for the last members of the Jewish community in Dresden were being issued on February 13, 1945, the Klemperers were saved by the Allied aerial fire-bombing that began that night, destroying much of the city.
>
> Klemperer saw the SED as excessively fanatical, but felt that the ongoing Soviet occupation was necessary to stamp out Nazism. He did not believe his fellow Germans could be trusted with a full restoration of sovereignty and self-determination so soon after the horrors of the Nazis. He eventually joined the SED, was made a representative of the Volkskammer and toured the country giving scholarly talks. A year after the death of his wife in 1951, he married Hadwig Kirchner (1926–2010), a fellow philologist, who, after Klemperer's death in 1960, managed his estate and his papers, publishing his diaries in 1995 to international acclaim.

The uprising exposed the levels of discontent in East Germany and the lack of resources available to the SED to forestall a similar event in the future. In response, the emphasis on Western interference as the official explanation for the cause of the 1953 Uprising provided an alibi for Ulbricht's austerity politics, and legitimized the creation of a more powerful security apparatus, as well as the wave of repression and show trials that followed.[64] Most notably, it resulted in a massive expansion of the Stasi. Created in 1950, the Stasi was initially the mistrusted junior partner of the NKVD and the Soviet Occupation Authority, but soon grew into its own.[65] In the early years of the GDR, the Stasi established itself as the key instrument for monitoring SED members—and thus essential to the mass purges engaged in eliminating those deemed to be opportunists or ideologically unsound. After 1953, the Stasi became crucial to targeting and identifying the "ringleaders" of possible future uprisings and implementing surveillance strategies to prevent their activities.

In addition to the Ministry for State Security, the armed forces of East Germany also expanded in the 1950s. Immediately after the 1953 Uprising, the SED created the paramilitary Combat Groups of the Working Class (Kampfgruppen der Arbeiterklasse), modeled after the Czechoslovakian communist militia units that had carried out the 1948 coup.[66] It drew its manpower from middle-aged party members across the GDR who were called on to volunteer to defend socialism. The social mobility of the early years had created a class of citizens materially committed to the continued survival of the GDR, and the SED looked to these citizens to fill the ranks of the militia. Following the Soviet declaration of GDR sovereignty, the SED also created the Nationale Volksarmee (NVA, National People's Army) to replace the KVP in 1956. That same year, the GDR signed the Treaty of Friendship, Cooperation and Mutual Assistance (better known as the Warsaw Pact), entering into the Soviet-led military alliance with Poland, Czechoslovakia, Hungary, Romania, Bulgaria, and Albania. Although a socialist military, the NVA still used uniforms modeled on the Nazi Wehrmacht, and most of its senior officers were veterans of service to the Third Reich. In a few short years, both the FRG and now the GDR had re-militarized (each with a sizable contingent of Nazi-era Wehrmacht veterans) as part of their integration into Cold War alliances.

Despite the near implosion of the GDR on his watch, Ulbricht managed to retain power, and he used the moment as an opportunity to further consolidate his position by purging the top echelons of the SED. In the wake of the Uprising, a faction led by Wilhelm Zaisser, head of the Stasi, and Rudolf Herrnstadt, editor of the *ND*, moved to have Ulbricht replaced. Backed by the head of the Soviet secret police, Lavrentii Beria, they mistakenly thought they could count on Moscow's support to remove Ulbricht and undo the austerity policies that had led to such disastrous unrest. But Beria was executed as a result of the Soviet Union's own internal post-Stalin power struggles. With the support of the triumphant Nikita Khrushchev, Ulbricht managed to hold on to power.[67] His position secure with the backing of Moscow, Ulbricht took revenge on his enemies by purging the faction that had sought to remove him from power, along with many others who had opposed him in the past, including his old KPD comrade Ackermann—summarily ending the latter's call for a gradual democratic path to German socialism. Ulbricht had already launched a campaign against "cosmopolitanism," enveloping those who had been in exile in the West, mostly Jews, by accusing them of being part of a "Zionist-imperialist conspiracy" (in parallel to the antisemitic Doctor's Plot in the USSR and the show trial of Rudolf Slánský, Jewish General Secretary of the Communist Party in Czechoslovakia). This purge was now extended to Jews within the SED who had sought Ulbricht's resignation, including Franz Dahlem and Paul Merker, who were accused of being agents of Zionism.[68]

Khrushchev's ascension to power in the USSR may have locked in the status quo in the GDR, but it also shook up the rest of the Eastern Bloc when he denounced the excesses of Stalinism in the 1956 "secret speech" to the Twentieth Congress of the Communist Party, which augured a process of de-Stalinization and a political "thaw" that led to the lessening of domestic political repression, including the release of thousands of Russians, Germans, and Eastern European political prisoners from the Gulags (labor camps), and a limited increase in pluralism. Other Eastern Bloc states echoed Soviet de-Stalinization by tearing down monuments to the dictator, moderating repressive measures toward internal critics, and asserting more independence from Moscow. In Poland, the previously purged and imprisoned Władysław Gomułka returned in 1956 to lead the Communist Party after bread riots in Poznań, while in Hungary that same year, a reform program by socialist moderate Imre Nagy escalated into a short-lived revolutionary uprising that was violently suppressed by a Soviet invasion. In the GDR, Ulbricht initially jumped on the opportunity to distance the SED from Stalin's crimes, but quickly pivoted to opposing the wave of liberalization that followed.[69]

The failure of the Hungarian Revolution gave Ulbricht the excuse he needed to put a stop to de-Stalinization and to delay even symbolic changes. Only in 1961 was East Berlin's prominent statue of Joseph Stalin removed and Stalinallee—a central show boulevard named after the dictator as a gift for his seventieth birthday—renamed Karl-Marx-Allee (a name it still carries today). Ulbricht also continued to consolidate power: in 1957, his close ally Erich Mielke—a survivor of exile in the Soviet Union, where he had fled in 1931 following his role in the targeted killing of two police officers in Berlin—was put in charge of the Ministry for State Security, which quickly expanded to around 17,000 employees. Under Mielke, as Jens Gieseke has written, "the spirit of Stalin survived like nowhere else in the GDR."[70] In 1958, Ulbricht launched another round of purges to finish off the last of the KPD old guard in the Politburo that had opposed his agenda. Among them, Karl Schirdewan, a proponent of de-Stalinization in the Politburo, was accused of factionalism. While many of those purged or imprisoned had hoped to restrain Ulbricht's ambitions, few sought his removal, and none were interested in major reform.[71] In 1960, with the death of President Wilhelm Pieck, Ulbricht initiated a set of reforms to the political structure of the GDR to further institutionalize his position. The presidency was eliminated and replaced by the Staatsrat der DDR (Council of State) as the new executive body alongside the new Nationaler Verteidigungsrat (National Defense Council), in charge of all security matters. Ulbricht was appointed the leader of both institutions, meaning that in addition to leading the SED as a political party, he also formally led the GDR as a state.

The Berlin Crises and the Building of the Berlin Wall

The existence of West Berlin, first at the center of the Soviet Occupation Zone and then of the GDR, had always been a catalyst for crisis. The relatively open sector borders allowed thousands of Berliners to commute daily from East to West, and vice versa, for work, socialization, and shopping. While this traffic helped to stimulate economic life in the city, much of which was still in ruins, it also created two major problems that the SED could not solve. The first was economic: people could purchase heavily subsidized basic goods in the East and sell them for a profit in the West. They could then bring back Western consumer goods to sell in the East. This constant black-market trading undermined the system of subsidies for everyday necessities and cut out state-run stores that were then deprived of sales revenue. Competition over wages in the city also distorted central planning for uniform pay according to production norms, since workers in the Eastern part of the city had to be financially enticed not to work in West Berlin.

The second, and more pressing, problem was emigration or *Republikflucht* (desertion of the Republic) in the SED's terminology.[72] East Germans who wanted to leave, but were not allowed to do so at a border crossing to West Germany proper, could go to the Western sectors of Berlin and catch a train or a flight to the Federal Republic. West Germany offered automatic citizenship to all ethnic Germans in the GDR and across Eastern Europe, and offered an immediate right to settle in the Federal Republic. The resettlement camp in Marienfelde, West Berlin, was one of the most popular sites for East Germans to claim their Western citizenship and begin the process of moving to the West.[73] There were a small number of migrants from West Germany to the GDR, primarily those who were ideologically committed to the socialist project, as well as desperate economic refugees who hoped to gain land from the mass expropriations conducted by the Soviets. In contrast to the journey West, emigrants to the GDR were screened by the Stasi and many were rejected on the grounds they could be socially or politically disruptive. However, emigration to East Germany was dwarfed—seven to one—by traffic in the other direction.[74]

Both of these problems were linked to the stagnation of the East German economy relative to that of West Germany. From the beginning, the GDR was smaller and less populous (eighteen million residents) than the FRG (fifty million). The GDR had also suffered greater structural harm through the division, both economically and demographically. The Silesian coal fields that once fueled its heavy industry were now part of Poland, and much of its traditional customer base was now living in the Federal Republic. The differential effects of reparations to the Soviet Union versus the generous aid from the Western occupiers only exacerbated these differences. This resulted in an economic system in the GDR plagued by bottlenecks of key production inputs, which were then aggravated by individual firms and factories hoarding goods and labor so that they could deliver on promises to central authorities to the detriment of the system as a whole.[75] As the SED imposed harsh working norms with little consumer compensation in return, West Germany was undergoing an "economic miracle" from a combination of Marshall Plan aid, reintegration into Western markets, and large American industrial orders driven by the Korean War (1950–3).

The SED sought to overcome these hurdles through Soviet-style economic planning. Building upon the wartime centralization of the economy and postwar expropriations, the SED sought to organize the economy around a central plan that would encompass targets for production and consumption and fix prices for most goods bought and sold. The First Five-Year-Plan (1951–5) prioritized the revival of heavy industry with a goal to double prewar industrial output. The decision to formally initiate the "construction of socialism" in the GDR at the SED's Second Party Congress in 1952 only intensified this focus on heavy production over consumer needs. In the face of the growing unrest in early 1953, the New Course introduced more consumer goods to placate the unruly population, but did not fundamentally change the focus on industrial development. The 1953 Uprising made the SED more cautious about the limits of the GDR population to handle rapid Sovietization without any immediate material rewards. The Second Five-Year-Plan, launched in 1956 under the slogan "modernization, mechanization, and automation," again emphasized the need to invest in heavy industry, including the nationalization of any remaining private industry into VEBs (Volkseigene Betriebe, People's Owned Industries) and the collectivization of farms into LPGs (Landwirtschaftliche Produktionsgenossenschaften, Agricultural Production Cooperatives). There were still some privately owned small businesses that could seek to maximize profit through whatever production methods they saw fit, but they had to abide by the price controls set by the central plan when selling their goods.

At the SED's Fifth Party Congress in 1958, Ulbricht announced the "main economic task" of reaching and surpassing West German levels of per capita consumption among workers by 1961. Industrial production in East Germany was finally hitting targets, and the West German boom had hit a slump, leading the SED to think victory was in sight. Buoyed by the successful launch of the world's first outer space satellite Sputnik by the USSR, SED officials presumed the Soviets would financially support this push and Ulbricht believed that by surpassing the Federal Republic, the GDR could orchestrate reunification on socialist terms.[76] A new Seven-Year-Plan was introduced in 1959 to realize Ulbricht's ambitious goals. But West Germany's drop in growth turned out to be a blip, not the beginnings of its collapse under the contradictions of capitalism. While West Germany averaged growth of 8 percent per year, the fastest in Western Europe, the new central plan for the GDR economy proved excessively optimistic, and the gulf between the two Germanies only grew larger.[77]

As the SED aimed to overtake the West, the issue of who controlled Berlin again entered the realm of high Cold War politics. In contrast to Stalin, who regularly entertained the possibility of reunification (at least in public), his successor Nikita Khrushchev accepted the division of Germany and saw the GDR as the vital frontline of the Cold War.[78] In 1958, a decade after Stalin's unsuccessful blockade of West Berlin, Khrushchev sought to pressure the Western powers into giving up their occupation rights to the city in an attempt to consolidate SED control over all of Eastern Germany. This would solve the issue of emigration and hopefully stabilize the GDR economy. But another blockade was out of the question: East Germany was too reliant on trade with the Federal Republic, and Khrushchev feared that a total break between the two countries would leave the GDR completely dependent on Soviet subsidies the USSR could ill afford. Instead, he issued an ultimatum demanding a general peace treaty—none had yet to be signed by any party to the Second World War—and for the Western Allies to remove its troops from West Berlin. Rather than renewing the blockade, Khrushchev threatened to sign a separate peace with the GDR, which would annul the occupation agreements and put all land and air routes between West Germany and West Berlin into the hands of the SED. The Western powers were unwilling to give up West Berlin, but agreed to hold talks, calling Khrushchev's bluff; in response, he dropped the ultimatum, keeping the status quo in place.[79]

Just as Khrushchev's gambit had failed, so too had the ambitions of Ulbricht's Seven-Year-Plan. The Soviets were unwilling to provide the SED with the foreign currency needed to pay for consumer imports like coffee, cocoa, and tropical fruit, and ongoing supply chain bottlenecks stalled various industrial projects, which meant much investment in development produced little significant economic benefit. Collectivized farms were producing far less than their independent counterparts, but the SED pushed ahead and ended private agriculture in 1960. The effect was both a massive drop in food production and the emigration of thousands of farmers to the West. By 1961, there were shortages not only of high-end consumer goods like televisions and cars or imported foodstuffs like coffee but also of basics like meat, butter, and potatoes.[80] Although the GDR had a positive birthrate and several hundred thousand people had migrated to East Germany out of ideological conviction or with the prospect of social mobility via the revolution, neither compensated for the massive ongoing outflow. Between 1945 and 1961, more than 3.5 million East Germans—one in six—fled the country.[81] In response, Walter Ulbricht lobbied Moscow to allow him to build a wall between East and West Berlin. Ulbricht argued that the porous border in Berlin was the root of all of the SED's problems: it disrupted central planning by forcing the SED to provide more consumer goods than the economy could afford; of all the "People's Democracies" in Eastern Europe, only the GDR had to realize socialism with the threat of an open border to a Western counterpart, putting it at a permanent structural disadvantage. Ulbricht issued dire warnings to Khrushchev that the GDR could collapse unless something drastic and permanent was done to stem the tide of emigrants.[82] While in June of that year, Ulbricht famously told a press conference that "no one has the intention of building a wall," behind the scenes, plans were underway to do just that.[83] By August 1961, the Marienfelde Camp in West Berlin was registering more than 1000 refugees every day. On August 12, 1961, it registered more than 2400.

On August 13, 1961, the SED deployed thousands of workers to construct a wall that would permanently divide the Western sectors of Berlin from both the Soviet Sector and the rest of the GDR. According to official rhetoric, this was an *antifaschistischer Schutzwall* (antifascist defense rampart), but for the rest of the world, it was simply: the Berlin Wall. East Germans reacted with widespread outrage, but compared to 1953, the SED and its security organs were prepared. Pre-emptive mass arrests rounded up all those seen as potential opposition ringleaders.[84] The Combat Groups of the Working Class were mobilized to border zones to prevent workmen and others from crossing to the West. Party members were sent to workplaces to hold educational events about why the wall was being built to skeptical audiences. According to the SED, the wall would protect East Germany from renewed ideological subversion by Western agents and the threat of "Day X," when revanchist Nazis would seek to conquer the GDR by force. Although this explanation satisfied few (including SED members who were accustomed to cross-border shopping in West Berlin themselves), there was little that anyone could do to stop it.[85]

Within days, a hastily built combination of barbed wire and brick had been erected along the whole of the border between the Soviet and the Western sectors. Emigration without official permission was criminalized, and violators could be shot on sight. This would evolve over the coming months and years into a multilayered array of concrete walls, fences, and sensors separated by open fields of fire

Figure 1.4 The hastily constructed initial cinder-block and barbed-wire version of the Berlin Wall, 1964. Hal Beral.

(which provided border guards with a clear shot, and the ability to release explosives and attack dogs) to operate as *Todesstreifen* (death strips). The border was not designed to be inherently impenetrable but to create a space where border guards could most effectively murder those attempting to cross. In places where the stationing of border guards was impractical, natural barriers—such as Berlin's many rivers, canals, and swamps—were used to the same lethal effect as evidenced by the many escape attempts that ended in drownings. On the sparsely populated German-German border, automated devices—such as mines and *Selbstschussanlagen* (automatic firing devices)—were also employed until they became too politically toxic. Illicit emigration declined massively (although, over the next twenty-eight years, more than forty thousand still managed), and almost all cross-border commuters in both directions lost their jobs. Families who lived on both sides of Berlin were now separated, instigating, among other things, dozens of custody disputes over children whose parents or guardians now lived on opposite sides of one of the hardest borders in the world.[86]

The construction of the wall stemmed the mass exodus of East Germans and stabilized the status of Berlin, but at a terrible human cost. In spite of the border fortifications, there were still many who attempted to flee, and at least 140 people were "shot dead, suffered fatal accidents, or committed suicide after a failed escape attempt across the Berlin Wall," with hundreds more killed at the land and sea borders of the two German states.[87] The majority of those deaths were incurred in the initial years after the wall's construction, as East Germans looked for weak spots in the border fortification—including several who drowned in the many waterways that made up the boundaries between East Germany and West Berlin. East German border guards were ordered to use lethal force to stop people from crossing the Wall and were explicitly instructed to use "firearms to deal with traitors and border violators." The so-called "order to shoot" instructed that those who entered the 100 meter exclusion zone at the border were to be "apprehended or destroyed."[88] Border guards who shot and killed GDR citizens trying to emigrate were awarded medals and bonuses. These orders were in effect until spring 1989.

The first person to die at the Berlin Wall was fifty-eight-year-old widow Ida Siekmann, who jumped out of her apartment window directly on the border with the French Sector and was fatally wounded when she landed on the sidewalk below. In response, the Stasi began emptying out and sealing up buildings that were directly on the border to prevent further such escapes. On August 24, 1961, Günter Litfin, a twenty-four-year-old tailor from Berlin-Weißensee, was shot to death in the Humboldt harbor (near the Charité hospital) while swimming toward West Berlin. The most globally infamous incident was the attempted escape of eighteen-year-old Peter Fechter in 1962: shot as he was climbing over the final barrier to West Berlin, he lay wounded and screaming in pain in the death strip for nearly an hour until he bled to death. Fechter's public execution was a global media sensation that deeply damaged the reputation of the GDR.[89] Some died trying to evade the Wall in the air, like Christel and Eckhard Wehage, who attempted to hijack an Interflug flight from East Berlin to Leipzig in 1970. Failing to gain access to the locked cockpit, they killed themselves onboard rather than face imprisonment upon landing.

The Berlin Wall was not just lethal for East Germans seeking to emigrate to the West. There were also two Poles: Franciszek Piesik, who managed to get to the outskirts of West Berlin by boat, drowned in the freezing cold water on the final stretch; and Czesław Kukuczka, who arrived at the Polish Embassy in East Berlin claiming to be strapped to a bomb and demanding the right to migrate to the West. He was shot in the back at the Friedrichstrasse train station checkpoint as he was about to reach West Berlin (the shooter was convicted fifty years later, in 2024).[90] In addition, eight GDR border guards were killed in the line of duty by deserters, escapees, escape helpers, West Berlin police, or friendly fire; they were posthumously made into celebrated martyrs with a monument erected to their memory by the SED in 1973 (and torn down, after reunification, in 1994).[91] There were also accidents, as when a border guard fatally shot thirteen-year-old Wolfgang Glöde while showing off his service weapon to a group of children. West Berliners were also among the victims: Hermann Döbler was killed by GDR border troops when he drove his boat too close to the border on the Teltow Canal. Although far from the standard image of

The German Democratic Republic

Berlin Wall victims seeking freedom, several young people, mostly the children of immigrant guest workers, also drowned after falling into the waters of the militarized border while playing on the banks of the Spree River in the West Berlin neighborhood of Kreuzberg.[92] Six-year-old Andreas Senk was the first such victim in 1966. He was followed by Cengaver Katrancı, Siegfried Kroboth, Giuseppe Savoca, and Çetin Mert—all between the ages of five and nine. West Berlin emergency services refused to help them, for fear of being shot themselves. In 1975, after Mert's funeral transformed into a mass protest by the West Berlin immigrant community, a treaty between East and West created a joint protocol for water rescues in the border zone that finally ended these drownings.

The West German government in Bonn was furious about the forced isolation of West Berlin, but their American allies privately welcomed the Wall as a solution to the Berlin problem, even as US President John F. Kennedy publicly denounced its construction.[93] There was, however, one final standoff between the superpowers over Berlin. At Checkpoint Charlie (designated specifically for the Allies, foreigners and diplomats, one of an eventual seven internal-Berlin border crossings), three months after the building of the Wall, an American was denied entry to East Berlin as per his treaty rights as a uniformed officer (though he was on his way to the opera, not to conduct official business). This prompted US forces to deploy tanks as a show of force; the Soviets responded in kind. After a tense few hours, the border guards relented, and Americans were allowed entry to East Berlin once more. The tanks on both sides withdrew to their respective bases. On a geopolitical level, the building of the Wall had thus ended the ongoing Berlin Crises that had pushed Cold War tensions to the precipice for more than a decade. West Berlin remained an "outpost of freedom" in the center of the GDR, but it was no longer a reliable escape route for East Germans.[94] After the final standoff, the free movement of uniformed Allied soldiers through the whole of Berlin remained unchallenged, and four-power occupation of Berlin persisted until German reunification.

From the Third Reich to the Berlin Wall

In 1945, the leaders of the KPD were optimistic that they could win over the German people; by 1961, it had become necessary to wall in the population of the GDR to prevent mass emigration and the collapse of the state. Anton Ackermann's early vision of a peaceful German path to socialism through elections and gradual change had summarily lost in favor of Walter Ulbricht's model of the GDR as an effectively one-party Stalinist dictatorship with an expansive security apparatus to quell dissent. The existence of the GDR continued to prove fragile, only narrowly avoiding destruction from a popular uprising in 1953 through the intervention of the Soviet Union. Even with the backing of the USSR, East Germany was unable to force the issue of West Berlin, and its solution of a wall to isolate the pocket of Western influence at its heart was a terrible blow to the SED's international reputation, its internal legitimacy, and its people.

CHAPTER 2
SOCIALIST SOCIETY AND ITS DISCONTENTS

East Germany has often been depicted as a totalitarian state where citizens were either cynical collaborators, meek conformists, or heroic dissidents. Historical scholarship has, however, complicated this image of how state socialism functioned in the everyday, demonstrating the limits on the power of the Party and its security apparatus and the agency of individual East Germans. The SED (Socialist Unity Party) also had to entice the population to support, or at least tolerate, its rule. Mass participation was necessary for the German Democratic Republic (GDR) to function, and rewards were offered for compliance through work and political engagement. Far from silent, East Germans complained, protested, and openly rebelled against authority. In some cases, the SED encouraged complaints from below so that the Party could gather information about the state of public opinion. But the active participation of citizens in East German society does not undercut its status as a dictatorship. While East Germans played some role in shaping the politics and society of the GDR, the public sphere was wholly controlled by the Party and all forms of opposition were strictly illegal. Those who ventured beyond the political boundaries set by the SED, or were merely suspected of doing so, were subjected to harassment, surveillance, and state violence. This chapter explores how the SED sought to integrate citizens into its political program and to elicit participation and compliance with Party goals and norms. In turn, it also examines how East Germans pushed back against the Party and the state in their everyday lives. These conflicts between society and the state highlighted the ongoing tension between the SED's claims to have created a society based on equality and the everyday reality of a country dominated by hierarchies of various kinds.

The German Democratic Republic

Organizing the People

Although the SED had abandoned any hope of gaining power through democratic means even before the founding of the GDR, it still aimed to rule through more than just brute force. As such, it created a complex array of parties, mass organizations and associations to integrate citizens into a dense web of social and economic relationships—and all of it within the apparatus of the state. Essential to the new East German society was the creation of a social elite to take the place of those purged during the Soviet occupation. At the top of the pyramid were senior members of the Socialist Unity Party—theirs were key positions that came with significant privilege and wealth in a society that was ostensibly based on equality. The top levels of the Stasi, military officers, senior bureaucrats, managers and administrators, judges, technicians and scientists, professionals, and the cultural elite all had access to a lifestyle that far exceeded that of the average East German. This included housing in single family homes or shared villas in leafy suburbs dominated by the social elite, such as East Berlin's Pankow.[1] Entry into the new elite gave one access to improved leisure opportunities like saunas in the cities or hunting lodges in the countryside, and far better access to imported luxury goods like Volvos and Mercedes from the West or caviar from the Soviet Union. Healthcare was both faster and better.[2] This privileged lifestyle was kept out of sight of the public eye and enjoyed privately. The top leaders of the SED mostly lived in the closed colony of Wandlitz, north of Berlin, where they were secluded from the population and guarded by an elite unit of the Stasi.[3] Greater access to such privileges was also available to those who served essential state functions, like officers in the NVA, or at the lower tiers of the "service class," such as teachers and local bureaucrats, upon whom the SED relied for the functioning of the everyday life of the state.

Membership in the SED became essentially mandatory for advancement in most fields of work. The upper ranks of culture, academia, law, the security services, and the government were dominated by SED members. Most were trained at the Karl Marx Party Academy in East Berlin, though some were still educated in Marxism-Leninism in Moscow. The SED was modeled off the Communist Party of the Soviet Union, with power concentrated at the very top levels of leadership, although joining as a regular Party member could also bring its own form of political influence and personal benefits. Party members throughout the country had the power to determine how exactly policies would be implemented at the local level, providing members with a degree of discretion in how rewards and punishments were distributed. Party members had special access to housing, consumer goods, and greater freedom of movement. In the early years, this did not mean luxury, but a fixed means of securing the basics of survival given the widespread shortages of food and shelter in the aftermath of the War. Party members were tasked with a constant flurry of meetings, events, and mobilization drives, not to mention far greater scrutiny of their opinions and lifestyle. Since so many were motivated to join the SED for material reasons over ideological enthusiasm, the Stasi conducted purges not as a form of arbitrary terror but a means of periodically clearing out those whom the leadership considered mere opportunists to thin the ranks of the privileged elite.[4]

If one was not interested in joining the SED, one could also move up the social ladder by joining one of the docile bloc parties that had been established during the Soviet occupation. The East German Christian Democrats (Christlich Demokratische Union Deutschlands, CDU) recruited churchgoers sympathetic to socialism—a fairly common view in postwar Germany, where unchecked capitalism was widely equated with the rise of Nazism. The Liberal Democrats (Liberal-Demokratische Partei Deutschlands, LDPD) recruited the few small business owners who were still allowed to operate within the mostly nationalized economy of the GDR. The National Democrats (National-Demokratische Partei Deutschlands, NDPD) targeted the middle class and the former Nazis who wanted to flip sides to the cause of socialism. These bloc parties had their own headquarters and daily newspapers; they were also carefully surveilled by state security. As a member, your requests and petitions had a better chance of being heard and acted upon by those in positions of real power. Senior bloc party members also held important positions in the state apparatus. Vincenz Müller, a former Wehrmacht General who had been a prisoner of war in the Soviet Union, was a leader of the NDPD and went on to become the Chief of Staff of the East German armed forces, the Nationale Volksarmee (NVA). Georg Dertinger of the CDU served as foreign minister from 1949 to 1953, and Johannes Dieckmann of the LDPD acted as president of the Volkskammer from 1949 to 1969. However, Dieckmann's role was purely ceremonial, and Dertinger was imprisoned for treason after a show trial in the wake of the June 1953 Uprising.[5]

Beyond party politics, East German society was ordered by one's membership in an overlapping assortment of mass and specialty organizations that formed the basis of social and political life. For most, this began from childhood with entry into the Ernst Thälmann Young Pioneers, before graduating to the Freie Deutsche Jugend (Free German Youth, FDJ) at the age of thirteen. Refusing to join the FDJ precluded access to youth-oriented leisure activities such as clubs, concerts, and sports leagues, and virtually prohibited access to higher education. There was also the voluntary youth group, the Society for Sport and Technology (Gesellschaft für Sport und Technik, GST), which mixed together activities around electronics, motorsports, and paramilitary training. Almost all workers—around 50 percent of the population—were part of a state trade union under the umbrella of the Freier Deutscher Gewerkschaftsbund (Free German Trade Union Federation, FDGB), which acted as a hub for the distribution of a collection of state benefits, including access to holiday spots around the country for East German workers. One could also be part of the Vereinigung der gegenseitigen Bauernhilfe (VdgB, Peasants' Mutual Aid Association) for the 20 percent of the country that worked in agriculture, the Kulturbund (the formally nonpartisan organization of the intelligentsia—around 1 percent of the country) or professional organizations like the Writer's Union or the Association of Jurists of the GDR.[6] If you were a writer for example, you needed the support and approval of the Writer's Union to be published with the state-owned publishing houses.[7] Dozens of associations were organized around various demographics, including the Demokratischer Frauenbund Deutschlands (DFD, Democratic

Women's League), the Verband der Jüdischen Gemeinden in der DDR (Association of the Jewish Communities of the GDR), and the Domowina (Home) for the Sorbian ethno-linguistic minority. Some groups mobilized the population around specific political goals, including the Society for German-Soviet Friendship (an almost obligatory organization and the second largest of all mass organizations with 6.5 million members, smaller only than the FDGB), the League for International Friendship (for solidarity with the Third World), and the Committee for the Protection of Human Rights, which campaigned for the release of political prisoners in the non-socialist world. Joining these groups demanded much time spent in meetings, events, and other official functions, but gave citizens access to work, benefits, and favors, but also friendships and community. Refusing to join organizations cut one off not from luxuries but the basics of life. It was also seen as a sign of political deviance, raising the suspicion of the state security services.

Working Life in the Worker's State

The workplace was central to all aspects of life in East Germany. For the SED, it was the main site for the recruitment of party members and the organization of the working class; for most East Germans, it was the primary site of contact with the state in terms of demands for labor and political participation, and it was also the main source of benefits and services. After the wave of nationalization in the 1950s, publicly owned enterprises (Volkseigene Betriebe, VEBs) ran not only the vast majority of the economy but also the social state. Large state enterprises provided healthcare through onsite clinics and childcare through kindergartens and summer camps, while some even had a cultural center and shopping outlets: "Plants in the GDR were much more than places of work, and the workplaces were much more than where one labored."[8] This power created the localized leverage to demand intense production and output from workers, who were often disgruntled and unhappy with conditions and compensation. The right to work—included in the GDR constitution—was paired with the duty to work. Although there was still unemployment in the GDR, those who rejected gainful employment were deemed antisocial and under suspicion of political deviance, subject to surveillance and imprisonment.[9] Illicit forms of earning money, such as engaging in sex work, were similarly targeted as antisocial, particularly because prostitution was supposed to only exist under the exploitative conditions of capitalism.[10]

In the first decades of the GDR, around half of East Germans were engaged in some kind of manual labor—a number that would stay relatively consistent throughout the GDR's history. The average working week was initially forty-eight hours, six days a week, with only Sundays off, and workers could be compelled to work overtime. Only in 1967 did this shift to a five-day week. There were also significant inequalities in earnings and benefits between different groups of workers in a labor system that emphasized individual performance and output in pursuit of collective goals. Other factors also increased the stratification of the workforce: heavy industry workers earned more than those in light industry. Those in skilled trades could take side jobs on the gray market (outside the rules of the centralized economy, but not explicitly illicit), and some even worked as independent contractors. White-collar workers, including engineers and managers, made more than blue-collar workers, although this disparity was not as great as in the West. Those who lived in East Berlin had better services and consumer options than those in major urban centers like Leipzig, Dresden, Rostock, or Halle, who—in turn—were better off than those living in the provinces.[11]

More broadly, the dynamics of working life in the GDR were shaped by the intersection of German labor traditions, imported models of economic management from the Soviet Union, and the pull of West Germany. The specter of the FRG provided a countermodel of the "social market economy" and contributed to the GDR's chronic labor shortages due to out-migration.[12] Most workplaces were run by a trifecta of officials—a manager, an official from the FDGB, and a representative of the SED. Workers were not legally allowed to strike (even if it was guaranteed in the 1949 constitution) or elect union officials. They could, however, form "production brigades," which

Socialist Society and Its Discontents

functioned as small voluntary collectives of workers that elected their own captains and cooperated with each other to try and collectively fulfill targets set by the central economic plan with the promise of bonuses.[13] These brigades built on longer traditions of labor cooperation in Germany, and, as such, they found wide local support.

Workplaces in the GDR were highly politicized spaces, where the Party sought to educate workers toward socialist ideals. Visits by senior SED officials were ritualized affairs with workers expected to play choreographed roles as patriotic socialists seeking to fulfill the national economic plan. During periodic mass consultations on major reforms or constitutional changes, factories organized collective letters of support signed by all employees to show the unanimity of the workplace. Solidarity drives were conducted at work so that the less enthusiastic would be subject to peer pressure. For example, when an FDGB union representative who worked at a fish processing plant on the Baltic island of Rügen was arrested in the FRG for subversive activities, his fellow plant workers were mobilized by the GDR Committee for the Protection of Human Rights to write protest letters to West German judicial authorities as part of a larger campaign for his release.[14] Donation drives to support the reconstruction of North Korea or to send humanitarian aid to Vietnam were also conducted in workplaces, and in some cases workers were docked pay as a form of involuntary contribution to an international cause. In addition to social services, worksites also acted as paramilitary extensions of the security state, with shooting ranges located near enterprises so that workers could conduct firearms training during breaks to prepare for a possible military conflict with the West.[15]

Collective achievement was essential to realizing centrally planned economic targets set by the Party, but so too was exceptional individual action. Already under the Soviets, state enterprises sought to transition from waged labor to piecework so that workers would be paid according to output. Continuing under the SED, managers embraced the concept of the "performance principle" to link individual productivity to individual benefits (to the strong objection of long-time communist workers).[16] Modeled on the iconic Soviet worker Alexei Stakhanov, the SED created the image of the *Held(in) der Arbeit*

(Hero/Heroine of Labor), who went above and beyond to overfulfill their output quotas as mandated by the central economic plan. In 1948, the example of Adolf Hennecke, a coal miner who produced 387 percent of his daily quota at the Karl Liebknecht mineshaft, became an icon in the GDR. His actions were mirrored in 1953 by Frida Hockauf, who over-fulfilled her work quota by forty-five meters of textile production. These achievements had been carefully prepared and orchestrated and were not actually possible for the average worker on a normal day, but exceptional figures like Hennecke and Hockauf were invoked by the SED to inspire workers to similar individual feats.[17] Up to fifty East Germans a year were awarded the title of Hero of Labor in recognition of their efforts, which came with a medal, a certificate, and a cash prize of up to 10,000 Marks. The ideal of everyday heroism at the workplace formed part of wider production campaigns, with elevated target outputs launched to commemorate symbolic events such as the anniversary of the end of the Second World War or Stalin's birthday. That being said, if the goals were not reached, deadlines were extended. As a result, in urban factories and in the countryside, "the never-ending campaigns meant that the public was never free from being mobilized for one goal or another without ever seeing the results of these efforts."[18] Over time, the impact of these calls for heroic labor diminished greatly and became part of the background noise of the workplace.

The line between worktime and leisure time was blurred as production bottlenecks due to poor equipment and substandard materials resulted in long shifts that sometimes involved little actual labor. Workers played cards, drank beer, or used work tools for private purposes while they were still on the clock.[19] Workplaces organized social events outside of work, such as summer festivals, and worker brigades often formed the basis for socialization when off the clock. East German workplaces also provided access to sporting activities as part of a broader SED goal of promoting health and physical development. To deliver this on a mass scale, the tradition of workplace-organized sports clubs was revived via Betriebssportgemeinschaften (BSG, Enterprise Sports Communities). While VEBs were supposed to offer a wide range of activities, football

Socialist Society and Its Discontents

Figure 2.1 "Hero of Labor" Otto Trinks receiving a bouquet of flowers for fulfilling his annual mining quota by October 20, 1952, at the "Wilhelm Pieck" combine in the town of Mansfeld. ADN.

was the most popular and tended to use up much of the allocated budget.[20] The FDGB was also tasked with providing its workers with vacation possibilities. The beaches of the Baltic coast were covered in FDGB-operated lodgings on offer to those who were eligible through their employment, and after 1961 some could even travel to Cuba on FDGB-owned and operated cruise ships.[21]

The workplace was a site of both conflict and compromise. There was a delicate balance between the leverage workers held over management, since their labor was needed to hit production targets and fulfill the plan, and the implicit threat of state violence that management could deploy against an uncooperative and unenthusiastic workforce. While workers ostensibly had a say in how state enterprises were run, being an FDGB member had practically no influence on day-to-day affairs. Workers often pushed backed informally against their bosses on issues of compensation for specific production goals as well as working conditions.[22] Those who had specialized skills or worked in essential industries could leverage their positions to make greater demands. For their part, managers could be arbitrary in disciplining workers, but most sought to avoid punishing workers for complaints about conditions so long as they avoided crossing the line into overt political opposition. The endemic labor shortages caused by mass emigration, especially before the building of the Berlin Wall, made most managers wary of losing anyone who they thought could be productively salvaged from even borderline sedition. Mild protest was written off as a form of political naiveté that required education rather than coercion.[23] While these tensions did on occasion erupt into open revolt, such as during the June 1953, Uprising, there was usually a delicate give and take with clear red lines beyond which neither side wanted to test the other. At the same time, the paranoia about economic sabotage meant that a simple industrial accident could be interpreted by the Stasi as a treasonous conspiracy against the state rather than a problem of incompetence, poor equipment, or plain bad luck.

Labor shortages also meant that integration of women into the workforce was both rapid and uneven. By 1950, 70 percent of women were active in the workplace, a number that rose to 90 percent by the collapse of the GDR—far greater than that of the Federal Republic, where barely more than half of women were employed in full-time positions. For the SED, socialism meant women were free to be both producers and reproducers, both workers and mothers. In the first decades of the GDR, women had to consistently demand that the state provide the goods and services needed to make that possible, by addressing chronic shortages of daycare spots for children at worksites and the lack of domestic consumer appliances that would lessen the burden of housework after long days at work.[24] Yet the experience of the workplace rarely offered the equality promised by state propaganda. The pay in female-dominated economic sectors was less, and few women were promoted into higher levels of management.[25] Female workers described workplaces rife with casually sexist displays (both during working hours and at work-related leisure activities),

Socialist Society and Its Discontents

Figure 2.2 Caroline Lange working on a Textima large format knitting machine to produce fabric for casual wear and undergarments. VEB Aprotex in the town of Limbach-Oberfrohna, District of Karl-Marx-Stadt (1989). Wolfgang Thieme, ADN.

discrimination, sexual harassment, and even sexual violence. Party officials were often complicit, defending male management against complaints of impropriety and impunity by female workers.[26] Male workers also vented their frustrations with management by sabotaging female coworkers who were viewed as proxies for the Party since the integration of women into the workforce was understood as an SED priority. Bullying junior colleagues was less risky than directly confronting those in charge, so women workers became the target of male dissatisfaction with the system. In this way, the workplace was a microcosm of the contradictions of GDR society as a whole.

Equality, the Family, and Sexuality under Socialism

East Germany also produced a wealth of contradictions when it came to gender norms and questions of sexuality. The communist movement promised the radical emancipation of women through the abolition of the bourgeois model of the family, in which an authoritarian patriarch ruled over his wife and children. Traditional gender norms were understood in socialist ideology as a reproduction of the oppression of the working classes. As such, gender equality was a legal reality from the outset in East Germany, far in advance of most Western countries. Yet, this emancipation on paper was not matched in reality. Especially in the early years of the GDR, most SED officials retained a socially conservative outlook. Women were introduced to the workforce in large numbers, but more out of necessity and usually without the material support needed to fulfill their ostensible duties at home and at work. Sexual norms under socialism were not as stifling as in postwar West Germany, but they remained focused on an ideal of heterosexual, child-producing relationships.

Already in 1946, the SED courted female voters by positioning itself as the most progressive party on the question of women's emancipation. At the GDR's founding, women's equality and the illegality of gender discrimination were explicitly written into the constitution (and in stronger terms than in the West German Basic Law).[27] In 1950, seeking to both increase the birthrate and continue the integration of women into the labor force, the SED passed the Law for the Protection of Mother and Child and the Rights of Women. The law codified how women were expected to both stand on the factory line and in line for groceries, a worker-citizen in society and at home raising the next generation. To facilitate this "triple burden"—employment, childrearing, and political engagement—the state promised to provide social services and state benefits to help cover the cost and logistical complications of having children (a promise that was not actually fully realized for several decades). The SED promoted its pro-natalist policies as a path to "freedom and prosperity," through the "natural and healthy delight of building families."[28] This was contrasted with the pro-natalism of the Nazis, which was aimed only at expansion and conquest, and the family policies of West Germany, which were aimed at the restoration of the patriarchy. Nowhere were men—and their role within the family—the focus of campaigns.

The SED placed intense symbolic value on the emancipation of women and the GDR's recognition of gender equality. In contrast to the conservative social turn of postwar West Germany, where women were widely excluded from the workforce and expected to be traditional housewives (a situation reflected in the stark divide between East and West in terms of both the availability of daycare and women's lifetime income that remains still today), the SED promoted the image of East German women as equal to men in education and the workplace. The 10 Mark note featured the control center of the Rheinsberg nuclear power plant being operated by a female engineer to highlight how women were at the center of the most advanced technological achievements of socialism. Portrayals of beauty pageants and glamorous lifestyles in Western media outlets were repackaged in GDR women's media with explanations of how these images "create an illusion of prosperity and distract readers from the depredations of American imperialism and military conflicts."[29] These images projected the message that women in the West had shiny luxuries, but women in the East had dignity and equality.

Although men were expected to renounce bourgeois patriarchy, this did not extend to the redistribution of domestic tasks, and the glorification of gender (near-)equality in the workplace was not matched by a normative shift in male behavior either at work or in the private sphere. The average East German man remained the patriarch at home, and held on to a self-image of the breadwinner who should not be expected to deal with domestic duties such as cooking, cleaning, or childrearing.[30] SED officials were forced to concede to a monthly "housework day"—originally an innovation of the Nazis—in which women were given a paid holiday to deal with chores at home to make up for this discrepancy between public and private gender norms.[31] Domestic violence remained a serious problem, but one that was publicly taboo; in private, Party officials focused on solutions that privileged maintaining cohesive nuclear families over protecting women from harm.[32] Reflecting a broader cultural trend, one of the bestselling books in the GDR was Maxie Wander's *Good Morning, Beautiful*—a collection of frank interviews with East German women, many of whom focused on the ongoing struggle for emancipation (in part due to the neglect by East German men) even after several decades of socialism.[33]

The question of women's access to abortion highlighted the contradictions of the new order. In the Weimar Republic, the Communist Party (KPD) had actively campaigned for the repeal of Paragraph 218—a law dating back to 1871 that remains on the books in reunified Germany today—which prohibited abortion, running on the slogan "Your Body Belongs to You!" Yet in the Soviet Zone of Occupation, the KPD backed a total ban on abortion on pronatalist grounds due to the massive population losses of the Second World War. Communist objections to abortion restrictions had always been framed around the dire condition of women exploited by capitalism, which meant that abortions could now be limited under the conditions of incipient socialism. However, in the wake of the mass rape perpetrated by the Red Army in occupied Germany and the endemic poverty following the war, the need for abortion access was greater than ever. Complications from illicit abortions (estimated at around two million a year in the immediate postwar) caused around 6,000 deaths per year in Berlin alone so the rules were relaxed to allow for exceptions in cases of rape, incest, or medical conditions.[34] Over the coming years, East German women regularly petitioned the government to liberalize access to abortion, both by working through the Democratic Women's League and by writing directly to Party officials. In the early 1970s, the SED reoriented its pro-natalist policies toward financial incentives and relaxed the abortion law, in line with international trends at the time. In response, the Party faced internal opposition from the Catholic Church and the Christian Democratic bloc party. In 1972, abortion access was nonetheless made available on demand until the twelfth week of pregnancy; the CDU was allowed, however, to (symbolically) vote against this law in the Volkskammer, making it the only non-unanimous decision of the East German parliament until 1989.[35]

Sex and sexuality were also central to the SED's vision of a new socialist society. Questions of morality, sexuality, and politics were intermingled as "the quest for a moral state linked political normalization to popular and official visions of respectability, gender identification, and preferred comportment."[36] The GDR was in many ways more liberal regarding sexuality than its Western counterpart in the early postwar decades, although it still echoed conservative moral values through the lens of socialist ideology. The strongest contrast was in norms surrounding premarital sex, which was strongly condemned in state-led campaigns in the Federal Republic, but practically encouraged in the GDR. Even in the 1950s, the primary message from state agencies in East Germany was that premarital sex was completely normal. An SED-sponsored sexual advice lecture told young people that "we as free people know that intercourse does not just service the propagation of the human race, but also furthers pleasure very significantly."[37] This advice had a clear political message: sex under socialism was understood to be superior to capitalist sex, because it could be based on true love. Taking part in the struggle for socialism would only improve romantic relationships.

Yet this open-mindedness only went as far as activities that were on the path toward monogamous, child-producing, heterosexual marriages. In the early years of the GDR, sex and sexuality beyond these limits were viewed as problematic and possibly politically dangerous. Efforts to revive nudist culture, which had been popular in the Weimar Era, were initially met with horror by the political and cultural elite of the GDR. Homosexuality was regularly used as a marker of deviance, and it remained a taboo. While queer bars had reopened in East Berlin after the fall of the Third Reich, they were closed down again by the Volkspolizei in 1950.[38] These venues were recreated again in a quasi-underground—including the queer salon run from the 1970s until the fall of the Berlin Wall by the trans woman Charlotte von Mahlsdorf, to cite the most famous example. Mahlsdorf operated a villa that was also home to her personal museum of items from the period of the founding of the German Empire. She was able to provide a replacement for the public sphere that was denied gay and lesbian East Germans. She was, however, also a Stasi informant, and her circle was heavily surveilled if not actively suppressed.[39]

Nonetheless, there was also a sexual revolution in East Germany from below, albeit with "elements of evolution and, like all revolutions, it was unfinished, uneven and stunted in places."[40] One of the fruits of the revolution was the increased tolerance for homosexuality. By 1957, consensual homosexual activities between adults were effectively decriminalized. In 1968, Paragraph 175 (dating back to 1871), the provision of the criminal code prohibiting homosexual sex between men was significantly reformed, a year before West Germany began to even lightly modify it. Although no longer criminalized, the state and society at large remained intolerant of public displays of homosexuality. By contrast, nudist culture was more successfully integrated into the mainstream as "free body culture" (*Freikörperkultur*, FKK) as enthusiasts demanded both the freedom to enjoy public beaches without clothing and to be recognized by the state as an officially sanctioned organized leisure group. Over time, the SED's attitude toward nudism shifted from suppression to celebration, eventually touting it as evidence of the natural freedom one could enjoy under socialism.[41]

Artists and Culture

The creation of art and culture in East Germany was at the center of a number of conflicting imperatives. Party officials tended toward a conservative view of art, and sought uncomplicated cultural products that would edify and appropriately educate the population of the GDR. Artists, even those with impeccable socialist credentials, often came into conflict with Party officials as they sought to explore and innovate in terms of both style and content.[42] In addition, both the Party and artists had to accommodate the general public's interest in popular cultural trends, often imported from the West and rife with possibilities for political incorrectness. Socialist culture was never fixed, but a constantly moving target, as official tolerance for the avant-garde waxed and waned over time and popular tastes evolved. New artistic forms and formats emerging from the West could not be wholly rejected or ignored, leading to an ongoing process through which they were absorbed and reimagined to the standards of a German socialist culture. Classic Westerns glorifying American expansionism were, for example, transformed into stories about heroic Native American resistance to imperialism (see also Dean Reed in Chapter 3).[43]

German communists viewed the classical Weimar culture of Goethe and Schiller as the humanistic core of the "other Germany" that had been trampled by Nazi atrocities, not merely the remnants of bourgeois society.[44] As such, the cultural elite of East Germany saw the reconstitution of German culture, which had been deformed and corrupted by the Nazis, as their primary purpose.[45] At a 1944 meeting of communist intellectuals in Moscow, poet Johannes Becher—founder of the Kulturbund and author of the lyrics to the GDR's national anthem—declared "our goal is to liberate the German people from all the reactionary detritus of its history, revealed in the crassest form in Hitler."[46] As with political antifascism, the mission of the cultural elite was conceived of in broad terms that could encompass the whole population, rather than a narrow group of the ideologically faithful. The SED positioned itself as the protector of German culture as a means of legitimizing the Party to the masses, but it was also prompted by an intense aversion among Party officials to contemporary artistic innovation. In the early GDR, "no one could say what a new Socialist art should look like since it had not yet been created, although politicians and conservative cultural functionaries claimed to know what it was not: anything related to modern art."[47]

The conservatism of party control over culture regularly shifted in the early years of the GDR. First there was the campaign by leading Party officials against "formalism" in high art—the emphasis of form over content as seen in movements like cubism or abstraction. This was held up as the antithesis to correct Soviet-style "socialist realism," which depicted politically inspiring scenes in a straightforward style untouched by modernist innovations. At the same time, modern socially conscious artists like Käthe Kollwitz, who had graphically depicted the poverty of the Weimar Era, were attacked for depicting workers too pessimistically and for the failure to use their art to depict the triumph of revolutionary forces.[48] Some of the artists who went on to become the "Leipzig School" of East German modern art in later decades—including Bernhard Heisig, Wolfgang Mattheuer, and

Werner Tübke—began their careers navigating these difficult waters. In 1959, the SED introduced the "Bitterfeld Way," which sought to close the gulf between the intelligentsia and workers by having artists collaborate with the working classes in the creation of their own art.[49] During a brief window after the building of the Berlin Wall in 1961, the SED relaxed its control over cultural production, and artists were given far greater latitude to openly discuss social and political issues. Yet by 1965, that window had once again closed. At the Eleventh Plenum of the SED's Central Committee, the so-called "clear-cutting meeting," Walter Ulbricht and his leading lieutenant Erich Honecker denounced the immorality creeping into East Germany society and the tolerance for imported Western "trash," including the Beatles and Elvis Presley. The intellectuals and artists of the GDR, in particular, were blamed for facilitating this corruption through their desire to copy modernist and pop cultural trends from the West rather than preserve the morals of the socialist youth.[50]

One point of pride for the SED was the number of cultural figures who chose to return from exile to the GDR. Having faced persecution by the House Un-American Activities Committee in the United States after the war, the playwright Bertolt Brecht and the composer Hanns Eisler both resettled in East Berlin. They were joined by non-German left-wingers also fleeing McCarthyism in the United States, including Afro-American baritone singer Aubrey Pankey.[51] Novelist Anna Seghers initially came back from exile in Mexico to West Berlin before moving to the East; the writer Heinrich Mann died in California before he could move to the GDR to take up a post as head of the Academy of Arts in 1950. Some returnees found great success in East Germany: Brecht and his wife, the star actress Helene Weigel, ran the Berliner Ensemble theater company together until his death (she continued to run it alone until her death in 1971). Others did not fare so well. Hanns Eisler wrote the music for the East German national anthem "Risen from the Ruins," but his attempt at an operatic new version of *Faust* drew harsh criticism from Ulbricht, who publicly denounced it as a "formalistic disfigurement" of Goethe's greatest work. He produced little more original music. The photomontage artist John Heartfield, who had produced political posters for the Communist

Socialist Society and Its Discontents

Party in Weimar and anti-Nazi art to international acclaim while in exile in Czechoslovakia and England, also suffered upon his return. Suspected of treason on specious grounds, he was able to work in set design for the theater but produced little original art in his remaining years.[52]

The moral panics that swept the West in the 1950s over the corrupting qualities of emerging popular art forms like jazz and rock music also hit the GDR, but with radically different conclusions. Western culture was viewed as a threat to the socialist project, but its undeniable popularity meant that it needed to be co-opted and assimilated into East German society. Just as in the West, rock 'n' roll was viewed by the authorities as degenerate and dangerous for young people and as a gateway to juvenile gangs. Youth crime was a major preoccupation given the explosion in the number of unsupervised children who had to survive on their own in the immediate postwar period and fears that young people could be organized into anti-socialist opposition through Western infiltration. As an alternative to rock music, the Lipsi was created as an upbeat, but not uncontrolled and chaotic dance step.[53] Young people responded with the chant "we don't want no Lipsi and no Alo Koll [a GDR band leader] / we want Elvis Presley with his rock 'n' roll."[54] In 1964, the Party did concede to demands for more pop music by creating the radio program DT-64 aimed at young people, but with the condition that the 60 percent of the music played had to have been produced in East Germany or other socialist countries (mirroring trends in other countries, such as Canada and France, for national content quotas to counteract growing US cultural hegemony). Unable to produce enough contemporary popular music at home, pop artists from the rest of the Eastern Bloc such as Polish singer-songwriters Czesław Niemen and Halina Frąckowiak got regular airtime and gained large followings.[55]

Rather than finding a replacement for jazz, its proponents in East Germany sought to distinguish between respectable forms and disreputable decadent varieties: traditional jazz was linked to a positive African American cultural tradition, while newer forms like bebop were denounced in terms that often reproduced the racist prejudices of both Nazi and Western critics.[56] In 1965, the eminent

American jazz trumpeter and singer Louis Armstrong was allowed to tour the GDR, where he was touted in the media as an outspoken advocate of racial justice in his native United States (even though the musician had a reputation for avoiding politics wherever possible).[57]

GDR authorities were most comfortable with international cultural exchange within the framework of carefully orchestrated events. In 1955, the Leipzig Week for Cultural and Documentary Film was founded as an international festival that would bring the world to the GDR and display East German film to foreign visitors.[58] The following decade in 1965, the Biennale of Baltic Countries (Biennale der Ostseeländer) was opened in the city of Rostock and held in the Kunsthalle, the only art museum to be constructed in the GDR. Under the slogan "The Baltic Sea has to be a sea of peace," the event displayed contemporary art from the GDR, Poland, the USSR, Finland, Sweden, Denmark, and the Federal Republic of Germany as well as Norway and Iceland.[59] While the last two were not actually located on the Baltic, they were included as the event was part of the SED's broader efforts to court the Nordic states diplomatically.[60]

While many artists chafed against the mercurial demands of the Party, there was no clean line between conformists and dissenters. The author Christa Wolf is emblematic of those who both aimed at socialist edification and drew the ire of authorities. Born to a family of expellees from the Eastern territory annexed by Poland, she joined the SED in 1949 and worked as an informant (*inoffizielle Mitarbeiterin*, IM) for the Stasi from 1959 to 1962. In 1963, she wrote *They Divided the Heavens*, which focused on the struggles of Rita, a young woman who falls in love with a man who becomes disillusioned by socialism; she is ultimately unable to convince him to return when he emigrates to the West. It was adapted into a film the following year by Konrad Wolf (no relation to Christa, but the brother of Stasi foreign intelligence chief Markus Wolf) to large audiences at home and critical acclaim abroad. Yet by 1965, Christa Wolf had been placed under Stasi surveillance, which would continue until the end of the GDR. In 1968, she faced lengthy struggles with state censors to publish her more subjective and experimental novel, *The Quest for Christa T*. For the rest of her career, Wolf was critical of the GDR, but still loyal enough to the socialist project that she never crossed the line into open opposition—nor did she quit the SED.⁶¹

The Wolf Family

Friedrich Wolf
Born 1888, Nieuwied, German Empire
Died 1953, Lehnitz, GDR

Markus Wolf
Born 1923, Hechingen, Weimar Republic
Died 2006, Berlin, FRG

Konrad Wolf
Born 1925, Hechingen, Weimar Republic
Died 1982, East Berlin, GDR

The story of the Wolf family encapsulates a history of communism in the twentieth century in three biographies. Father Friedrich Wolf was born to a Jewish merchant family and became a committed communist. A playwright, novelist, and doctor, he was an advocate of naturopathic medicine and abortion legalization in Weimar Germany. When the Nazis came to power in 1933, he fled to Moscow, along with his sons. In 1936, Friedrich traveled to Spain to work as a medic for the International Brigades, fighting on the side of the Republican forces, while Markus and Konrad stayed in the Soviet Union and attended the German expatriate school. After the fall of the Spanish Republic, Friedrich was interred in a French concentration camp, returning to the USSR in 1941. During the Second World War, Friedrich was a founding member of the anti-Nazi National Committee for a Free Germany (which organized German exiles and POWs); Markus joined the Comintern and received training in underground political action; Konrad joined the Red Army. In 1945, Konrad was among the first Soviet soldiers to reach Berlin; Markus followed soon thereafter as part of the Ulbricht group. Upon his return, Friedrich helped found DEFA and participated in the literary cultural revival of the Soviet Zone.

In the GDR, all three had eminent careers. Friedrich was named the first East German ambassador to Poland (1949–51) and helped found the Academy of Arts before dying of a heart attack in 1953. Markus joined the Stasi in 1951 and rapidly advanced to become its second-in-command and head of foreign intelligence, nicknamed the "Man Without a Face" for the lack of photographs of him in circulation (the first, published in the West German magazine *Der Spiegel* in 1979, ended his ability to travel internationally). Konrad studied film in Moscow and became one of East Germany's most renowned filmmakers, with credits including the adaptation of Christa Wolf's *They Divided the Heavens* (1964), a fictionalized version of his own experiences as a soldier in *I Was Nineteen* (1968) and the still-popular *Solo Sunny* (1979) about a young singer struggling to conform to the East German system, before dying of cancer at age fifty-six. Markus was pushed into retirement in 1986, reportedly for his philandering, his relationship with a woman who had previously attempted to flee the GDR, and his desire to complete a book begun by his late brother Konrad about their experiences in the Soviet Union. Surprisingly self-critical, *The Troika* was published simultaneously in both Germanies in 1989. He subsequently took a reformist line in 1989 calling for liberalization at the November 4 Alexanderplatz demonstration, where he was booed by many. After reunification, he was initially convicted of treason (later reversed), then convicted of lesser charges for which he received a suspended sentence. He died in his sleep in a reunified Berlin in 2006.

Socialist Society and Its Discontents

The tension between artistic vision and the demands of the Party was similarly evident at DEFA, the East German film studio. Founded in 1946, it produced the first postwar film *The Murderers Are Among Us* about a woman returning from the concentration camps forced to confront a society of ex-Nazis in the ruins of Berlin. Many of the GDR's top filmmakers split their careers between conventional work portraying socialist realist heroic narratives and more critical work.[62] Kurt Maetzig directed a conventional antifascist biopic on KPD leader Ernst Thälmann and followed it with *The Rabbit Is Me*, which looked at the disillusionment of East German youth.[63] While the film was produced, it was banned as part of the larger crackdown on culture that took place in 1965 and never screened. *Traces of Stones* featuring the popular singer and actor Manfred Krug as the leader of a group of unruly workers bucking against the strictures of the everyday in East Germany met a similar fate. The film was banned, and director Frank Beyer, who had previously made a quintessential antifascist film *Naked among Wolves* on the (communist-led) resistance in the concentration camps, was barred from filmmaking for several years.[64]

Although Erich Honecker, as Ulbricht's favored deputy, had been one of the leading conservatives behind the crackdown on the cultural scene in 1965, he ushered in an era of liberalization when he took over in 1971, declaring: "When one starts from the firm position of Socialism, there can be [...] no taboos in the realm of art and literature. This concerns the question of content, as well as style."[65] The film *The Legend of Paul and Paula*, about a chaotic love affair between a working woman and an ambitious young party functionary, was almost banned, until Honecker screened it and personally decided to allow it.[66] Featuring surrealistic fantasy sequences and a soundtrack by the GDR prog-rock band the Puhdys, the film became a huge hit and remains popular today, including as former Chancellor Angela Merkel's favorite film. Similarly, the television crime show *Polizeiruf 110* (Police Call 110—the emergency services phone number in the GDR), created in 1971 to compete against the popular West German *Tatort* (Crime Scene), also highlighted the new era of relative openness by acknowledging that petty criminality, interpersonal violence, and alcoholism still existed under established socialism—all of which was normally depicted as a relic of the pre-socialist era.[67] These critical perspectives were, however, balanced out by the end of each episode, which demonstrated the capacity of the system to find culprits and to repair the damage they had done to society. Both *Tatort* and *Polizeiruf 110* are still in production, alternating in the same Sunday evening timeslot.

Consumerism and Material Cultures

From the start, the ability of the GDR's economy to produce things that could be used and enjoyed by the population was understood as an essential test of the SED's legitimacy. The material goods provided by the state—and those that it could not provide—were a central aspect of East German complaints about the everyday under "real existing state socialism." The socialist project's capacity to deliver a good life to the average German was judged not only in comparison to the hardship of late-Second World War and the Soviet occupation era but to life in West Germany.[68] In examining the history of consumption in the GDR, it is useful to consider three different perspectives: first, the utopian visions produced by the SED; second, the reality of what was delivered to the average East German; and third, the subjective experiences of East Germans as consumers and what consumer products meant to them.[69]

The means of production in the GDR were owned by the state, but consumption was a matter of private expenditure. The cash economy remained in place, and although basic goods were highly subsidized, East Germans still had to buy most of their own food, pay rent on their state-owned apartments, and purchase tickets for public transit and many cultural events. Goods could be purchased at a variety of stores: the *Konsum* chain emerged from the postwar cooperatives that proliferated across the country, while the *HO* (*Handelsorganisation*, Trade Organization) chain was directly state-owned and operated. There were also *Centrum* shopping malls in most major cities with specialist departments for different products. In the 1960s, two specialty stores for higher-quality goods were created, with *Exquisit* selling clothing and higher-end fashion and *Delikat* focused on foodstuffs. Both stores were intended to widen consumer choice, but also to soak up as much money held by East Germans as possible to cut down on inflationary pressure in an economy with fixed prices. Also established at this time was the *Intershop*, which only accepted Western currencies and initially sold only to visitors and those transiting through the GDR. East German money had little value outside of the country, due to strict capital controls and official exchange rates disconnected from actual value. As a result, the SED had limited "hard currency" from foreign trade that could be used to acquire goods that were only available abroad like oil, tropical fruit, coffee, cocoa, and specialty machinery. From 1974 onward, East Germans who were able to acquire hard currency from relatives or working in the West were also able to purchase from the Intershop, which stocked Western cigarettes, liquor, and home electronics.

That being said, access to most goods was less a matter of cost, but of availability. Even after the end of rationing, the SED prioritized price stability, which meant that fluctuating patterns of production and consumption produced constant shortages in stores, much to the consternation of the public. In contrast to SED proclamations of socialist superiority, especially after the launch of the first Soviet satellite Sputnik in 1957, a popular rhyme among East Germans went "There's no cream, there's no butter, but on the moon the red flag flutters."[70] The GDR economy was plagued by gluts and shortages, so standing in line for hours for specific products before they sold out was commonplace, made worse by store staff who would set aside items for friends or barter. The Genex mail order catalog allowed West Germans to send care packages—from food to automobiles—to relatives in the GDR, paid for in Deutsche Marks and provided by an East German state agency at a mark-up. Regular supplies of easily traded goods like coffee or blue jeans provided vital "currency" for bartering in the gray market.[71] The rise of luxury shops created a widening division in consumer culture between those who had access to hard currency or foreign goods—often from generous relatives in the West—and those who had to survive on what was available at the local HO for East German Marks.[72]

Access to food was an overriding preoccupation in the early years of the GDR. In the immediate postwar, many in the Eastern Zone were fed by factory canteens, which authorities saw as an essential tool not only for keeping their workforce functional but also reducing rates of absenteeism. After the GDR's founding, this policy was expanded to include a school lunch program, so that most East Germans received at least one daily meal directly from a state enterprise or agency. The availability of basic foodstuffs like meat, bread, potatoes, and dairy products improved steadily until 1958, when the rationing of butter, sugar, and meat was finally abolished—a full eight years after the end of rationing in West Germany. Access to "luxury" foodstuffs like tropical fruit, coffee, and cocoa would continue to lag massively behind the FRG. The ability of the state to provide these goods, as well as seasonal necessities such as Christmas *Stollen* and champagne on New Year's Eve, became an ongoing test of the legitimacy of the SED.[73]

In the area of consumer goods, the SED had to overcome the Stalinist focus on mass industrial production in order to compete with the differentiated consumer culture developing in West Germany. This focus on industrialization in the early years meant that there was no specifically consumer-oriented economic development. Instead, state enterprises responsible for industrial production were mandated to also devote a small percentage of their productivity to consumer goods. This resulted in VEB Robotron, which produced computing equipment alongside knitting needles, and the Simson Schwalbe, a popular motor scooter manufactured by VEB Vehicle and Hunting-Weapons Plant in Suhl, which also produced rifles. Furthermore, in the 1950s, the "1,000 small things in goods and services" campaign aimed to diversify the range of products available to East Germans. This dovetailed with the "chemistry program," which sought to overcome shortages in raw goods by turning to synthetics like locally produced plastics, which became the material of choice for socialist consumer goods. The SED aimed to link together advancements in science and technology under the umbrella of rational economic planning to demonstrate the superiority of the socialist system over its capitalist rival. Although plastic had a negative connotation in the West as cheap and inauthentic, in the GDR, plastic goods had a reputation as modern and durable, with consumers objecting to their scarcity, not their construction.[74] Indeed, many of these items continue to dot eBay and flea markets to this day, maintaining their durability and popularity into the twenty-first century.

Similarly, the incorporation of fashion into socialist production and mass culture is emblematic of the push and pull between state and society. East Germans were not shy about complaining to state authorities about the style and quality of clothing. As one petition (Eingabe) to authorities about an unpopular line of sweaters read: "here in Hoyerswerda, we do not have so many small square women."[75] As a result, fashion in the GDR was often defined by personal modifications to available products, and many took up making their own clothes both out of a sense of individual style and, in some cases, as a form of rebellion.[76] On the part of state officials, complaint letters were used for market research to determine what the population wanted, especially given the transitory nature of what is deemed fashionable. There were also efforts to direct the population's tastes, most notably through *Sybille*, a "magazine for fashion and culture"—colloquially known as the East German *Vogue*—which included only clothing produced in the Eastern Bloc and available in state stores in the GDR, and popular home sewing and knitting magazines. Rather than focusing on stimulating sales or dictating trends, these magazines explored how the women of the GDR could style themselves and individualize the fashion produced primarily by local state industries.

Shifts in SED economic policy in the 1960s started to pay off over the course of the decade and allowed the GDR to begin catching up to the West in terms of certain key consumer goods. While automobile ownership lay outside the reach of the vast majority of East Germans, between 1960 and 1970, the percentage of households with a television jumped from 18.5 percent to 73.6 percent, ownership of both refrigerators and washing machines from around 6 percent to nearly 54 percent. More than just mere appliances, these goods represented a new form of consumer modernity that East Germans had felt acutely denied in recent years, and finally helped lighten the household burden of East German women.[77] By the 1970s, the state began to pour more money into providing consumer goods and expanding the luxury shops under Erich Honecker's "Unity of Social and Economic Policy" program—albeit mostly financed by ever-growing foreign debt.

But these programs did not solve East Germany's issues with shortages. The chronic lack of goods like coffee or bananas became symbolic of the GDR's inability to compete with the West. When global coffee prices skyrocketed in the 1970s, the SED had to roll out Kaffee Mix—a mix of half coffee and half chicory or pea flour that was detested by most East Germans as a tangible manifestation of their inequality with Western consumers.[78] While hated poor quality staples were one issue, other SED consumption projects were marred by their own success. Limited resources meant that supply could rarely keep up with demand for genuinely popular items. One such example was fast food. State agricultural and nutritional authorities were intent on expanding East German consumption of chicken (since it was cheaper than red meat and seen as healthier than pork), and the solution was the Goldbroiler rotisserie chicken restaurant. Goldbroiler soon became so popular that the chain could not expand quickly enough to keep up with demand, and customers soon complained that locations were overcrowded and undermaintained.[79] Similarly, the Trabant automobile became an East German icon, but supply never came close to keeping up with demand. Made from fiber resin that was relatively cheap to produce, it had a two-stroke engine that was simple enough for most East Germans to maintain themselves. Almost three million Trabants were produced, but with a population of around fifteen million, there was eventually a thirteen-year waiting list to buy a new one.[80]

The material aspects of life in the GDR and the relationship of East Germans to their things and their homes created a distinct lived experience to that in West Germany. The material culture of East Germany was not dictated purely from above by the SED nor generated from below by the demands of the population. Despite the general imbalance of power between the Party and the people, the widespread culture of complaint around consumer goods "created a unique culture, something purely East German, a combination of state and society but representing the power of neither one over the other."[81]

Socialist Society and Its Discontents

While derided as backward in comparison to the West, the material remnants of the GDR have formed the basis for a sustained nostalgia culture—from iconic plastic egg cups shaped like a rooster to midcentury modern furniture. The consumer goods of East Germany "no longer embody the dreams of a prosperous present and a hopeful socialist future, they now serve as repositories of private histories and sentimental reflections."[82]

East Germans Outside of the Norm

Having moved from oppositional communist movement to actually running a state, the leaders of the SED had to contend with the reallife population of the GDR, which meant engaging with those who did not inherently conform to the ideals of German socialism. The largest group outside the SED's norms was not a minority but rather a majority: of eighteen million people living in a state grounded in atheism, nearly 90 percent of the population considered itself Christian in 1949. In parallel, a small Jewish population remained in the country, having survived Nazi persecution or having returned from exile to help rebuild. Initially in the thousands, the community dwindled to only a few hundred by the 1980s. And there were the Sorbs, a small Slavic ethnic and linguistic minority group numbering around 80,000, concentrated in the coal-mining region of the Lausitz (Lusatia) on the border with Poland. Although the Afro-German community that had existed in the Weimar Era did not survive the Third Reich in Eastern Germany due to persecution and emigration, non-white racial minorities from the Global South began to arrive in the GDR via migration as students, refugees, and contract workers in the 1970s.[83] Finally, there were also the disabled and elderly in a country built around the valorization of being an able-bodied worker. In a state founded on the ostensible total equality of the citizen under a unifying ideological vision of atheistic Marxism-Leninism, how did the state accommodate difference?

Christianity was tolerated, but also steadily suppressed during the early decades of the GDR. The founding constitution recognized a range of religious freedoms, but these existed primarily on paper. The organized churches—primarily Protestant, but with a sizable Catholic minority in Western Thuringia and a smattering of free churches like the Moravian Brethren—were allowed to operate, but the SED applied sufficient financial and social pressure to make the existence of institutional religion difficult.[84] Certain denominations, like the Jehovah's Witnesses and Christian Scientists, were outright banned. Rather than abolishing the more mainstream churches altogether, SED officials intended for them to slowly wither away. Adults who were already Christians and worked within key state institutions were put under pressure to discontinue their affiliation with organized Christianity in order to advance their careers. To reduce future numbers, one of the key tools was the *Jugendweihe*—a secular socialist confirmation ritual. Originally established by free thinkers in the nineteenth century, the Jugendweihe was instituted as a ceremonial coming of age for the socialist citizen during which, as with a Christian confirmation ceremony, young people around the age of fourteen were invited to affirm their commitment to atheistic Marxism-Leninism. At the ceremony, East German youth were given a book entitled *Outerspace, Earth, Man*, which "offered a five-hundred-page scientific discussion of the universe, the planet, and the history of humankind," from an atheistic and socialist perspective.[85] Churches refused to allow their members to take part in both confirmation and the Jugendweihe, as they believed the core values of the two ceremonies to be contradictory.[86]

For most church officials, their relationship to the state was one of animosity, but there were elements within the Christian community in the GDR that supported socialism. The Christian Democratic Party of the GDR, one of the bloc parties that followed the lead of the SED within the National Front, acted as an official mouthpiece for Christian socialists who saw collaboration as the most effective way to preserve their faith within the boundaries set by a state that was broadly hostile to organized religion. Some within the church hierarchy, most notably Bishop of Thuringia Moritz Mitzenheim, openly embraced socialism and positioned themselves as reliable partners to the SED in communicating with the wider Christian community. The

Figure 2.3 Three girls who have just completed their Jugendweihe in Berlin-Friedrichshain. Each received a certificate and a copy of *Outerspace, Earth, Man* at the ceremony (1958). Erich Zühlsdorf, ADN.

Protestant and Catholic Churches were also still influential enough to mobilize Christians around the country to demand more rights for freedom of belief as part of a mass consultation for the new "socialist constitution" in 1968. But protests from the Christian churches were just as often ignored. In that same year, the University Church of Leipzig, where Johann Sebastian Bach once played, was demolished over the objections of the Church and the wider community to make way for a new higher education complex.[87] By the 1970s, the structural pressures placed on Christians by the SED meant that Christians had become a distinctive minority group as active church membership dropped to a few hundred thousand. In 1972, despite protests by the Catholic Church and even the open opposition of the Christian Democratic bloc party, the SED went ahead with the liberalization of abortion access.[88] After this, the Catholic Church largely retreated from public life and any engagement with politics; its dwindling membership sought to keep their heads down and avoid conflict with the state in order to maintain their individual access to worship and Christian community.[89]

The Protestant Church, by contrast, found a space of compromise with the SED. In 1968, most of the Protestant churches in East Germany broke from the existing pan-German institutional structure to form the League of Evangelical Churches of the German Democratic Republic (Bund der Evangelischen Kirchen, BEK). In 1978, the leaders of the BEK held a summit with Erich Honecker and came to an agreement with the state that recognized it as a "church *in* socialism"—rather than for or against it. The SED aimed to avoid a situation as in neighboring Poland, where the Catholic Church had become the vehicle for political opposition and provided crucial institutional support for the activities of human rights campaigners and union organizers. To forestall a similar fate, the SED acknowledged the legitimacy of the church as an institution and promised not to exert further pressure on Protestants to quit their faith. In exchange, the Protestant churches were not to speak out against the SED publicly and were not to become a "disguised opposition party." Social groups that did not fit the socialist norm were able to find refuge under the protection of the Church; however, the Church hierarchy now also policed their activities. Beliefs that could be perceived as anti-state or anti-socialist had to stay carefully within the church, and all hand-printed publications were always stamped "for inner-church use only." This politically neutralized the Church but also created a safe space that eventually fostered many of the dissident elements that would emerge in the late 1970s and evolve into an organized opposition to the effective one-party rule of the SED in the 1980s.[90]

The Jewish population of East Germany was not large in 1949, and it declined further in response to the wave of antisemitism that subsequently swept across the Eastern Bloc. Beginning in the Soviet Union with Joseph Stalin's targeting of Jews as "rootless cosmopolitans," it intensified following the creation of the state of Israel in 1948 as Jewish communists faced accusations of being agents of Zionist imperialism.[91] In the Soviet Union, this manifested in the Doctor's Plot, and in Czechoslovakia in the show trial of Rudolf

Slánský and other former leading Communist Party members. In East Germany, Paul Merker was the most prominent victim of this purge, accused of being part of an international Zionist conspiracy spun off from the accusations leveled in the Slánský trial. The fact that Merker had been in exile in Mexico rather than Moscow was suspicious, as was his support for a German path to peaceful reunification. Merker was removed from the party in 1952; another Jewish old communist, Franz Dahlem, was similarly purged the following year.[92]

While Jewish Party members were more likely to be targeted in the purges during this period, Jewish communists were not uniformly removed from power. This era also saw the elevation of Jewish SED members to important posts, including Minister of Justice Hilde Benjamin, Information Minister Albert Norden, and Politburo member Hermann Axen. After the wave of antisemitic paranoia died down, other Jewish SED members similarly rose to leading positions, including Minister of Culture Alexander Abusch and Klaus Gysi, who served as Minister of Culture and later State Secretary for Church Affairs. The purge also did not touch several prominent Jewish cultural and intellectual figures including Ernst Bloch, Stephan Hermlin, Stefan Heym, Anna Seghers, and Arnold Zweig. Markus Wolf was able to ascend through the Stasi to run its foreign operations, and his brother Konrad Wolf became one of East Germany's most famous film directors. To succeed in the GDR while being Jewish, however, required them to put their identity as socialists first and to obfuscate their Jewishness as a background trait of no import in the day-to-day. Once Zionism was equated with imperialism, emphasizing one's Jewish identity was perceived by East German authorities as a reactionary political tendency.[93]

The Holocaust was not a taboo subject in the GDR but public discussion of the suffering of Jews at the hands of the Nazis was filtered through the official narrative of antifascism, which emphasized the organized opposition against the Third Reich and centered the actions of communist resistors.[94] Initially, the Association of Victims of Nazism rejected classifying Jews as a recognized victim group (that would then be eligible for financial compensation) on the grounds that they did not collectively fight the Nazis. After debate at the highest political levels, however, it was decided to recognize those persecuted on racial grounds as one group among many targeted for destruction by the Third Reich.[95] The centrality of genocidal antisemitism to Nazism was downplayed in East German memorials, which instead emphasized the heroism of resisting antifascists.

While not targeted for destruction by the Nazis, the Sorbs had been persecuted culturally, including a ban on their language. Once in power, the SED implemented a program for the protection of the Slavic minority of the Lausitz (which today straddles Brandenburg and Saxony), which followed the Soviet model of minority cultures under the slogan of "national in form, socialist in content." For the SED, protecting the Sorbs was an opportunity to demonstrate their humanitarian character in contrast to the brutality of the Nazis, as well as showing their Eastern European allies that they had been instrumental in saving a Slavic minority group from total assimilation. In 1945, the Sorbian cultural organization Domowina was re-established in the city of Bautzen, and the 1968 constitution of the GDR guaranteed the protection of the Sorbian language and support in the free development of their national culture.

When this support extended to mandatory bilingualism, however, the SED unleashed a backlash among Germans and Sorbs alike. Germans objected to state support for minority languages and outright rebelled against forced bilingualism for their own children living in majority-Sorbian towns. Even among ethnic Sorbs, this decision provoked protest from those who regarded their minority status as backward and actively sought assimilation into the larger German-speaking community. Protests against bilingualism were treated as anti-socialist, and the Stasi began to regard it as a possible marker of fascist tendencies. Ultimately, efforts to revive Sorbian culture for the future through state mandate proved too divisive: compulsory bilingualism was dropped in 1964, leading to a steep drop in young people learning the Sorbian language, although SED support for cultural institutions like a state theater and an ethnological museum continued.[96] In parallel, internal migration of Germans to Sorbian regions due to industrial development—like the Black Pump energy complex near the city of Hoyerswerda—also

Socialist Society and Its Discontents

contributed to a long-term decline in Sorbian self-identification and knowledge of the Sorbian language.

Racial differences were officially celebrated with the SED formally embracing an antifascist vision of antiracism as a repudiation of Germany's imperial and Nazi legacies. According to East German state ideology, all races were equal, and prejudice was a tool of imperialist and capitalist rule and an indication of fascist tendencies. The SED's anti-imperialism served to sever the GDR from Germany's colonial past (including the Herero genocide) and its present-day racial prejudices.[97] Propaganda did not reject racial difference but displayed it positively through images of Europeans together with African and Asian comrades interacting as equals.[98] In practice, racial prejudice remained widespread and was a common problem faced by non-white residents in East Germany, from stores discriminating against foreigners, to stereotypes deployed in workplaces and interpersonal violence. Some Black revolutionaries, like the African American communist Angela Davis, were lionized as the vanguard of the socialist revolution and elicited thousands of letters of support from East Germans as part of a nationwide solidarity drive.[99] But aside from Davis, GDR media tended to focus on violence and oppression enacted on Blacks internationally from Africa to the US South as part of the larger depiction of racist capitalist imperialism but rarely included the perspectives of Black people or showed them as agents of political change.[100] The existence of Black East Germans was more complicated in the everyday.[101] The children of East German women and male African, Asian, and Middle Eastern students, refugees, and contract workers almost always grew up in the GDR without their fathers who returned to the home countries for political, social, or economic reasons.[102] These children found themselves citizens of a country that assumed itself to be both homogeneously white and ethnically German, and one in which openly discussing racial difference among Germans was off-limits.[103]

Beyond religious, ethnic, and linguistic difference, the GDR also upheld a vision of the normative body under socialism that was at odds with the reality of a population that also had disabilities and injuries. Images of the strong and healthy family of workers and farmers were a staple of SED media and public art, reflecting a society where physical productive and reproductive capacity was an ideal. These norms celebrating healthy bodies partly explain the eventual support of nudist culture (and toleration of homosexuality) so long as it reinforced this aspect of state ideology. Efforts to redesign public spaces, public transit, and housing developments to allow for greater accessibility, including ramps for wheelchairs and other basic measures, were met with resistance on the grounds of cost and efficiency.[104] How to broadly accommodate those with disabilities also proved difficult. The ideal of integrating deaf East Germans, for example, into existing organizations and leisure activities designed for those who could hear conflicted with early demands from within the deaf community itself for separate, but still socialist, organizations, and events specifically designed around their needs. Fearing that deaf East Germans would become alienated and emigrate to the West or take refuge in the Church, the SED eventually relented and overcame its fears that such an organization could become politically unreliable due to its separatism.[105] Those who no longer fit the physical ideal of productivity due to old age had similar issues. The retired were practically encouraged to emigrate so that their pensions would be paid out by the Federal Republic. But not everyone left, so the SED was forced to find a place for an aging population that had ceased working within the socialist project. This problem was enhanced by the GDR's competition with the West, which made the social welfare of elderly workers a matter of comparative and competitive legitimacy.[106]

Protest and Opposition

Beyond complicated questions of personal identity, gender, and access to economic opportunities among others, the population of the GDR cannot—at any point in its history—be cleanly divided between conformists and dissidents. Most existed along a spectrum of support or opposition to the SED party line, which varied depending on the time, the place, and the subject matter at hand. There were those who were wholly dissatisfied with SED rule, but had no interest in openly defying the state; those—a small minority—who were willing to openly challenge it and risk the consequences; and many somewhere in between. Furthermore, among those most harshly punished for political dissent in East Germany, there were many who saw themselves as deeply committed to the socialist cause. Nonetheless, organized political opposition to displace the SED from power was virtually eliminated in the immediate aftermath of the 1953 Uprising (see Chapter 1), as street demonstrations were met with swift crackdowns by the security services. That being said, protest conducted according to specific terms—particularly in the form of petitions and letters of complaint—was legally and politically possible in the GDR.

There were some groups, mostly based in the West, who sought to undermine SED rule through various covert means, but they were never in a position to seize political power. The West German SPD maintained an Ost-Büro to gather information on the GDR and had an extensive intelligence network sustained by those who remained loyal to the SPD in spite of the merger with the KPD in the Soviet Zone in 1946. While it had no capacity to actively destabilize the SED, it did act as a convenient pretext for the SED's removal of politically inconvenient figures like Foreign Minister Georg Dertinger, a member of the CDU-Ost who was accused of conspiring with the SPD Ost-Büro after the 1953 Uprising. Among the few active resistance organizations were the Kampfgruppe gegen Unmenschlichkeit (KgU, Fighting Group against Inhumanity) and the Investigative Committee of Free Jurists (Untersuchungsausschuß Freiheitlicher Juristen, UfJ)—both based in West Berlin and supported by the American CIA. The KgU engaged in actions ranging from the distribution of fake postage stamps printed with anti-SED propaganda to plans for industrial sabotage and attacks on state infrastructure. Mostly made up of anti-Nazis and anti-communist liberals, it was infiltrated by the Stasi and ended operations—along with most CIA covert action programs fomenting active resistance in the GDR—in 1959.[107] The UfJ, by contrast, focused primarily on intelligence gathering and documenting human rights abuses in the East. Its head, Walter Linse, an ex-Nazi who had been tasked with Aryanizing property in the city of Chemnitz, was kidnapped by the Stasi in 1952 and delivered to the Soviets, who executed him in Moscow in 1953.[108]

The SED understood dissent among the Party elite and intelligentsia as an especially serious threat. In particular, long-time communists in the Party hierarchy who had fled the Nazis to the West were, upon their return, alienated by a Germany under the rule of a small clique of those who had survived exile in the Soviet Union.[109] After the 1956 anti-Soviet Hungarian Uprising, which originated from within the ruling party elite, SED leadership feared that counterrevolution could be brewing in its own ranks. A group of idealistic philosophers in the orbit of Wolfgang Harich set out to reform the GDR—with disastrous results. Harich was a committed communist who believed that East Germany along with the rest of the Eastern Bloc needed to embark on a path toward democratic socialism. He and a group of like-minded intellectuals drew up a plan to replace Walter Ulbricht and other key officials and implement free elections, freedom of expression, and the rule of law after a peaceful reunification with West Germany to form a new neutral state. After pitching his manifesto to key SED officials who rejected its publication, he leaked it to Western media, resulting in the arrest of Harich's entire circle. The crackdown on the intelligentsia that followed led to thousands fleeing the GDR. After a show trial on charges of counterrevolutionary conspiracy, Harich was sentenced to ten years in prison, most of which he spent in solitary confinement. Another member of the group, Walter Janka, had been jailed by the Nazis, fought in the Spanish Civil War, and then lived in exile in Mexico. He was charged with counterrevolutionary conspiracy and sentenced to ten years in prison, some of which he spent in Bautzen in the same facility where he had previously been imprisoned by the Nazis.[110]

In the 1950s, de-Stalinization and the ensuing consolidation of power under Walter Ulbricht led to an SED purge and attempts to re-educate hundreds of loyal, if idiosyncratic, intellectuals. Those who sought to grapple with the complications and contradictions of rule under real existing socialism found themselves accused of "ideological revisionism." Economic theorist Fritz Behrens was removed from his academic positions for proposing that moderating

Socialist Society and Its Discontents

central planning through market functions could be a solution to poor economic growth and the chronic overproduction of unpopular goods. In 1958, there was a purge of legal academics who had been recruited and trained under the socialist system and had gone on to suggest that the power of the Party could be constrained or limited by legal institutions. Several leading legal academics were removed from their posts and sent to serve as mayors of provincial villages, as a means of re-education. The philosopher Ernst Bloch was fired from the University of Leipzig and deemed a revisionist threat to the youth of the GDR because he questioned whether the socialist revolution had fully reconciled the interests of the individual and society. None of these men were closet liberals but rather sought a more humane socialism and predictable state system less dominated by the arbitrariness of Party leaders.[111]

The post-Stalin wave of socialist nonconformists was effectively suppressed by the end of the 1950s, but other disaffected intellectuals would follow, most prominently Robert Havemann. Imprisoned by the Nazis for his resistance activities, Havemann later became a professor of chemistry at Humboldt University in East Berlin and served as an SED representative in the Volkskammer. When he began to criticize the dogmatism of the party in 1963 however, he lost his professorship and was expelled from the SED. Like those before him, Havemann rejected the status quo of East German state socialism without endorsing Western liberal anti-communism. He sought to create a socialism with greater freedom of expression and political pluralism, even the creation of a socialist opposition party. Viewing the dictatorship of the SED as a transitional phase away from capitalism, he saw these freedoms as a means of pushing forward the revolution toward its ideal endpoint: full communism in which the state would wither away, as prophesized by Karl Marx. A marginal figure in the 1960s, Havemann would serve as an inspiration for the generation of cultural and intellectual dissenters to come.[112]

While the SED showed little tolerance for ideological deviation among party members and the intelligentsia, everyday complaints remained endemic. Daily interactions in the workplace were rife with conflict and negotiation, albeit asymmetrically; managers always held the implicit threat of state violence over the heads of their workers. For most regular citizens, there was only one functional mechanism for voicing complaints: the petition (*Eingabe*).[113] All East Germans could send in individual petitions to any official they pleased, be it a local party leader, the head of a regional company, or even Walter Ulbricht himself. So long as petitions were framed as constructive contributions to the development of socialism, they were accepted, if not necessarily acted upon.[114] Letters to GDR state institutions were sometimes hostile, but in practice, Party and state officials used the petition system as a means of gauging public opinion, supplementing reports from the bloc parties and mass organizations.[115] Petitions provided valuable data about what consumer products were unpopular and why, which organizations were not producing according to the demands of the central plan, and which officials were seen as inefficient or corrupt. Without market pricing mechanisms to indicate consumer preference, the petition system became an essential part of the informational structure of a modern centrally planned consumer economy.[116]

Protest did at times have some effect, particularly when it came with the added force of the Churches and Christian East Germans more widely. Plans to reform family law in 1954 met with such a massive upheaval from the population (amid rumors that the communist state intended to abolish marriage or allow polygamy) that the SED backed off of the project for more than a decade.[117] Unique among Warsaw Pact states, the SED created an option for conscientious objection after introducing universal male compulsory service (eighteen months) in the NVA in 1962. Responding to protests from the Churches, East Germans were given the choice to become a *Bausoldat* (construction soldier), living in barracks and performing uniformed, but unarmed service on arduous labor projects under military discipline. Conscientious objection came with long-term social consequences, marking citizens as dissidents and cutting them off from educational and employment opportunities.[118] The mobilization of Christians across the GDR as part of a referendum on the creation of a new socialist constitution in 1968 also bore some fruit. A mass consultation—the *Volksaussprache*—was organized in

Socialist Society and Its Discontents

anticipation of the vote, with thousands of petitions submitted to a state commission with comments on the contents of the constitution, a draft of which had been published in the national media. Hundreds of thousands of small meetings were held across the country during which party officials took questions and then responded, for the most part, with prepared talking points. Facing a curtailment of the constitutional right to religious freedom, the Catholic and Protestant Churches launched a massive letter-writing campaign. These petitions framed the issue carefully, arguing that the SED was about to exclude good Christians who wanted to be part of socialism but could not renounce their faith. As these protests coincided with the SED's campaign for international diplomatic recognition during the International Year for Human Rights, the constitutional commission agreed to add one more right protecting freedom of conscience in order to placate the protests and appear responsive to the people. Nonetheless, the addition was superficial, and did nothing to alter the everyday life of East German Christians.[119]

Repression and Surveillance

Over the course of the GDR's first decade, the SED developed several institutions for internal security and the repression of enemies of the state—or at least those perceived as enemies. The Volkspolizei (founded in 1949) handled everyday infractions, while the Stasi (founded in 1950, see Chapter 1) dealt with extraordinary crimes, policed the border, monitored economic activity, and cracked down on ideological deviance across society and the Party. A militia, the Combat Groups of the Working Class (Kampfgruppen der Arbeiterklasse, in 1953), and the NVA (in 1955) were also tasked with suppressing open revolt. But it would be a mistake to think of the GDR as a state ruled only by fear and the threat of violence. Over time, systems of control moved away from overt coercion for the vast majority of the population. In its place, the SED relied primarily on social pressure, incentive structures, and mass surveillance over direct violence. This interconnected system was not just the work of professional agents or informants but also encompassed widespread social denunciation. As such, the "Stasi was not above society but part of it."[120] Although the two organizations are not directly comparable, the Stasi was far larger than the Nazi-era Gestapo: at its peak, the East Germany agency had 91,000 employees, while in 1944, the Gestapo had only 31,000 personnel to cover the whole of the Nazi empire including the occupied territories.[121]

During the occupation, the Soviets were generally distrustful of allowing Germans to take control of internal security. The first security organization run by Germans in the Soviet Zone of Occupation was the Main Administration for the Protection of the Economy (Hauptverwaltung zum Schutze der Volkswirtschaft), founded in 1948 and focused on sabotage—the blanket term for almost all disruptions to production. Two years later, it evolved into the Ministry for State Security, increasing in size and responsibilities.[122] In early years, terror and mass arrests were used to round up suspected Nazis, war criminals, and opponents of the Soviet military occupation authority. But there was never a uniform persecution of all non-socialists, and these measures were matched by the creation of the bloc parties and tolerance for non-socialist institutions like the Churches. When the Soviets transferred control of the special camps—housing the remaining suspected Nazi criminals who had not yet been prosecuted—to the SED in 1950, it held mass trials with practically no procedural oversight, leading to an additional 4,092 convictions and 49 executions.[123] Even into the early years of the GDR, the SED continued to exercise the option of sending political enemies to the USSR to be executed (including as a means to discipline the bloc parties) or held in labor camps. Defectors from the Stasi to the West were regularly kidnapped in West Berlin and returned to the GDR to be executed on charges of treason. As in other Eastern Bloc states in the Stalinist era, the SED's ranks underwent purges, but these were less lethal and less thorough than their equivalents in Poland, Czechoslovakia, or Hungary.[124]

The mass arrests in connection with the building of the Berlin Wall in 1961 represented the last real wave of terror in the GDR, as methods evolved toward systems of social control, surveillance, and psychological disruption. By the late 1950s, the SED had introduced "conditional sentences" and "public censure" for criminal charges to move away from imprisonment as the primary tool of the judicial system. The police and the judiciary shifted to an educational tone of benevolent social correction.[125] The carrot and stick of state benefits and their potential revocation in response to dissenting behavior allowed the SED to reward compliance and punish deviance without the need for direct violence. Those who openly opposed socialism and the SED were obvious candidates for repression and surveillance, but many other factors could trigger the interest of the Stasi or its informants. Active church membership, personal or family connections to Nazis and members of the SS (Schutzstaffel, the Nazi paramilitary organization that ran the concentration camps and was responsible for numerous crimes against humanity including carrying out much of the Holocaust), contacts in the West, owning a telephone, nonconformist sexual habits or forms of dress and grooming (including hippie and punk subcultures), consuming foreign media, refusing to join mass organizations or take part in armed military service—all of these could raise red flags. Sometimes those whose politics were deemed vague or opaque were investigated since they could hypothetically pose a threat. Seemingly benign leisure activities like camping could be seen as connecting to nature in the socialist homeland or as an anti-social anarchic activity that represented political resistance through individual self-determination.[126] Those under surveillance for such minor issues may have had no idea anyone was taking a particular interest in them. For others, the Stasi used heavy-handed forms of surveillance to create an atmosphere of constant stress and psychological distress. There were also those who convinced themselves that they were under surveillance and self-censored or took countermeasures against being recorded even though the Stasi had no interest in them. As a result, there was a pervading sense that someone could always be watching and that the potential existed for more drastic surveillance with or without one's knowledge.

Stasi agents moved into positions in state agencies across the country to provide a source of intelligence on what was happening outside the open informational channels provided by local SED members and bloc party officials, who were also tasked with keeping tabs on public opinion. The Stasi thus functioned in tandem with the SED party apparatus, both serving and policing it. In the countryside, where the SED had difficulty effecting policy due to poor communication and sparse infrastructure, the Machine Tractor Stations (Maschinen-Traktoren-Stationen, MTS) that provided farmers with equipment, became a hub for Stasi intelligence gathering. In cities, the Soviets initially built on the existing Nazi surveillance system grounded in neighborhood associations by creating a network of "block and house leaders" who reported to the occupation authority. In the GDR, this developed into the "confidence man" (*Vertrauensmann*) system, where each building had a designated supervisor to keep tabs on tenants and maintain a "housebook" in which everyone reported all visitors to their homes.[127] The Stasi also developed a widespread network of informants: first referred to as "secret informants" and then after 1968 as "unofficial collaborators" (IMs), the Stasi drew on approximately 10,000 informants in the early 1950s, 100,000 IMs by 1968, and—after another large expansion of the Ministry for State Security—around 180,000 after 1975.[128] IMs were regularly recruited from within the cultural scene, as it was seen as a breeding ground for possible dissent.[129] Some IMs were recruited to spy on specific individuals or social milieus as part of an organized intelligence gathering operation. Most, however, were given little direction as to their targets or mission aside from a vague sense of defending the GDR from its enemies.[130] Among those who volunteered, the motivation for becoming a Stasi informant ranged from an idealistic sense of socialist patriotism to cynical efforts to instrumentalize the security services to their own ends. Others were blackmailed into participating or became IMs to avoid punishment after being denounced by others for some crime, real or imagined.

A range of specific crimes and offenses beyond the standard criminal code could bring down the wrath of the state. *Sabotage* was a particular fixation, especially in the early years, and was loosely interpreted to cover a diverse array of offenses that related in some way to economics; for political crimes, the key term was *Boykotthetze*. Taken from Article 6 of the GDR Constitution, this referred to

Socialist Society and Its Discontents

"agitation to boycott the democratic institutions and organizations" of East Germany. In practice, it was used to prosecute all forms of political dissent, including reform ideas from within the SED that offended party leadership. Within the Stasi itself, there were a number of abbreviations and special terms for behavior that was to be curtailed or surveilled. Hostile-negative (*feindlich-negative*) subjects were a concern, as was political-ideological diversion (*politisch-ideologische Diversion*), which could develop into political underground activity (*politische Untergrundtätigkeit*). Another key area of responsibility for the Stasi was the prevention of *Republikflucht*—flight from the Republic. If someone did successfully emigrate without permission, their family, friends, and coworkers would be interrogated to see if they had been given any warning or had assisted in any way.

In addition to punishment through imprisonment if one was convicted of a crime, there was the threat of investigative detention (*Untersuchungshaft*). There was no system of guaranteed *habeas corpus* where those placed under arrest had to be brought before a court, so detention without charge as part of an investigation was a standard tactic against both suspected criminals and dissenters. During their detention, individuals were subject to repeat interrogations while being held in total isolation, and often subjected to psychiatric medications as well as long periods of sleep deprivation and forced standing.[131] In the absence of guaranteed rights for defendants, individuals did not have access to independent legal counsel and arrests were not subject to independent judicial review. Prisoners, including those convicted of political crimes, could be put to work as a form of punishment. Given the widespread shortage of workers, the SED was loath to let anyone sit idle. Conditions at prison camps were usually not significantly worse than in the outside world and nothing like the Nazi forced labor programs that worked prisoners to death.[132] However, it remained a scandal in 2012 when it was revealed that the Swedish furniture giant IKEA contracted with factories in the GDR worked by political prisoners in the 1980s. Those who were placed in either investigative detention or in prison for political crimes or as "asocials" could have their children taken away from them and adopted by a family that was considered politically reliable.[133]

Adults were the main focus of the Stasi and the mass surveillance system, but young people were also closely watched by teachers, state officials, and within the Thälmann Pioneers and the Free German Youth for signs of deviance. Schools were understood as centers for the raising of the next generation of socialist citizens and one of the primary institutions of social engineering.[134] Children were both idealized as the future of the socialist project and feared as dangerous, chaotic, and corruptible.[135] In the immediate postwar years, these fears stemmed from the proliferation of youth gangs—often just collections of orphaned children trying to survive deprivation in the ruins of the Third Reich. At the 1950 trial of Werner Gladow, the leader of a youth gang who was convicted on several counts of murder and robbery, the defendant was portrayed as the symptom of the corrupting power of American culture, and prosecutors demanded the death penalty by guillotine to demonstrate that "Berlin is not Chicago."[136] Cases of multiple murderers like Gladow were rare, although fears of more commonplace youth deviance and defiance of state authority led to the creation of a network of "special homes" (*Spezialheime*) for young people who were deemed "difficult to educate" where they were subjected to military-style disciplinary practices, as well as routine physical abuse. The most extreme option was a closed work camp (*Jugendwerkhof*) such as Torgau, where young people were drilled with relentless work projects and extreme forced physical training.[137] Around half a million young East Germans spent time in a special home or work camp between 1949 and 1990.

Overall, the Stasi and the repressive elements of the East German security apparatus were essential for the SED to secure power and police ideological nonconformity—but they were not omniscient. Official paranoia could generate threats from completely mundane behavior, and industrial accidents were often transformed into "economic sabotage." Informants allowed the Stasi to infiltrate and disrupt groups with possible "counterrevolutionary" tendencies, but most IM reports were filled with trivia that violated the privacy of colleagues, friends, and family, while contributing little or nothing to the actual security of the state. On a social level, however, it created an atmosphere of fear and distrust. The full extent of the IM networks in the GDR was not known until after the fall of the Wall but the widespread existence of informants and social surveillance was a known fact of life. For most East Germans, the Stasi existed as a hypothetical problem, however, rather than an actual presence in the day-to-day. In general, "in the post-Stalinist period, it became possible for individuals to lead lives relatively distanced from the regime and its instruments of repression as long as they learned to consciously or unconsciously accept their place and the limits of their agency."[138]

Socialist Society and Its Discontents

By the mid-1960s, the SED had created a society that was thoroughly dominated by state- and Party-led institutions and organizations. But that was not enough to realize a totalitarian state where the population obeyed orders without question or ceased to think for themselves. While the East German party state was able to create a powerful system of incentives and punishments to direct GDR citizens toward specific goals—economic productivity, ideological orthodoxy, social norms of gender, sexuality, and spirituality—it also allowed for limited spaces of pluralism, even as it used the coercive power of the state to apply pressure on those who occupied them. East Germans also took advantage of all the tools available to them to complain and protest against the demands of the state, while also being conscious of the limitation of how far they could push such dissent. Although it was possible not to conform to the norms of the state, such a refusal resulted in a difficult and lonely existence, pushed to the margins of society, and cut off from state institutions and social organizations that provided for everyday wants and needs.

The lives of individual East Germans under these conditions varied greatly; there was no singular experience of everyday life in the GDR. There were those who took part in the rituals of socialist life as a pragmatic means of belonging to society, advancing in their careers and gaining various social, cultural, and material benefits, without having strong feelings toward the ideology to which they formally adhered. For others, life in East Germany was unbearably oppressive, relentlessly politicized, and extremely alienating through its devotion to an ideology that often clashed with lived reality. In response, some sought to risk everything to escape, while others retreated to social niches and understood their daily existence as a political performance for the sake of getting by. There were also those who thrived under the structure of the socialist state, finding purpose in the visions of antifascism propagated by the SED and the drive to rebuild Germany in the wake of the Third Reich. For a minority, the GDR provided a genuine sense of mission. Many facets of East German society contained contradictory elements that have often produced conflicting memories of the state that have persisted to the present day. Some persecuted by the Nazis found the GDR to be a safe haven after years of terror, while others found themselves imprisoned by both regimes. Accepting the diverse reactions of East Germans toward the demands of the state does not diminish its dictatorial character, but at the same time, the fact that the GDR was a dictatorship did not always mean constant terror and tyranny to those who lived through it.

CHAPTER 3
EAST GERMANY AND THE WORLD

The German Democratic Republic (GDR) is often understood in terms of its isolation from the world, alone behind the concrete and barbed wire of its border wall to the West. The GDR had few friends beyond its "fraternal socialist" neighbors when it emerged from the Soviet Zone of Occupation in 1949; the Federal Republic of Germany (FRG) had imposed a diplomatic blockade by threatening to cut trade and aid to any state that recognized the GDR. But East Germany as a state and society was always intrinsically connected to the world beyond its borders—through its relationship to West Germany, as part of the Eastern Bloc, and through the GDR's connections to the Global South via diplomacy, trade, and migration. Unlike other socialist countries in Europe, the GDR had a direct point of comparison to judge the results of its development against that of a capitalist rival. There was no West Poland or West Hungary against which to directly evaluate the economic outcomes or political rights of the original. At the same time, the GDR owed its existence to its position as a "frontline" state in the Cold War, and its political fate was tied up with the other "socialist fraternal states" of the Eastern Bloc. The SED (Socialist Unity Party) also put great stock in courting the newly decolonized states of the Global South and providing aid to fellow socialists and national liberation movements. These efforts went beyond high-level diplomacy to include mass mobilization at home. The SED sought to legitimize itself through its support for international causes—from the Vietnam War, and the anti-apartheid movement in Southern Africa, to the resistance to right-wing authoritarian regimes in Latin America—which made global politics part of everyday life for East Germans. Finally, the economy of the GDR was inextricably tied up in global commodities markets, and its need to purchase goods in the global marketplace forced the SED to take out huge loans from banks in the capitalist world.

Division and Interconnection between the Two Germanies

The division of Germany, and of Europe more broadly, was an ongoing process, not only a single event in 1949 that founded the two German states. The new boundary lines cut through long-standing communities, whose economic, social, and family links were not immediately erased by the establishment of two German states. Moreover, a clean break was not desired by the FRG, which claimed to be the sole legitimate German state and claimed sovereignty over the GDR's territory and its population.[1] Not to be forgotten, at the center of the GDR was the greatest barrier to disentangling West from East Germany: the city of Berlin, which remained under four-power occupation by the United States, the United Kingdom, France, and the USSR. The policies of the SED and the experiences of the people of the GDR were understood in direct comparison to those of the Federal Republic, both by contemporaries and in historical analysis. Both states also actively intervened in the affairs of their opposite: West Germany (and the United States) sponsored resistance groups operating in East Germany, and Western NGOs highlighted human rights violations against would-be emigrants and political prisoners. In the early years, the Stasi conducted kidnappings in West Berlin, and in later decades provided funds to both the peace movement and neo-Nazis in the Federal Republic.[2] In this way, the history of the GDR's existence can never truly be separated from that of the FRG.[3] Beyond that, their interconnections were also physical and material, as people and goods continued to flow between the two countries, and the more the SED sought to seal itself off from the West, the more people on the ground organized to maintain contact.[4]

At first, the long and mostly rural border along the length of the two German states allowed for significant unauthorized traffic across the boundary outside of formal border checkpoints. By 1952, the SED had decided to further demarcate and secure the German-

German border to remake the landscape into a more permanent physical boundary, launching Operation Vermin along the length of the border zone: homes were demolished, and forests were cleared so that patrol paths and kill-zones could be created along the length of the frontier. The Stasi also politically vetted all those living close to the border with the West and forcibly relocated anyone suspected of the intention to defect or cause problems for border enforcement. Farms were cut apart, as were many communities, such as the twin town of Sonneberg and Neustadt bei Coburg, which had been linked by a river and was now divided by an international border, or the village of Mödlareuth, which was sliced in two, with the Western side in Bavaria and the Eastern side in Thuringia.[5] The border regime was imposed not just from above but also from below as locals negotiated with agents of the state over how to make these spaces both secure and still economically functional. Division was not just an international political project but also a local one, as distinct communities were being created on both sides of the border that diverged from one another through their daily practices.

The construction of the Berlin Wall in 1961 proved to be the most difficult task, because of its location deep inside the GDR and its continued legal status as a city under four-power occupation. All phone lines between West Berlin and East Germany were severed to isolate the city; water and sewage tunnels were barred to stop human traffic, but could not be sealed entirely for practical reasons. Public transit was more problematic, as some lines cut across the new border between East and West. Stations passing through the GDR were closed and armed guards stationed on the platforms to prevent East Germans from trying to hitch a ride on a passing train. After one of the guards in the tunnels escaped to the West while on duty, the stations were also walled up. The division of public enterprises created bizarre situations, such as the status of the S-Bahn rail system, which was owned by the Soviets, who claimed it as part of the Nazi Reichsbahn rail network (which they had seized) only to gift it back to the GDR. As a result, East Berlin authorities were responsible for the operations and maintenance of a train network that also operated across West Berlin. The borders of West Berlin were particularly chaotic, since

Figure 3.1 Ariel view of the still visible death strip at the former border between two Germanies, Rhön Mountains, 2016. Aldo Pavan.

the city had authority over a handful of tiny exclaves, home to a few hundred people, that now lay in the Brandenburg countryside in what was GDR territory, only accessible by roads through a foreign country or by helicopter. While the East German People's Police (Volkspolizei) tried to occupy the largest of these exclaves, Steinstücken, to force its annexation, they were forced to back off in the face of American protests. A series of land swaps to eliminate certain exclaves and to provide permanent walled road connections to others finally resolved the issue in 1972.

Controlling all forms of mobility between East and West, however, was impossible. At least 40,000 East Germans managed to illegally emigrate after the building of the Berlin Wall—some through elaborate escapes, including multiple efforts to tunnel underground to West Berlin. Stasi informants often disrupted these plans, and confrontations between border guards and escape helpers ended in casualties on both sides. One of the most famous examples was Tunnel 57, dug by West Berlin volunteers between April and October 1964, which opened into the basement of an apartment building in East Berlin. The project was cofinanced by the editor of the West German magazine *Stern*, who purchased the exclusive rights to the story. While over one hundred East Germans had hoped to use the tunnel to cross the border, only fifty-seven made it through before they were interrupted by border guards and the Stasi.[6]

But the German-German border also had to be managed for other reasons. In addition to human activity, there was also the problem of natural forces, which had little interest in respecting the border. Wind patterns moved East, while the Elbe and the Werra rivers ran West, meaning that pollution from either country was a problem for the other, requiring bureaucratic coordination for systems of compensation.[7] Trade also continued. For the GDR, maintaining economic ties with the West was a matter of practicality and survival. Many businesses in the East had long-standing relationships to firms in the West, and exports were vital to bringing in hard currency. Even though West Germany took part in a Western embargo on the export of high technology to the Eastern Bloc, the GDR economy was dependent on the Federal Republic as a source for key goods in the fields of machinery, chemicals, and metals. For officials in Bonn, maintaining trade with the GDR was seen as a necessary precursor to realizing reunification. In 1951, the Berlin Agreement between the FRG and the GDR created an arrangement for international payments between the two countries, with West Germany offering "swing credits" to facilitate trade—a financial system that allowed the GDR to maintain regular trade imbalances and to clear its debts periodically in large amounts when the funds were available. The West German Trust for Intra-Zonal Trade handled the day-to-day instead of the Ministry for International Trade since Bonn refused to grant the necessary administrative recognition to East Germany.[8] This logic was extended when West Germany joined the European Economic Community, the predecessor to the European Union. Bonn successfully negotiated a provision that inter-German trade was considered "non-foreign" and thus not subject to the tariffs and duties that applied to all other imports.[9]

The entangled relationship between East and West was also a matter of competing identities. For West Germany, this meant portraying itself as a Western state grounded in the values of parliamentary democracy and the social market economy—in contrast to the GDR, an illegitimate Communist dictatorship. West German elites believed they needed to create a "defensive democracy," to avoid a repeat of the collapse of the Weimar Republic, and organizations deemed a threat to the democratic constitutional order could be banned. This occurred first with a ban on the neo-Nazi Socialist Reich Party in 1952 and then the Communist Party of Germany (KPD) in 1956. The West German KPD and all affiliated organizations, like the Free German Youth (FDJ), were banned and thousands were arrested and jailed for continued participation in groups viewed as fronts for SED subversion in the FRG.[10] East German communism was positioned not just as a rival but as a threatening antithesis to West German democracy.

In the GDR, the SED promoted a new identity for its people based on the shared values of antifascism, state socialism, and the centrality of the alliance with the Soviet Union. These abstract concepts were often inscribed onto physical spaces: Communist martyrs and socialist heroes of the past replaced the names of Nazi and Imperial era luminaries on public squares. Workplaces were similarly rebranded after communist figures like a textile plant named after Clara Zetkin—a German communist feminist icon who had died in Soviet exile and was buried in the wall of the Kremlin near Lenin's Tomb—or a chemical tube factory named after Friedrich Engels, the revolutionary philosopher and intellectual collaborator of Karl Marx.[11] In East Berlin, the construction of Stalinallee (later renamed Karl-Marx-Allee), complete with a statue of the Soviet leader himself, began in 1949 as a grand boulevard lined with apartment buildings clad in fine Meißen porcelain tiles, which was to provide a space for military parades and major events. In the center of the city, the Prussian-era Stadtschloss (City Palace), heavily damaged in the war, was demolished and an equestrian statue of Kaiser Wilhelm removed. They were replaced by the Palace of the Republic (Palast der Republik), which housed the Volkskammer as well as several high-end restaurants, a disco, and a bowling alley. Today, the City Palace is back—reconstructed in 2020, after the Palast der Republik was itself torn down (its steel was recycled and used to build the Burj Khalifa skyscraper in Dubai).[12] Near the border with Poland, the first planned socialist city of Eisenhüttenstadt (renamed Stalinstadt between 1953 and 1961) was built to provide housing for a massive steelwork modeled on the Soviet Magnitogorsk. In the south, the city of Chemnitz was renamed Karl-Marx-Stadt in honor of the seventieth anniversary of the philosopher's death in 1953 (and then Chemnitz again in 1990 after a referendum). The enormous monument of the philosopher's head installed in 1971 still stands in the center of town.

Figure 3.2 Karl Marx monument in Chemnitz, 2023. Photo courtesy of the author.

The German Democratic Republic

Just as West Germany contrasted its democracy against the dictatorship of the GDR, the SED sought to highlight its own virtues against the sins of the Federal Republic. The SED consciously constructed and portrayed East German social advancements against the negative example of the West. Propaganda chief Albert Norden, in particular, sought to use the specter of resurgent fascism in West Germany to demonstrate the righteousness of the SED to East Germans and to win over Western Social Democrats to the side of the GDR.[13] In response to the banning of the KPD, the SED created numerous ad hoc committees to mobilize East Germans to campaign for the freedom of specific prisoners, and in 1959, it created the Committee for the Protection of Human Rights to fight for the release of political prisoners in the West. These campaigns highlighted the renewed imprisonment of communists (who had previously been jailed by the Nazis) as evidence of the ideological continuity between the Third Reich and the Federal Republic under Chancellor Konrad Adenauer.[14] When the Berlin Wall was constructed in 1961, the SED named it the "anti-fascist defense rampart" and claimed that it was a necessary defensive measure to protect the GDR. To add weight to these accusations, Norden published the *Brown Book*, documenting the ongoing participation of Nazi Party members in positions of power and social prominence in West Germany. The SED held show trials (in absentia) for Adenauer's chief of staff Hans Globke, who had been a key legal bureaucrat in the Nazi regime, and Minister for Expellees Theodor Oberländer, for his role in the 1941 Lviv Massacre. This propaganda was politically damaging to the individuals targeted but failed to convince average West Germans to see the GDR as the better Germany.[15]

In the 1970s, under SED leader Erich Honecker, focus shifted from portraying the GDR as superior to the West to reimaging East Germany as a separate nation as part of a policy of *Abgrenzung* (demarcation) — of truly separating East Germany and the Federal Republic. This process was initiated in the late 1960s with the collapse of the last joint-German institutions in law, sports, and religion. For the first time since 1949, the GDR introduced formal rules on citizenship.[16] Honecker told the Central Committee that division was no longer a temporary condition but a permanent reality: "The GDR is not part of the FRG, and the FRG is not part of the GDR."[17] The quest for a separate East German identity now extended to the total rejection of the earlier rhetoric on reunification. In 1974, Honecker altered the text of the constitution to remove all references to reunification as a goal. On a cultural level, demarcation sought to wall the GDR off from "everything harmful that is meant to be smuggled into our country—narcotics and ideological perversions, pot and heroin, nationalistic reaction and social-democratism!"[18] Relations would improve between the two states during Détente, as Cold War tensions lessened, but on the terms of separate national groups reaching a peaceful coexistence.[19]

For most East Germans, however, there was little internalization of a newfound national spirit proud of the GDR as a socialist state under the SED. As purely ideological messaging found little purchase, the SED tended toward appeals to local patriotism, a sense of connection to community, and the fostering of an ideal "socialist home" (Heimat). As a result, the self-identification of many East Germans moved from the level of the state to that of their local community, which provided stability, but ultimately proved too weak a foundation for loyalty to the socialist system when it came under increased strain in the 1980s.[20] This problem of whether the GDR was a separate nation would ultimately also come to define the lines of division among dissidents: Was the purpose of the opposition to improve the GDR—or end it and reunite the German nation under the banner of one state?

East Germany in the Socialist World

The integration of East Germany into the Soviet Bloc was as complex as the SED's efforts to separate it from the West. The GDR was founded as an extension of Soviet foreign policy, and the ruling SED was politically dependent on the USSR as sponsor and occupier. From the beginning, the GDR-Soviet relationship was strained by both the legacy of the Nazi's genocidal war and the mass rapes conducted by the occupying Red Army as well as the Soviet dismantling and reparations program, which nearly destroyed the East German economy before it really began. In 1953, a popular uprising against the SED had been put down by Soviet tanks, and the subsequent invasion of Hungary during its incipient democratic revolution in 1956 confirmed that Moscow would not allow its Eastern European allies to abolish socialism at home. East German elites were able to operate with independent initiative on the international stage, but only within the limits set by Soviet foreign policy.[21] While the occupation of the GDR formally ended in 1955, the two countries signed an agreement authorizing the permanent stationing of Soviet forces in East Germany. In the following year, the GDR joined the Warsaw Pact military alliance—the USSR-led counterpart to NATO in Eastern Europe—so Soviet forces maintained a massive presence on East German soil, which only ended in 1994.[22] The "socialist constitution of the GDR"—promulgated in 1968—formally committed the country to the "comprehensive cooperation and friendship with the USSR and the other socialist states," in perpetuity. The oft-repeated SED slogan "to learn from the Soviets is to learn how to win!" was made into a defining legal principle of the state.

The GDR's economic relationship to the USSR and the rest of the Eastern Bloc was one of strategic dependence.[23] East Germany needed raw goods to fuel its industrialized economy, particularly cheap oil and grain from the Soviet Union. In return, it provided finished goods for the rest of the socialist market via the Council for Mutual Economic Assistance (CMEA)—a more expansive economic counterpart to the Warsaw Pact. Since Eastern Bloc states used soft currencies internally that were of little value for international trade, exchanges within the CMEA were based on the equal value of goods, not cash. The integration of East Germany into the Soviet-led alliance of socialist states in Eastern Europe was, however, marked by distrust.[24] Many of the "socialist fraternal states" had been occupied by the Nazis and had recently deported their ethnic German population. The GDR normalized relations with Poland in 1950 and affirmed the Oder-Neisse river line as the new boundary between the two countries and Poland's annexation of former German territories east of that line (to the protest of West Germany). Poland and Czechoslovakia remained wary of the GDR due to the atrocities committed by the Nazis, but also because authorities feared that expelled Germans would attempt to reclaim their lost land and property.[25] The new border between the two countries was closely policed with regular clashes over issues from cross-border shopping to the use of fishing spots and offshore drilling rights.[26] The equality of the fraternal states was also undermined by the GDR's greater relative wealth, which allowed it to import "contract workers" from Poland, Hungary, and Cuba beginning in 1965 to fill the manpower shortage caused by mass emigration.[27]

To overcome this latent distrust, the Soviets engaged in pan-Eastern Bloc initiatives to demonstrate the cooperation and comity of the fraternal socialist states of Eastern Europe. One project involved the collective construction of the Friendship Pipeline, completed in 1963, which shipped oil from Kuibyshev in the USSR to East German refineries in Schwedt and Leuna, as well as to Bratislava and Budapest. Another was the Soviet Interkosmos program, which sent cosmonauts from socialist and other friendly nations to outer space—including the first German in space, Sigmund Jähn, who flew on Soyuz 31 in 1978.[28] Everyday contacts also created new spaces for positive exchange on an individual level. Many East German metal workers had fond memories of working on the pipeline with comrades from across the Soviet Bloc. Cross-border informal trade (sometimes illicit) also helped bring together East Germans with their Polish neighbors, while cross-border shopping at times aggravated relations in border communities with East Germans complaining that foreigners had emptied their stores of particular goods that were already in short supply.[29] State-sponsored cultural exchange programs among socialist states were created in the early years to encourage a sense of shared socialist fraternity, but East German officials began to sour on the project over time, as they feared ideological deviation in fellow socialist states could infect the intelligentsia in the GDR.[30] Tourism within the Eastern Bloc was also popular (especially since travel to the West was not possible for many). When visa-free travel became possible to most of the Eastern Bloc in 1972, many jumped at the opportunity to take a road trip and go camping in Czechoslovakia, Hungary, Poland, and Romania.[31] The Bulgarian Black Sea coast served as the East German alternative to a beach vacation on the Spanish island of Mallorca, which had become the emblematic destination for the middle-class West German.³² Most popular, though not most accessible, were the Free German Trade Union Federation (FDGB)-operated cruise trips to Cuba. The Caribbean island was a non-Warsaw Pact country, but still a fellow socialist state, which was exoticized in the GDR as a land of revolutionary hedonism with its many sunny beaches. The on-board voyage featured bingo, dancing, political lectures, and plentiful Cuba Libres made from Cuban rum and the East German Coca-Cola replacement Vita-Cola.³³

Although the Warsaw Pact was formally a defensive alliance, its only deployments were to invade member-states in order to forestall anti-socialist revolutions. The crushing of the Prague Spring in 1968 put the GDR constitutional provision for the "close brotherhood of

Figure 3.3 GDR cosmonaut Sigmund Jähn (right) with Soviet cosmonaut Valery Bykovsky (left) at their landing site near Zhezkazgan, USSR, with the capsule of Soyuz 31, September 3, 1978. ullstein bild, Germany.

arms with the armies of the Soviet Union and other socialist states" to the test. Czechoslovakian leader Alexander Dubček had initiated a program of liberalization under the slogan "socialism with a human face," which had elicited great concern among party elites in both Moscow and East Berlin and prompted Ulbricht to personally entreat Dubček to reconsider. When the latter refused to back down, Soviet leader Leonid Brezhnev assembled Warsaw Pact forces to undo the "counterrevolution." While the GDR's National People's Army was prepared to take part in the intervention, it was ordered to stand down by Moscow in order to avoid the catastrophic optics of another German attack on Czechoslovakia so soon after the Nazi occupation. The invasion by hundreds of thousands of Warsaw Pact troops from the USSR, Poland, Hungary, and Bulgaria on August 21 resulted in the deaths of 137 Czechoslovakians and Dubček's removal from power. The so-called "Brezhnev Doctrine" made it clear that Moscow would not abide a counterrevolutionary state within the sphere of the Warsaw Pact. It also showed that the SED was a willing enforcer of Soviet domination across the region—in contrast to Romanian leader Nicolae Ceaușescu, who refused to take part in the invasion. Until the bitter end, the SED elite remained among the most committed opponents of liberalization in the Eastern Bloc.[34]

The GDR was also caught up in the international ideological conflicts within the larger communist world, particularly the split between Beijing and Moscow. The People's Republic of China (PRC) had been founded in the same month as the GDR, and relations were initially positive. SED officials saw the PRC as both a potential market for East German industrial goods and a source of raw materials, and Chinese officials saw the GDR as a technologically advanced partner that could help with modernization.[35] The PRC also used the GDR to showcase its socialist bona fides by sending massive pavilions to the Leipzig Trade Fair to demonstrate that they were the equals of their European counterparts.[36] Yet, even before the Sino-Soviet split, tensions had already emerged in the 1950s: East German experts sent to China were resented for their better living conditions as foreign visitors, and in turn, the East Germans saw China's rapid technological advance as a threat rather than a boon to the global socialist project.[37]

The German Democratic Republic

De-Stalinization created a further wedge between the Eastern Bloc and the PRC, which under Mao Zedong sought to claim the leadership of the global socialist project from the "revisionists" in Moscow, who, he believed, had betrayed the revolution. Within the GDR, Maoist agitators began to propagandize against the Soviet line, and the Stasi found itself fighting against ideological infiltration from both the capitalist West and the socialist East.[38]

Decolonization Diplomacy

In the 1950s, the GDR was a lonely country. Recognized as an independent state only by its Eastern European socialist allies, North Korea and the PRC, East Germany was largely shut out of the international community. Neither German state was a member of the United Nations, but the Federal Republic was often able to secure observer status at the UN's associated organizations, including UNESCO, the World Health Organization, and the International Labour Organization. The West German Hallstein Doctrine (named after Walter Hallstein, the FRG's State Secretary of the Federal Foreign Ministry) threatened to cut diplomatic ties as well as aid and trade to any country that established relations with East Germany. This was by no means an empty threat: although Yugoslavia had broken from the Soviet Bloc, relations had improved after Stalin's death and Tito recognized the GDR in 1957. In retaliation, the Federal Republic severed its own diplomatic ties with Yugoslavia.

During this period, the conflict between the United States and the Soviet Union intersected with decolonization in Africa and Asia, making the Cold War go global.[39] In addition to military conflicts in Korea and Vietnam, the independence of so many countries that had been part of the British, French, Dutch, and Belgian empires presented the superpowers with an opportunity to demonstrate the superiority of their system through development aid. This was replicated between the two German states: West Germany sought to establish its global political and economic clout and step out of the shadow of the Third Reich, while the GDR hoped to use the moment to break out of its diplomatic isolation. Lacking West Germany's financial means (an essential consideration for most postcolonial states seeking to rapidly modernize), the SED appealed to shared anti-imperial values in its attempt to convince the decolonizing world to take their side against the FRG.[40] West German offers of economic development aid were met by competing East German offers of anti-imperialist solidarity—in the form of technology, expertise, and ideological guidance.[41]

East Germany's international outreach was initially concentrated on the Middle East, where British influence over its protectorates was beginning to wane. The SED believed the Arab states were the easiest potential allies to be tempted away from working with West Germany. While formally nonaligned in the Cold War, Arab nationalism was on the rise across the region, and, with it, a strong anti-imperial sentiment directed toward the West. The SED also sought to exploit the conflict with Israel: the two Germanies split on policy toward Israel, with West Germany (which claimed to be the legal successor state to the Third Reich) seeking international rehabilitation for the crimes of the Nazis through a package of reparations directed at the newly founded state.[42] In 1952, four years after Israel's founding, it made a payment of three billion Marks, which was meant to compensate survivors and cover the costs of Jewish refugees from Europe. By contrast, the SED followed the Soviet line that Zionism represented an extension of Western imperialism and backed the Palestinians and neighboring Arab states in their conflict against Israel. As an antifascist state that did not have any official legal continuity with the Third Reich, the SED also argued that it carried no responsibility for the Holocaust and thus no obligation to make reparations.[43]

Yet this ideological alignment was not enough to convince Arab states to recognize the GDR and risk losing access to West German trade and aid. Since many international forums were closed to the GDR, the SED sent Prime Minister Otto Grotewohl personally on a tour of the region, and delegations traveled to trade shows and industrial exhibitions to show off East German technical prowess and values.[44] In 1953, the GDR managed to establish a trade agreement with Egypt—one year after the revolution that brought Arab nationalist leader Gamal Abdel Nasser to power. Yet the Egyptians made sure this stopped short of actual diplomatic recognition in order to preserve relations with the FRG. Just as Nasser would later play the United States against the Soviets over assistance for his ambitious Aswan High Dam development project, the GDR provided a useful foil in negotiations with West Germany.

The SED subsequently shifted focus to sub-Saharan Africa as more countries began to gain independence. In 1960 alone, seventeen countries in Africa gained independence, and their new leaders, often emerging directly from their country's anticolonial movements, looked beyond their former imperial rulers for development aid. But as with Egypt, what exactly constituted "diplomatic recognition" versus open trade and maintaining friendly relations was a gray area. In 1958, Guinea under Ahmed Sékou Touré declared unilateral independence from France and signaled that it would sign a trade agreement with the GDR. But Bonn quickly dispatched one of its top officials to Guinea, threatening to cut ties and withhold generous development aid; in response, Guinea quickly backed away from diplomatic recognition.[45] The GDR had somewhat better luck when the island of Zanzibar declared independence from the UK and it became the first African country to recognize the GDR. The SED responded by sending large numbers of experts to aid with development and construction projects.[46] However, only months later, Zanzibar merged with Tanganyika, which did not recognize the GDR, to form Tanzania. Under Julius Nyerere, Tanzania embraced African socialism, but remained nonaligned in the Cold War, working with all sides for the sake of improved aid and trade conditions. East German experts and advisers remained influential on Zanzibar, but Nyerere only allowed the construction of a consulate (and not an embassy) in Dar es Salaam. This partial transgression of the Hallstein Doctrine resulted in Bonn cutting off military assistance and refusing to negotiate future aid deals. Despite this minor victory, the SED struggled for influence against competing Chinese solidarity programs and Western aid agencies, all of which were able to considerably outspend the GDR.[47]

Since the SED's attempts at bilateral diplomacy had failed to realize diplomatic recognition across the decolonizing world, Ulbricht turned to directly courting the United Nations instead. In 1966, the GDR formally applied to UN Secretary General U Thant to join the body as an independent country. Yet, all admissions had to be approved by the UN Security Council, which included the Soviet Union—but also the United States, France, and the United Kingdom as permanent members with veto power. The Western powers rejected the admission of the GDR without some kind of equivalent arrangement for the FRG, and the Soviets did not even bother to bring the question to a vote judging it a foolish and doomed initiative. Not a single country in the UN General Assembly saw fit to publicly support it. The issue of German membership was not a case in isolation, but one that had implications for other divided countries at the UN, especially the question whether the PRC or Taiwan had the right to sit as a permanent member of the Security Council representing the nation of China.[48]

The quest for recognition was more than just a high-level diplomatic game, but deeply intertwined with domestic developments in the GDR. This most visible example of the SED merging domestic and global politics was the creation of a new constitution in 1968. The original GDR constitution had been largely modeled on the Weimar constitution and resembled the text of a liberal parliamentary democracy. The new "socialist constitution of the GDR" was meant both to mark the completion of the "construction of socialism," which had been announced by Walter Ulbricht in 1952, and to commemorate the realization of a "socialist people's community," as part of the march through the stages of Marxist historical development on the path to full communism. The first article of the new constitution now affirmed the GDR as "the political organization of the working population in town and country, who are jointly realizing socialism under the leadership of the working class and its Marxist-Leninist party," namely the Socialist Unity Party. To demonstrate that the new constitutional order—and the leading role of the SED—had popular support, a draft of the constitution was publicized so that the citizens of the GDR could offer feedback during a mass consultation, followed by a referendum in order to give it the official approval of the people.

Having failed in his first, direct, application to the UN, Ulbricht now sought to weave together the domestic constitutional reform process with an appeal to the international community: the SED promoted the new constitution and the referendum on its adoption as the GDR's contribution to the United Nations' commemorative "Year for Human Rights," which had been instigated by Jamaica. The SED pledged to sign the UN's human rights covenants (once it was made a member of the organization and was eligible to do so) and held up the adoption of a new "socialist constitution of the GDR" via a popular referendum as clear evidence of East Germany's compliance with international law and its readiness to join the international community as an equal. The referendum ultimately passed with 94.5 percent in favor—a low result for an East German popular vote, which usually produced numbers above 99 percent through the social engineering that made citizens seeking to vote against do so publicly by placing their ballot in a specifically designated urn. The symbolic victory of the SED at home, however, had no real impact abroad, where material and geopolitical considerations trumped ideological theater.[49] Despite its many disparate initiatives, the SED did not have the political influence or economic power necessary to break out of its diplomatic isolation alone.

Figure 3.4 Free German Youth mass rally at the Leipzig Staatsoper in support of the socialist constitution on the day before the referendum on its adoption, April 5, 1968. Günter Weiß, ADN.

Everyday Internationalism and Cross-Border Migration

International affairs were part of the everyday life of East Germans—even for those who had not actually met someone from a foreign country before. State media in the GDR regularly broadcast international news stories, including the triumphs of various socialist movements around the world. While most East Germans could not travel to the West, they did get a daily barrage of stories about its failings—from the political oppression of the left to the racist treatment of its citizens and the epidemic of drug abuse among young people. More directly, East Germans could take part in global politics through solidarity activism, without ever leaving their workplace. Foreigners also came to the GDR, as tourists and students, but also as refugees fleeing political persecution and as guest workers from socialist states in the Eastern Bloc and the Global South.

State-sponsored solidarity campaigns were a ubiquitous part of life in the GDR.[50] The FDGB organized solidarity drives where workers were asked to make voluntary donations to support allied movements around the world.[51] Postage stamps often included a solidarity donation—an additional amount added to the cost that would be donated to various causes. The earliest major campaigns were in aid of Greek communists and the reconstruction of North Korea; later campaigns focused on other world events like the liberation of Vietnam or the fight against apartheid in South Africa.[52] Children's magazines asked their readers for small donations to international causes from postrevolutionary Angola to socialist Chile.[53] The truly enthusiastic could join a solidarity committee: the Afro-Asian Solidarity Committee was founded in 1960, and related organizations proliferated to support more specific causes—the plight of Palestinian refugees, the struggle for Vietnamese liberation, justice for the torture victims of the Greek military Junta, the fight for the Nicaraguan revolution. After Augusto Pinochet's coup brought down the socialist government of Salvador Allende in 1973, East Germans took part in mass campaigns to pressure the Chilean military Junta to free Luis Corvalán, the imprisoned head of the Chilean Communist Party. Nelson Mandela and the struggle of the African National Congress

(ANC) in South Africa were also a popular cause for decades, remaining a potent source of mobilization in the GDR after citizens in other Eastern Bloc countries had lost interest.[54] East German state and party organs also tried to maintain contacts with sympathetic or ideologically allied groups in the West.[55] The civil rights movement in the United States was of great interest, as it represented the "other America," the one on the *right* side of history. The campaign to free imprisoned African American communist Angela Davis was widely popular in East Germany and generated thousands of letters of support through a state-organized mass solidarity campaign.[56]

East Germans could also connect to the rest of the world through visitors who came to the GDR. The border was designed to prevent citizens from leaving, but it also conversely facilitated the controlled movement of people from the rest of the world in and out of East Germany.[57] Visitors from abroad came to the bi-annual Leipzig Trade Fair, which sought to compete not only with the global reach of West German fairs in Frankfurt am Main and Hannover but also with competitors in the rest of the Eastern Bloc. Organizers drew on Leipzig's long history as a trading hub to promote the city as a new space for trade and exchange beyond the inequalities of Western colonialism.[58] Mass international political events were also held in the GDR: East Berlin hosted the World Festival of Youth and Students in 1951 and 1973. While the initial event was a rather dour affair with mass parades of young people carrying portraits of Joseph Stalin, the second was a more hedonistic affair dubbed "Red Woodstock." It featured performances by East German rock bands and celebrity appearances by international figures like Angela Davis and Yasser Arafat, chairman of the Palestinian Liberation Organization (PLO).[59] In 1975, East Berlin also hosted the World Congress of Women—a socialist alternative to the United Nations' World Conference on Women, held in Mexico City that same year.[60]

The relaxation of border controls over the course of the 1970s also brought millions of tourists from the nonsocialist world to the GDR. The SED had struggled to develop a tourism industry in the 1960s, in large part due to high prices, a lack of suitable hotels, and the bureaucratic complications of booking trips via the official East

German state travel agency.⁶¹ But in the 1970s with West Germans now able to travel to the GDR with greater ease due to new treaties, East Berlin became a popular destination to see the Palace of the Republic and the nearby Television Tower, which, at 368 meters tall, was the fourth-tallest free-standing structure in the world at the time of its construction in 1969. Turkish guest workers in West Berlin, who had fewer restrictions on their travel to the GDR than those with West German passports, were also frequent visitors to East Berlin, where entertainment—as well as flights home from East Berlin's Schönefeld airport to visit family—was cheaper.⁶²

There were also socialist refugees—"political emigrants" in the terminology of the SED—who were granted asylum in East Germany. The first group to arrive immediately after the Second World War were communists fleeing the royalist victory in the Greek civil war.⁶³ By 1961, around 1,300 Greeks had claimed asylum in the GDR.⁶⁴ They were joined by veterans of the Spanish Civil War who could not return to the Franco dictatorship, and a small number of American soldiers stationed in West Germany who defected to the GDR.⁶⁵ Fleeing persecution after Pinochet's coup, more than 1,500 Chileans, around one-third Communist Party members, arrived in the GDR.⁶⁶ While the far-right military regimes of Southern Europe and Latin America drove most of the refugee traffic to the GDR, there were also those seeking refuge from other socialist regimes. Inspired by Maoist China, the Khmer Rouge revolution in Cambodia in 1975 resulted in a radical program of land collectivization and the genocidal mass killings of the urban and educated population, resulting in 1.5 million to 2 million dead. As the Khmer Rouge also targeted socialist dissenters, the SED allowed Cambodians who were already in the GDR as students or for training to remain as refugees.⁶⁷

The SED also provided a place of temporary refuge for activists, fighters, and terrorists and a wide range of groups under the umbrella of solidarity with the anti-imperial struggle, including members of the PLO, the Algerian National Liberation Front (FLN), the People's Front for the Liberation of Palestine (PFLP), the Abu Nidal Group, as well as anti-apartheid organizations like the ANC and its armed wing uMkhonto we Sizwe, the Zimbabwe African People's Union (ZAPU), and the South West African People's Organization (SWAPO) from what is now Namibia.[68] The PLO was allowed to open an office in East Berlin in 1973, the first of its kind in the Eastern Bloc. Active fighters in guerrilla campaigns against apartheid were sent to East Germany for military training and medical treatment, and the ANC was given access to East German printing facilities to produce its party organ *Sechaba*. While some of their partners, like SWAPO, were not perfectly ideologically synchronized with the SED, both sides were pleased to publicly affirm their partnership as a meeting of like-minded anti-imperialists practicing solidarity.[69] The GDR also acted as a "strategic hinterland" for those involved in international terrorism to hide out, plan, and regroup, including the Red Army Faction (RAF) and other far-left West German terrorist groups, as well as Ilich Ramírez Sánchez—better known as Carlos the Jackal—who lived in East Germany under Stasi protection and surveillance for several years.[70] Crucially, the SED also maintained a red line that none of this support be directly used to organize terror attacks within Europe, afraid of endangering the gains from the relaxation of Cold War tensions—the era of Détente—with the West.

Figure 3.5 Dean Reed performing on GDR television, May 1986. ullstein bild, Germany.

Dean Reed

Born 1938, Denver, Colorado, USA
Died 1986, Zeuthen, GDR

Born and raised in Colorado to a conservative American family, Dean Reed's origins made him an unlikely pop culture icon of East Germany. In the late 1950s, his music label tried to market Reed as the next Elvis Presley, but he failed to deliver any real hits. On a South American tour, he turned to left-wing politics and learned Spanish. Deported from Argentina after a military coup in 1966, he moved to Europe, where he featured in some spaghetti westerns, appeared in commercials, and toured the Eastern Bloc as a singer.

In 1973, he decided to settle in the GDR after acting in a film there and marrying an East German woman. In the GDR, his musical performances were almost all covers of hit Western pop songs or socialist anthems sung in (strongly accented) German and Spanish. Along with Canadian singer Perry Friedman, who had also settled in the GDR, Reed popularized North American folk music for East German audiences. As an actor, he was the lead in the Western *Blood Brothers*, where he played a US cavalryman who deserts after participating in the Sand Creek Massacre and befriends a Cheyenne warrior played by the German-Serbian actor Gojko Mitić, the so-called "chief Indian" of DEFA films, who regularly played Native American roles, including the lead in adaptations of Karl May's Winnetou series of pulp novels. In *El Cantor*, a TV movie from 1978, Reed played the Chilean socialist musician Victor Jara, a personal friend who had been murdered during the coup against the government of Salvador Allende. Around this time, Reed began to work as a Stasi informant under the code name IM Victor.

By the 1980s, Reed's films and albums had begun to flop, and he became increasingly disillusioned with everyday life under state socialism. In 1986, seeking to raise his profile in the United States, where he had never renounced his citizenship

> and continued to file taxes, he gave an interview to the TV news magazine *60 Minutes*. He expressed his desire to return to Colorado and run for Senate, but, after defending the Berlin Wall and the Soviet invasion of Afghanistan, he received an outpouring of hate mail. Later that year, Dean Reed's body was found in a lake near his residence in a leafy suburb of East Berlin, where much of the cultural elite lived. He had committed suicide at the age of forty-seven. His death was covered as a tragic accident in the GDR media; evidence of his suicide note sent to his SED handler was covered up.

There was some migration to East Germany out of ideological conviction—primarily from the cultural scene, like American singer Dean Reed (the so-called Red Elvis), who made a career in East Germany as an actor and entertainer. The main group of foreigners in East Germany, however, were visiting students from the Global South who first started arriving from Nigeria and North Korea in 1951, to be followed by thousands from India and across Africa and the Middle East. Educational programs for Third World students were usually part of a larger bilateral relationship connecting trade and solidarity. Students would be educated in ideological and technical matters in the GDR, which the SED hoped would both foster goodwill and orient the sending countries in a socialist direction. Technologies and machinery, up to entire factories, that students and apprentices had been trained on could be exported to the sending countries in exchange for goods and raw materials.[71] The more practical education programs were often connected to the "contract worker" program. Unable to offer the kind of wages that attracted Italians, Greeks, Yugoslavs, and Turks to West Germany, the SED sought to leverage ideological alliances and development projects. The first agreement on contract workers was signed with Poland in 1965 and Hungary in 1967. Between ten and thirty thousand Poles migrated annually to work for their wealthier socialist neighbor, and many crossed the border bridge daily to work in twinned cities like Frankfurt an der Oder/Słubice or Görlitz/Zgorzelec. Additional contingents of contract workers arrived in the GDR in response to global geopolitical developments. Post-revolutionary Cuba's growing partnership with the Soviet Union and the Eastern Bloc and the victory of the Algerian National Liberation Front in its war of independence against France created new opportunities to recruit workers from states that looked to East Germany as a partner in economic modernization. The victory of socialist North Vietnam and the independence of Angola and Mozambique in 1975 following the collapse of the Portuguese Empire did likewise.[72]

Foreigner visitors who arrived in the GDR as part of organized tours or major international events had a more controlled and orchestrated experience than those who came as refugees or contract workers. Under the surveillance of the Stasi, visitors to the World Festival or the Leipzig Trade Fair were restricted to specific spaces that showed the GDR at its best. Usually staying in one of the Interhotels built specifically for foreign visitors in major cities, the version of

Figure 3.6 Mozambican worker-trainees at VEB Fischfang Rostock, 1984. Sindermann, ADN.

East Germany they experienced was a privileged one with access to imported luxury goods that could be purchased with hard currency. Political refugees had a more difficult time. Many Chileans found the lack of democracy in the GDR challenging after the much more open socialism of the Allende government.[73] Contract workers were not meant to integrate into broader society and were housed in special barracks and residence halls and generally segregated from the rest of the population. Residency in the GDR was completely dependent on employment: if a female contract worker became pregnant, they were given the choice to go back to their home country or get an abortion.[74] While they came to the GDR to earn money, the SED also restricted what contract workers could take out of the country and tried to limit access to scarce goods like watches and motorcycles.

There was also the issue of xenophobia and racism. Contract workers describe friendships and relationships with East Germans, but also experiences of a society that was deeply distrustful of outsiders—of any race or nationality.[75] SED propaganda regularly depicted racial difference through the theme of solidarity: imagery of white Europeans standing together with Africans and Asians was meant to show the absence of racial hierarchies and the equality of all peoples.[76] On the ground, however, non-Germans often faced racial discrimination in institutional settings and from the wider population. Fears of shortages transformed into xenophobia as some shops barred Vietnamese customers who were perceived as taking precious goods from Germans.[77] Foreign students, particularly those from Africa, faced racist discrimination in everyday life and in connection with the romantic relationships they formed with East Germans.[78] The African American singer and performer Aubrey Pankey, who had migrated to the GDR for political reasons, found himself typecast and complained to the SED that he was only offered minor parts that matched his race.[79] There were also regular outbursts of racist violence. In 1975, in Erfurt, a violent pogrom against Algerian workers raged for four days, with crowds up to 300 strong calling for their expulsion and murder. In Merseburg, in 1979, two Afro-Cuban contract workers, Delfín Guerra and Raúl Paret, were killed by a mob that chased them into the river Saale.[80] The racist violence that took place across Germany in the early 1990s, including violent mob attacks on foreigners in the former GDR (Hoyerswerda in 1991 and Rostock-Lichterhagen in 1992) and arson attacks against non-ethnic Germans in the West (Mölln in 1992 and Solingen in 1993), had roots in both German states pre-dating reunification.[81]

From Ostpolitik to the Helsinki Accords

At the end of the 1960s, the GDR finally emerged from its diplomatic isolation, and subsequently joined the United Nations, and was recognized as a sovereign country almost universally. These developments did not come about because the SED found a new strategy of diplomatic engagement but because the politics of the Cold War shifted radically in Europe and globally during this period. The German-German relationship was fundamentally altered by the West German turn to the "Neue Ostpolitik" (New Eastern politics), which sought engagement over the isolation of the GDR. At the same time, there was a thaw in the relations between the United States and the Soviet Union, known as the period of Détente. Rather than breaking through West German opposition directly through appeals to the Global South, the GDR gained widespread recognition due the changing nature of the larger Cold War conflict.

The arrival of Social Democrat Willy Brandt, first as Foreign Minister and then Chancellor of West Germany, on the international scene had wide-ranging effects on East Germany and Cold War Europe. The West German policy of diplomatically blockading the GDR by threatening postcolonial states was already under pressure, since smaller states now knew they had leverage in negotiations, as any recognition of the GDR could be an embarrassment. For Brandt and other members of the Social Democratic Party (SPD), the belligerent stance of the Christian Democratic Party (CDU) since 1949 was counterproductive and isolation only furthered the division of Germany. With Ostpolitik, Brandt and his SPD allies aimed at "change through nearness": rather than trying to destroy East Germany and state socialism through isolation, the GDR could be reformed from within through exchange and openness.[82] The Social Democrats believed that the Eastern Bloc needed to evolve slowly toward change as the crushing of the Prague Spring had demonstrated that rapid moves toward liberalization or democratization would be suppressed with violence.

On the flipside, it was harder for the SED to demonize the Social Democrat Willy Brandt than the CDU leaders of the early Federal Republic, many of whom had played to communist stereotypes: Konrad Adenauer was an austere, conservative Catholic and Ludwig Erhard a cigar-smoking capitalist. They were followed by Hans-Georg Kiesinger who was even better for propaganda purposes as a former Nazi Party member. By contrast, Willy Brandt had been an anti-Nazi resistance fighter, and, after the fall of the Third Reich, became part of the pro-Western and anti-communist wing of the SPD. He had been mayor of West Berlin when the wall was erected in 1961 and then became Foreign Minister under Kiesinger in an SPD-CDU coalition government from 1966 to 1969 where he began his program of Ostpolitik. In 1969, he was elected chancellor, leading a social-liberal government—the first postwar West German government not led by the Christian Democrats.

Willy Brandt

Born 1913, Lübeck, German Empire
Died 1992, Unkel, Federal Republic of Germany

Herbert Frahm was raised by a single mother who worked as a department store cashier. A youth socialist activist, he fled to Norway in 1933 and changed his name to Willy Brandt to evade Nazi persecution. After working as a journalist covering the Spanish Civil War, he fled to neutral Sweden after the German occupation of Norway in 1940. Returning to Germany in 1946, he began to rise up the ranks of the Social Democrats in West Berlin, in part due to financial support from covert American sources. He was elected governing mayor of West Berlin in 1957 and held the position through the construction of the Berlin Wall. Ascending to lead the federal SPD, Brandt lost two elections against the CDU; in 1966, he finally gained enough support to force a grand coalition between the two rival parties and was appointed Foreign Minister. In this role, he began to implement the *Neue Ostpolitik* that sought increased engagement with the GDR and the Eastern Bloc.

In 1969, Brandt became the first post-war SPD chancellor by forming a slim majority government with the FDP. Continuing with Ostpolitik, Brandt presided over the collapse of the West German diplomatic blockade of the GDR, the acknowledgment of the Oder-Neisse line as the new German-Polish border, and the improvement in relations with the Eastern Bloc via personal diplomacy. In 1970, he was the first West German leader to travel to Poland since the Second World War; while visiting a memorial to the Warsaw Ghetto Uprising, he famously fell to his knees in an act of genuflection.

In 1972, Brandt almost lost a vote of no confidence in his government, but was saved (as it was later revealed) by the Stasi bribing two members of the CDU/CSU. However, Brandt subsequently lost his parliamentary majority after several defections to the CDU in protest over his Ostpolitik. He nonetheless won re-election with more votes than in 1969, leading the SPD to becoming the largest party in parliament for the first time since 1930. His time in office was marked by a major expansion of the welfare state and new domestic programs, including the strengthening of the education system and social security programs.

While Brandt was in office to sign the Basic Treaty between the GDR and the FRG, he was soon forced to resign when it was revealed that his personal assistant was a Stasi agent. Günter Guillaume and his wife had migrated to the FRG in 1956 with orders to infiltrate the SPD. Rising steadily through the ranks, he had become Brandt's personal secretary in 1972. By 1974, West German intelligence had gathered enough evidence to

> arrest him for espionage. The Guillaumes were released back to the GDR in a spy exchange in 1981.
>
> Brandt remained chairman of the SPD until 1987 and chaired the Independent Commission on International Developmental Issues, which published its report in 1980. In 1989, even as many on the left in West Germany were skeptical of reunification, Brandt was an enthusiastic proponent of reunification, declaring, "Now, what belongs together will grow together." He died in 1992. In 2003, Brandt's son Matthias played Guillaume in a TV movie about his father's downfall as chancellor.

While Brandt was still foreign minister, the Hallstein Doctrine had effectively collapsed when Iraq decided to recognize the GDR and extend full diplomatic relations in 1969. Iraq, along with several other states, had already cut ties with the Federal Republic in retaliation for its recognition of Israel in 1965, and there was little foreign aid at stake, so Bonn had no real leverage to use against Baghdad. Shortly afterward, Cambodia, which had been studiously trying to maintain nonalignment by treating both Germanies as equally as possible offered to allow the GDR to establish a consulate to balance out privileges already meted out to West Germany. Bonn sent mixed messages in response, not only seeming to want to avoid cutting ties but also appearing high-handed toward the Cambodian government. Taking offense at its diplomatic treatment, the government in Phnom Penh chose to break off relations with West Germany and offer full recognition to the GDR. Before the year was out, South Yemen, Sudan, Syria, and Egypt also joined in recognizing East Germany.[83] Yet this wave stopped at six countries, and other nations remained cautious about aligning themselves to the GDR.

In Bonn, officials were upset about the demise of the blockade, but it did not stop momentum for further engagement with the Eastern Bloc when Brandt became chancellor. In 1970, West Germany signed treaties with both the Soviet Union and Poland to normalize relations and affirm the new postwar borders.[84] Brandt accepted an invitation from East German Prime Minister Willi Stoph to visit the city of Erfurt in the GDR. Brandt was welcomed by East German crowds and the SED was surprised by his popularity among the population. Later that year, Brandt traveled to Poland, where he fell to his knees in genuflection in front of the monument to the Warsaw Ghetto Uprising, creating an iconic image of reconciliation. East-West engagement rapidly delivered a series of diplomatic agreements. In 1971, the United States, the United Kingdom, France, and the Soviet Union signed the Four Power Agreement on Berlin, reaffirming their mutual occupation rights over the city. A Transit Agreement between East and West Germany paved the way for a controlled opening of cross-border traffic and communication. While it did little to make East Germans more mobile, West Germans could now travel to West Berlin on GDR highways. It was also possible, even for those who had previously fled the GDR, to more easily travel to East Germany, so families that had been separated by the Berlin Wall could once again meet in person.[85]

Much of this progress came from shifts within West Germany, but also as a result of political changes within the GDR and the socialist bloc writ large. The split between the Soviet Union and the PRC worsened at the end of the 1960s, leading in some cases to armed border clashes between the two communist superpowers. Under Leonid Brezhnev, the Soviet Union sought to balance out the rising power of China by relaxing tensions with the West leading to the era of Détente. Just as the rise of the SPD-led government under Willy Brandt in the West led to important changes in Cold War diplomacy, so too did the fall of SED leader Walter Ulbricht in 1971. Ulbricht considered himself one of the elder statesmen of the global socialist movement: he had known Lenin personally, had outlasted Stalin and Khrushchev in power, and was the only head of an Eastern Bloc state to have survived in that position from the postwar until the end of the 1960s. Poland and Romania had seen several leaders rise and fall to internal political intrigues, while Hungary and Czechoslovakia had both been invaded to suppress revolutions led from within the socialist establishment. Ulbricht regarded himself as having built a socialist society from the ashes of the Nazi regime and as such viewed Soviet leader Leonid Brezhnev as a relative newcomer who should heed his wisdom. For his part, Brezhnev resented Ulbricht's high-handed attitude, especially since he regarded him as a subordinate to Moscow.

From within the top echelons of the SED, Erich Honecker took advantage of these tensions between East Berlin and Moscow to oust Ulbricht from power. Honecker had joined the KPD during the Weimar Era, and under the Nazis, he was jailed for his participation in communist underground activism.[86] Liberated from prison by the Soviets, he joined the Ulbricht group and cofounded the Free German Youth, which he then led as chairman for more than a decade. In the wake of the 1953 Uprising, Honecker had supported Ulbricht against those in the Politburo who sought to replace him and was rewarded for his loyalty with a series of important positions over the coming decades. While Ulbricht sought to forestall his fall from power by evicting Honecker from the Politburo in 1970, the Soviets intervened, and Honecker was reinstated. Seeing Ulbricht as a spent force who was insufficiently deferential to the Kremlin, the Soviets then demanded Ulbricht step down from his role as general-secretary of the SED for "health reasons," and Honecker was handed the reins of power. When it came to the leadership of the GDR, the last word still came from Moscow. Ulbricht was allowed to stay on as leader of the Council of State until his death in 1976, but he was barely a figurehead. Under Honecker, the key figures within the SED were his wife Margot, who was Minister of Education, Günter Mittag, who was in charge of economic affairs, Joachim Hermann, chief propagandist in charge of the media, and Erich Mielke, the head of the Stasi. This group would dominate East German politics until shortly before the fall of the Berlin Wall in 1989. Honecker accepted the Soviet strategy of engagement with the West and peaceful coexistence, but he also promoted the strict demarcation (*Abgrenzung*) of East German culture from that of West Germany. The rise of Honecker marked the end of SED ambitions toward German reunification on socialist terms.[87]

Margot Honecker

Born 1927, Halle, Weimar Republic
Died 2016, Santiago de Chile, Chile

Along with Minister of Justice Hilde Benjamin (in office 1953–67), Margot Honecker was one of the few women at the top levels of power in the SED and the GDR, serving as Minister of Education from 1963 to 1989.

Margot Feist was born to a family of communists. Her father Gotthard was imprisoned in various concentration camps during the war, and afterwards quickly moved up the ranks of the FDGB. Margot joined the KPD in 1945 and quickly made her mark within the FDJ. At twenty-two, in 1949, she was in charge of the Thälmann Young Pioneers and a representative in the first Volkskammer. When she became pregnant with FDJ chairman Erich Honecker's child, he quickly divorced his second wife to marry Margot. As Minister of Education, she was responsible for the much-hated authoritarian educational system of the GDR and its system of correctional youth camps. Widely reviled among the population, she received the moniker "the purple witch" because of the blue-rinse hair dye she used.

Margot Honecker resigned from her position as Minister of Education on November 2, 1989, shortly after her husband Erich had been ousted as General Secretary of the SED and a week before the opening of the Berlin Wall. After fleeing together to Moscow, Erich was extradited to Berlin to stand trial, while Margot fled to Chile, where daughter Sonja already lived, married to a Chilean communist. She did not make a public appearance between the fall of the Berlin Wall and a 2008 ceremony in Managua, Nicaragua, where she was honored by President Daniel Ortega for her support of the Sandinista movement. She continued to defend her actions and those of her husband as necessary and just to sustain the socialist project until her death in 2016.

The German Democratic Republic

Ostpolitik reached its zenith in 1972 with the signing of the Basic Treaty between the GDR and the FRG, which provided for mutual recognition of each other as sovereign states, but stopped short of full diplomatic relations as foreign countries. Rather than exchanging ambassadors, both countries would have a permanent representative in each other's capital.[88] East German recognition of the Federal Republic was not a great ideological hurdle, but West German conservatives challenged the legality of the treaty on the grounds that it violated the Basic Law's provision to seek reunification. The Constitutional Court ruled that "the German Democratic Republic belongs to Germany and cannot be seen as a foreign country in relation to the Federal Republic of Germany," but it did not disallow the treaty as it had stopped short of accepting the GDR as a recognized foreign state.[89] This agreement between the two Germanies paved the way for a series of diplomatic events. First, in 1973, the two German states were finally admitted as members of the United Nations. This was exceptional for the era as the UN admitted countries on the basis of "one nation, one seat." Only shortly before, Taiwan had been de-recognized by the body and replaced by the People's Republic as the representative of "China."[90] The two Korean states would not be admitted until 1991. In other words, the division of Germany was no longer a problem to be solved by the international community but simply a fact accepted by all.

The final step in the normalization of German division was the Helsinki Accords of 1975. Also known as the Final Act of the Conference on Security and Cooperation in Europe, the Helsinki Accords were a treaty between thirty-five countries in North America, Western Europe, and Eastern Europe (NATO, the Warsaw Pact, and the neutral and nonaligned countries alike), that served as a peace treaty to settle the Second World War. Negotiations had begun in 1972, and over several years, diplomats had negotiated a carefully worded agreement that recognized the borders created by the Soviet Union in the East, including the Oder-Neisse line between the GDR and Poland, and the annexations of German territory to Poland and the USSR. Signatories pledged to only alter borders through peaceful means and included provisions on human rights norms as a basis for continued relations and increased cross-border exchange and travel.

For the SED, the agreement was an essential conclusion to nearly twenty years of fighting for recognition as a country equal to the Federal Republic in the eyes of the international community.[91] But those signing the Helsinki Accords did not all agree as to the meaning of its contents. For some in the West negotiating the agreements, like US Secretary of State Henry Kissinger, the point of the agreement was to lock in peaceful coexistence between the superpowers, not to improve the lives of people beyond the Iron Curtain. Talk of human rights was purely decorative for the self-described practitioner of *Realpolitik* over idealism (or as others would describe him, an unindicted war criminal).[92] For Erich Honecker and the SED elites, the human rights provisions were in line with other agreements they had signed at the UN, which they saw as part of the international organization's broader anti-colonial politics that emphasized the inviolability of state sovereignty from outside interventions. The greater concern was the agreement's provisions on freedom of information and cross-border mobility—which raised red flags for Stasi chief Erich Mielke and others, who saw this as a Trojan Horse for Western infiltration. Ultimately, Honecker decided that the net benefits of the agreement were worth the risk, since it would finally provide international recognition of the GDR and its borders. The impact of the Helsinki Accords would prove double-edged: Honecker was right that it ushered in universal recognition of the GDR, but Mielke was also right that it provided leverage for Western intervention in the internal affairs of the East Germany. In the short term, it fulfilled the decades-long ambitions of SED diplomacy; in the long term, it proved to be a major liability.[93]

Debt, Consumer Socialism, and the Global Market

Over the course of the 1960s, the SED had been able to increase the standard of living in the GDR and improve access to consumer goods, but it remained unable to solve its chronic economic problems. East Germany always had a centrally planned economy, but *how* it was planned evolved over time. To address ongoing supply bottlenecks in the production process of many industries, the New Economic System was introduced in 1963. Inspired by new innovations in cybernetics and information systems, State Planning Commission chief Erich Apel sought to create a system of production that would allow more flexibility for industries and ministries with regard to how they met targets. Yet, the reforms only went so far: economically inefficient plants were not closed, nor were prices on scarce goods allowed to rise. As a result, the state continued to invest in industries that generated systemic losses and even though prices for consumer goods remained steady and affordable, there were widespread shortages putting them still out of reach of the population.[94] Facing pressure from within the Politburo, reforms needed to be closely controlled to prevent economic decentralization from spilling over into political liberalization. Fearing that things could get out of hand, Ulbricht rolled back much of the economic experimentation (along with the thaw in the field of arts and culture) by 1965. As part of this turn back to central planning, an economic treaty was prepared between East Germany and the USSR that formally subordinated the GDR within the larger Soviet economic system. Planning chief Erich Apel committed suicide on the eve of the treaty's signing from despair over the failure of his economic reforms.[95]

In the late 1960s, Ulbricht shifted to a new model called the Economic System of Socialism, which moved even further toward recentralization and ended the last vestiges of the experiments in flexibility from earlier in the decade.[96] East German production was increasingly organized into *Kombinate*—large vertically integrated concerns consisting of multiple People's Owned Industries (VEBs) that were meant to handle all aspects of production of specific goods under one roof. This approach was based on faith that the scientific-technological revolution of socialism would allow for centrally planned strategic investment in certain key fields. East German scientists had been trying to keep pace with Western countries in the development of new technologies like lasers, semiconductors, and microelectronics, but they were often underfunded, and political support was sporadic. In the late 1960s, with the construction of engineering marvels like Berlin's *Fernsehturm* (television tower), there was a swell of optimism that East Germany could combine technological know-how with the rational planning of socialism to compete with the West.[97] The 1950s' vision of overtaking the Federal Republic across the board was abandoned in favor of "overtaking without catching up" (*überholen ohne einzuholen*). This new slogan encompassed the hope that the GDR could selectively excel in key fields like synthetic fibers, complex engineering, and microelectronics, which could then compete in export markets. To invest in these areas, Ulbricht had to arrange for substantial loans from Western banks to cover the costs of importing specialized equipment that could not be produced at home or purchased from within the Eastern Bloc.

The economic system underwent further reforms after Erich Honecker replaced Ulbricht in 1971. Honecker continued Ulbricht's centralization and, in 1972, completed the process of "eliminating capitalism" by nationalizing the remaining privately owned small businesses in the GDR—almost 12,000 in total, which until then had been crucial in filling the gaps of the planned economy.[98] In contrast to his predecessor, however, Honecker had no illusions that the GDR would be able to outperform the Federal Republic in order to realize unification on East German terms. He expanded Ulbricht's strategy of taking out large loans from the West, but with a focus on spending sufficiently on high-tech production to pay back the interest and provide enough consumer goods to keep the population content. Honecker's new scheme, the "Unity of Economic and Social Policy," sought to increase consumer goods, massively expanded the state apartment tower construction program (the equally hated and beloved *Plattenbauten*—prefab concrete panel apartment buildings—that still dot the landscape in the former East Germany today).[99] He also instituted wide-ranging pro-natalist spending programs including improved social services for women (including dealing with the chronic problem of underfunded childcare) and financial bonuses for young families.[100] Although he faced resistance from SED economic experts who feared the consequences of the long-term debt burden,

Honecker refused to debate the matter and sidelined those who raised the specter of runaway debt. For Honecker, providing the population with a baseline of housing, services, and consumer goods was the necessary foundation for political stability and the legitimacy of the SED. He continued to believe that investments with foreign loans would eventually create enough exports to manage East Germany's chronic foreign currency shortages.[101] This ushered in a new era of "consumer socialism" and made the GDR into what has been called a "welfare dictatorship" in which Honecker created an implied social contract between the SED and East Germans: the legitimacy of his rule and of the socialist project writ large was to be judged by its capacity to consistently deliver the needs of everyday life to individual citizens.[102]

Ulbricht's economic plans had already led to an accumulated debt of two billion Deutsche Marks by 1970; Honecker's plans made it skyrocket to eleven billion by 1975. By 1976, the GDR was faced with a payment crisis, as its foreign currency reserves dwindled as it tried to service its ballooning Western debt load. The response by the SED was to seek alternatives to paying global prices on the open market by turning to trade and solidarity with the Global South. In the early years of the GDR, the foreign policy priority for the SED had been breaking out of the West German diplomatic blockade by gaining recognition beyond the Eastern Bloc. As East Germany was increasingly recognized as a sovereign state, it was possible to shift foreign policy priorities to solving strategic international trade problems instead. But ideology did not map perfectly onto the economic needs of the GDR and the world itself was not neatly divided into socialist friends and capitalist enemies.

The task of acquiring foreign currency for the GDR economy, beyond what could be generated through normal exports, was handled by the Commercial Coordination Office (Kommerzielle Koordinierung, KoKo), which mixed foreign trade and international espionage. Run by Alexander Schalck-Golodkowski from its founding in 1966 until the end of the GDR, KoKo emerged from programs to smuggle in strategic goods to East Germany that were under embargo from the West, like key industrial raw inputs and advanced technology. KoKo eventually operated more than 150 front organizations to generate foreign currency wherever possible. This included dealing in legal markets, like oil, but also making arrangements for the West German government to pay for certain East Germans (along with other ethnic Germans across Eastern Europe) to emigrate to the Federal Republic in exchange for hard currency.[103] It never lost its early black market role in the GDR economy, becoming responsible for evading import embargoes on goods like computer technology from the West. Through KoKo's involvement, the GDR's international trade often worked through channels that could move back and forth between illicit markets and the legitimate business world.[104]

Arms supplies and military aid had been a major element of GDR diplomacy and solidarity as early as the 1960s and helped smooth the way for the mass recognition of the GDR by Arab states in 1969.[105] In the 1970s, the SED expanded its exports of arms and materiel to deal with problem of oil imports. Unlike the Federal Republic, East Germany had avoided the worst consequences of the global 1973 oil shock brought on by producing states restricting production and driving up prices, since the GDR was supplied with cheap oil from the USSR via the Friendship Pipeline. In fact, the crisis produced increased profits for East Germany as it was able to sell refined gasoline to West Berlin, providing a major source of hard currency that helped fuel the boom in consumer socialism under Honecker and relieved some of the need for Western bank loans.[106] Yet deliveries from the Soviets were limited and shrinking, right as the demand for refined petroleum products—from gasoline to plastics—was increasing. The initial country targeted by the GDR to expand its petroleum sources was Libya, which under Colonel Muammar Gaddafi had become a radical socialist Islamic state and had subsequently nationalized its oil industry. Gaddafi had ambitions of regional expansion and put Eastern Bloc arms to use the following year when he intervened in the civil war of neighboring Chad.

In addition to oil, the other main commodity the GDR sought to source directly was coffee. Two years of bad harvests in Brazil led to a doubling of the price of coffee in 1976, causing a huge, sudden, drain on the SED's foreign currency reserves. The East German population saw the provision of coffee as a basic responsibility of the planned economy, not an optional luxury, and ersatz coffee products introduced to help deal with shortages were widely detested.[107] One solution was found in Mozambique, which had recently gained independence from Portugal and was led by the socialist Liberation Front of Mozambique (FRELIMO).[108] A deal was struck, trading arms needed to fight an anti-communist insurgency in exchange for coffee and the creation of a contract worker program. Sights were soon set on Ethiopia, which was ruled by the Marxist-Leninist military regime, the Derg, that had taken control in 1974, overthrowing Emperor Haile Selassie. Although it was a fellow socialist state, Somalia had invaded Ethiopia in 1977 prompting wide-ranging aid to the Derg from the Soviet Union and its allies. As part of a larger program of international cooperation and development with Ethiopia, the SED was able to work out a trade deal exchanging arms for coffee.[109] A more future-oriented deal was struck with Vietnam in connection with a contract worker scheme. The GDR paid for the construction of a massive coffee plantation system to help rebuild the economy of the war-torn country in exchange for receiving a generous percentage of the harvest each year. Ironically, due to the long-term development needed for coffee production, the first batch of deliveries was not possible until 1990 (by which time the GDR no longer existed).

But ideology and economic interests did not always map neatly onto one another. The GDR's relationship with Ba'thist Iraq—the first nonsocialist country to recognize East Germany in 1969—was fraught with complications. Both sides had a strong interest in trade and exchange: Iraq offered the promise of cheap oil and a substantial market for arms exports, while the GDR could offer military technology and educational opportunities to support the growing Iraqi managerial class. The main priority for the Ba'th, however, was tech and training for its security forces, which were notorious for their brutal violence toward the Shi'a majority population, the Kurdish ethnic minority and political dissenters, including the Iraqi Communist Party. Iraqi communists faced violent repression at home, but Ba'thist-aligned students even attacked Iraqi Communist Party (ICP) students studying abroad in East Germany. The conflict resulted in an extraordinary Stasi operation to protect ICP members on GDR soil from Ba'thist violence, which soured relations, and put a hold on major economic and military exchange.[110]

By contrast, cooperation with Japan—one of the wealthiest non-socialist states in the world—flourished in this era on the basis of mutual economic interest. For the East Germans, Japan was a capitalist, but not Western, country that had a familiar reliance on large vertically integrated corporate structures and an emphasis on state paternalism. For Japan, partnership with the GDR revived older ties from the Nazi era, but without the political baggage of Axis atrocities, due to East Germany's official antifascism. Both nations shared a proclaimed goal of international peace and cooperation while being key strategic allies to rival Cold War superpowers. On a practical level, Japan was a source of high-tech know-how, and they in turn saw the GDR as a useful gateway to Eastern Bloc markets. Symbolic of this era of collaboration was the International Trade Center in East Berlin. Designed by a GDR architect, the Center was paid for and constructed

Figure 3.7 The Interhotel "Merkur" in Leipzig, designed by the Kajima Corporation of Japan. Opening in 1981, it featured a conference center, 450 rooms, 10 restaurants and bars including "Sakura," a Japanese-themed restaurant. There was also a Japanese garden with waterfalls, ponds, and lanterns. Friedrich Gahlbeck, ADN.

The German Democratic Republic

by the Kajima Corporation, with the expectation that they would be repaid through hard currency paid by Western corporations to rent space in the building. After the success of this initial partnership, Japanese firms spent the next decade in East Germany building its most prestigious new buildings, including new "luxury" Interhotels in East Berlin and Dresden meant to accommodate the increased tourism post-Helsinki.[111]

East Germany and the World

By the late 1970s, the GDR was able to overcome West German pressure and gain almost universal recognition as a legitimate state, yet it continued to struggle to integrate into the global economy. While the SED was far more vocal than West German officials in proclaiming its solidarity with Afro-Asian states in the anti-imperialist struggle, the smaller, poorer, and more isolated GDR could not compete with the appeal of its Western counterpart. The FRG's superior relative economic status and integration into Western political structures made it far more appealing as a trading partner and potential ally. East Germany's diplomatic success at escaping isolation came mostly in response to the relaxation of tensions between the Soviet Union and the United States and internal shifts in West Germany that paved the way for a new Ostpolitik of engagement over isolation. Even once it had gained recognition as a sovereign state, the GDR was still left with the glaring problem that its currency was worth very little internationally and its economy could not function without ever-increasing debt to the West. Globally, the binary logic of the Cold War was in the process of breaking down in the late 1970s, and with it, the basis for the existence of the GDR as a state socialist dictatorship. The successes of this era thus proved to be short-lived, as East Germany entered into a phase of crisis and collapse over the following decade.

CHAPTER 4
STAGNATION, COLLAPSE, AND REUNIFICATION

In 1987, GDR leader Erich Honecker made his first official visit to West Germany, where he was ceremoniously received as a fellow head of state by Chancellor Helmut Kohl. The following year, East Germany came in second in the medal count at the Olympic Games in both Calgary and Seoul, bested only by the Soviet Union. On the international stage, East Germany presented itself as a successful socialist state that could stand as an equal to the West. Yet, these superficial victories belied the imminent collapse of SED rule—and with it the entire German Democratic Republic. In 1989, the Socialist Unity Party's capacity to rule rapidly slipped away as the streets filled with citizens demanding change in mass demonstrations not seen in East Germany for thirty-six years. Erich Honecker was forced to resign in the face of a new crisis of emigration to the West (this time through gaps opening in the Iron Curtain between East and West elsewhere in Europe), and his successor, Egon Krenz, proved equally incapable of turning the tide. On November 9, the Berlin Wall was opened, and by the following month, the SED had renounced its monopoly on power, putting the German Democratic Republic on a path to democratic elections the following year. By the fall of 1990, the GDR ceased to exist when it was absorbed into the Federal Republic of Germany.

What accounts for this paradox of seeming long-term stability and yet rapid collapse that took place in 1989? There were many structural factors: the declining political legitimacy and economic performance of the East German state, the regional transformation of Eastern Europe by reform communists, shifts in international affairs due to economic globalization, and the decline of revolutionary politics. At the same time, contingent events in the fall of that year also determined how these structural problems translated into a mostly peaceful transition from state socialist dictatorship to a social market economy under a parliamentary democracy in under a year. Specific decisions by key actors and groups in 1989 allowed this transition to occur without mass bloodshed—in contrast to events in China and Romania. Likewise, the path to unification via the creation of five new federal states rather than continued GDR independence or some kind of hybrid confederation with West Germany was also far from predetermined. This chapter thus examines how these structural problems crossed with a short-term crisis to bring about the opening of the Berlin Wall, the collapse of SED rule, a peaceful democratic revolution, and finally reunification with the Federal Republic of Germany.

Economic Decline and Political Fallout

By the 1980s, Erich Honecker's plan to jump-start the GDR economy with Western loans was clearly not working. Debt to Western banks stood at eleven billion Deutsche Marks (DM) in 1975; only five years later, that number had more than doubled to twenty-five billion DM. In 1989, it peaked at around forty billion DM. To keep the peace domestically, Honecker had consistently prioritized maintaining access to consumer goods and social services. As revenue failed to meet spending needs, these priorities drew funding away from investments in state enterprises, leaving many hollowed out and unproductive after years or decades of neglect.[1] Investment oriented toward efficiency and innovation was increasingly concentrated in a few risky bets placed on high-tech projects—especially the development of a homegrown microchip industry. As a result, the SED was unable to spend enough to keep the population happy, but continued to borrow so much that it was on the path to bankruptcy with an industrial base in rapid decline.

The conditions of the early 1970s were ideal for Honecker's economic and social ambitions. The relaxation of Cold War tensions—the era known as Détente—and subsequent relative stability across Eastern Europe had promoted trade, while the GDR's reselling of cheap Soviet oil to the West had long been an easy source of foreign currency. Post-collectivization, East German agricultural production was finally booming, which allowed for significant exports on top of supplying the domestic market. All of this fell apart by the end of the decade. Détente collapsed over the Soviet invasion of Afghanistan in 1979 and a failed arms control treaty to limit further deployments of nuclear weapons in Europe. Instead, the NATO defense alliance decided to implement the so-called double-track solution: a fresh round of negotiations on arms control was requested with the Soviets, but in the meantime, the United States would deploy a new generation of tactical nuclear missiles to West Germany to counter Soviet missiles stationed across the Eastern Bloc. While West German Chancellor Willy Brandt had pursued a policy of constructive engagement with the East (see Chapter 3 on *Ostpolitik*), he had been forced to resign (see bio on page 128), to be replaced by the Social Democrat Helmut Schmidt, who took a more confrontational stance with the Soviet Union and approved the stationing of nuclear arms in the Federal Republic despite mass popular protests (also encouraged by the Stasi) against the decision.[2]

These renewed tensions between East and West were intensified by the political crisis in Poland, where martial law was imposed in 1981 to crush the independent trade union Solidarność.[3] In response, the SED cut off visa-free travel between the GDR and its socialist neighbor, fearing the spread of the "Polish disease" of mass worker unrest. As the Polish economy worsened, deliveries to the GDR of raw goods needed for industrial and consumer production were disrupted or canceled altogether. New harbor facilities were quickly built on the Baltic Island of Rügen to create a direct sea connection from the GDR to the USSR in case a revolution in Poland cut off the land route. Coordination of trade between the socialist states through the Council for Mutual Economic Assistance (CMEA) had never been efficient, but it now became deeply dysfunctional.

The global commodities market, which had been a boon to East German finances in the early 1970s, also turned against the SED by the end of the decade. After coffee prices shot up in response to poor harvests in Brazil, the SED was forced to find alternative sources through trade deals with Ethiopia, Mozambique, and Vietnam (see Chapter 3).[4] The Iranian Revolution in 1979 set off a new oil crisis, but this time, the SED could not take advantage of it by reselling Soviet oil to the West, as it had previously done, since the Soviet Union, facing its own deepening financial crisis, had cut off deliveries of cheap oil to its Eastern Bloc allies. SED officials were dismayed by the Soviet decision, but warnings of dire consequences were ignored. In response, the SED implemented a crash program to cut petroleum usage across the GDR by converting rail and home heating oil systems to electrification. However, the main alternative to imported oil was locally mined, low-quality, brown coal that was even worse for the environment. The nuclear energy industry in the GDR had never been able to replace the need for fossil fuels, and nuclear plants suffered from ongoing issues with fuel supplies and Soviet reluctance to share state-of-the-art technology with East Germany.[5] The chemical industry was tasked with producing gasoline from coal stocks in a process that generated huge quantities of toxic by-products.

The environmental effects of East German industry were becoming increasingly noticeable to the public. The air quality in GDR cities was particularly poor due to coal-oven heating in homes and the pollution from cars like the Trabant, which generated far more exhaust fumes than larger cars in the West due to its inefficient engine design. By the end of the decade, East Germany had the worst air quality in Europe, with the "chemical triangle" between Halle, Merseburg, and Bitterfeld suffering most of all. East German agriculture also contributed to the larger picture of ecological degradation: the era of cheap oil and feed imports from the Soviet Union had allowed for a massive increase in pork production for the global export market. Once the price of feed and fertilizer shot up, East German factory-farmed pigs became a financial liability that also created lakes of toxic animal waste.[6]

First Walter Ulbricht and then Erich Honecker had placed their hopes for the East German economy on the high-tech sector. Both believed that rational planning could allow the GDR to develop selected areas of the economy that would develop export goods to sell to the West. The hard currency generated by these sales could then be used to pay off the loans taken out at Western banks to pay for the initial investment. The largest of these projects was for the development of a globally competitive microelectronics sector—despite the fact that the SED knew it would be competing against rival producers in tech leaders like the United States, Japan, and West Germany.[7] A further obstacle to this plan was the Coordinating Committee for Multilateral Export Controls—a trading agreement among NATO states plus Japan and Australia established early in the Cold War—which had embargoed the export of strategic goods and high technology to the Eastern Bloc. Billions in hard currency were poured into East German high-tech projects, including paying high mark-ups to smuggle in restricted technology with the collusion of firms like Siemens (West Germany) and Toshiba (Japan). The project eventually resulted in the U61000, a 1-megabyte microchip produced by VEB Microelectronics Research Center in Dresden. The chip was promoted as a technological marvel at the Leipzig International Trade Fair and awarded a gold medal for best new product of 1988, but it was an economic failure. It cost so much to produce that it was uncompetitive on the world market and required so many expensive foreign inputs that it would have cost less to simply import finished chips from the West. The culmination of Ulbricht's 1960s vision of a scientific-technical revolution that would allow the GDR to overtake without catching up proved to be a costly illusion that diverted funds from other, more productive, initiatives at a time of severe economic decline.[8]

The failure of the microchip program and other ventures meant that hard currency needed to be secured by less illustrious means. East German prisoners were put to work making goods for Western corporations, including sofas for the Swedish giant IKEA.[9] The GDR health ministry agreed to allow Western pharmaceutical companies to test experimental new drugs on East Germans who would otherwise have had no access to newer medications. Garbage from West Berlin was transported across the Wall to a landfill near the town of Zossen.[10] One of the loudest signals of the desperation for cash was the increasingly shady activities of the Commercial Coordination (*Kommerzielle Koordinierung*—KoKo) run by Alexander Schalck-Golodkowski (see Chapter 3). Tasked with acquiring foreign currency by any means necessary, KoKo's activities became increasingly illicit. During the

Iran-Iraq War (1980–8), the bloodiest war of the late twentieth century, and in direct contravention of international embargoes, the GDR supplied weapons to both sides of the conflict.[11] While the SED described East Germany as a "peaceful state" (*Friedensstaat*), it continued to grow its arms exports as one of the few products made in the GDR that nonsocialist customers were interested in buying. The Wieger automatic rifle, an East German alternative to the Soviet AK-47, was developed specifically to be sold to Third World clients.[12] While East Germany was sending guns to anti-apartheid liberation movements and supporting the African National Congress, it was also trying to broker arms deals with apartheid South Africa for profit.[13]

There had always been inequalities between different types of workers, but these were now made worse due to chronic economic problems, leading to widespread resentment in GDR society. Those working in tourism, or with well-off Western relatives, or other means of accessing hard currency maintained their access to "luxury" and imported goods that could only be purchased at Intershops, which did not accept East German Marks. In addition, a lack of investment in industrial equipment meant that some machinery was increasingly dangerous to use, and labor shortages pushed many into constant overtime, creating a widening gap in wages between workers depending on their specific positions or worksites.[14] For many workers, the cultural rituals of the workplace, such as celebrating "Heroes of Labor" to spur on productivity during the postwar drive for reindustrialization, were now a source of alienation. For the younger generation, "the focus on heroism only further highlighted the distinction between a (fictive) past in which communism seemed to have meaning and a stagnant present filled with empty slogans."[15]

By the 1980s, housing had also become a major point of embitterment. Most petitions written to the SED in that decade contained complaints about substandard living conditions. The Honecker spending boom of the 1970s was in many ways epitomized by the construction of large, prefabricated high-rise housing colonies (the so-called *Plattenbauten*) that encompassed more than 1.5 million apartment units. The WBS-70 model building, which provided around half a million of those units, became emblematic of the GDR in the Honecker era. For most who lived in suburban developments like Halle-Neustadt or Berlin-Marzahn, they were associated with "upward mobility, new beginnings, and general happiness."[16] There were invariably complaints about new developments, many of which were so rushed that they were surrounded by fields of mud when tenants moved in, but the real problem was that too little money was being spent for the maintenance of existing *Altbau* (pre-First World War) housing stock. As a result, "60 percent of all workers were reportedly still living in turn-of-the-century housing, with the bathroom on the floor landing, coal heating, and without hot running water."[17] This had political implications as GDR citizens witnessed not only a net loss of habitable housing each year as ever more Altbau rotted away but also how access to new housing with modern amenities became the privilege of the few, not a guarantee for all. Already in the 1970s, some citizens had begun to occupy apartments without state permission, and illicit squats only became more common over the following decade, especially among the growing dissident counterculture.[18]

Petitions to the SED and state agencies began to take on a harder edge in the 1980s. East Germans made clear in their letters that shortages very much called into question the political legitimacy of the SED. As one pensioner who had been waiting years for a telephone line wrote in a petition, officials were treating this delay as a problem of production shortages, which "fails to recognize that it diminishes the rule of law, deeply violates civil rights, and discredits the social system of the GDR."[19] East Germans had always complained about the quality of domestically produced condoms (brand name Mondos, produced by VEB Plastina), but the emerging HIV/AIDS epidemic and an explosion in global latex prices meant that not even these were available any longer. As one petitioner wrote, "The GDR always wants to change the world and make it a better place, but not even being able to buy condoms? That's a sign of impotence."[20] While state and party officials were supposed to reply to every petition, many offices became completely overwhelmed; the backlog was then made worse by those people writing to complain that they had not yet received a reply to their previous letter. Some citizens began to openly declare that they would not take part in elections unless their demands were met. Others found that the only way to get anything done was to work outside normal channels, including SED officials who now began to improvise, ignore the central economic plan, and implement their own projects off the books. In one case, officials in Leipzig managed to construct a massive bowling alley without the permission or even knowledge of their superiors in East Berlin.[21]

The political fallout of the failing economy was also felt at the international level. To deal with their inability to service the GDR's ever-growing debt obligations, the SED turned to an unlikely savior: Franz Josef Strauss, the conservative minister-president of Bavaria in West Germany. In 1982, a conservative-liberal government under Helmut Kohl had taken power in Bonn. While the Christian Democratic Union (CDU) had opposed Willy Brandt's normalization of relations with the GDR, its Bavarian sister party, the Christian Social Union (CSU), had been even more hardline. The CSU and the (Beijing-aligned) Albanian Communist Party were the only European political parties to oppose the signing of the Helsinki Accords (see Chapter 3). As leader of the CSU, Strauss had been a staunch anti-communist for decades, but the economics of the Cold War had changed. The GDR was now an important customer for West German goods and a steady supplier of agricultural goods at low prices to West German firms. The idea of East Germany going broke was politically appealing in theory, but would have enough downstream economic effects to be disastrous in practice. As such, Strauss traveled to East Berlin to meet with Honecker and arrange for a partial West German bailout of the SED's loans from the private banking sector.[22] Two new loans, around a billion DM each (nearly one billion euros total), were arranged on favorable economic terms. Strauss emerged as a key economic broker between East and West, facilitating insider deals to political allies and using his influence in East Berlin to direct GDR state purchasing to Western firms he was connected to. While this forestalled bankruptcy, it also gave West German politicians an immense amount of leverage over the SED. The GDR's finances were now increasingly determined by political and economic actors in the West.[23] The lack of financial control was not an ideal outcome, but in comparison to Poland, which defaulted on its foreign loans in 1981 shortly before declaring martial law, or Romania, which enacted a program of extreme austerity to deal with its financial problems, it appeared to the SED as the only option. Crucially, the structural problems that created the debt in the first place remained intractable, and the competitiveness of GDR exports on the global market—the key to generating hard currency to paying off foreign debt—continued its steady decline through the 1980s.[24]

Since the founding of the GDR, creating and securing a border that would be recognized as legitimate by the world had been a top priority. Now as the Helsinki Accords had realized this legitimacy, the SED was starting to lose its capacity to control border policy. The Helsinki Accords had created an ongoing process of summit meetings among the signatories to discuss the implementation of and compliance with the terms of the agreement. The SED found itself under pressure from reformist Eastern Bloc colleagues, as well as Western states, to allow more freedom of expression and travel. The FRG continued to pay for the release of East German citizens to the West, but also to use its financial leverage to *de facto* bribe the GDR to approve more petitions from those who wanted to emigrate. Simultaneously, West Germany also made demands about who should *not* be allowed to cross the border. Since West Berlin legally remained under four-power occupation and was not technically part of the Federal Republic, the only people actively monitoring the border were East German guards: West German authorities did not want their own immigration and customs checks in place in Berlin alongside those of the GDR, since that would create the impression of a "counter-wall." This meant that, for years, foreign students in the GDR could freely travel to West Berlin even as their German compatriots could not. By the 1980s, however, those seeking to claim refugee status in West Germany had discovered the "Berlin Gap": they could take cheap Interflug flights to East Berlin's Schönefeld Airport and then simply take a bus to West Berlin, where they did not need to show papers to get to Western Europe. In 1986, West Germany suddenly threatened to cut off its short-term "swing" credit, used to finance cross-border trade, to force the GDR to police the border on their behalf and keep out further migrants to the FRG.[25] Even control over border policy was thus gradually ceded to the West.

The German Democratic Republic

Cultural Production, Consumption, and Subcultures in Late Socialism

In the early years of the GDR, culture was granted a central place in the socialist project. Artists were crucial to the revival of a German culture corrupted by the Nazis, and were expected to play a guiding role in the building of socialism. In the midst of the material deprivation after the Second World War, the SED invoked the glorious future—both material and intellectual—that would come through hard work and faith in the Party. By 1971, the transition from Ulbricht to Honecker brought about important changes in both culture and consumption, as Honecker declared the cultural *Abgrenzung* (demarcation) from West Germany to be a core task of the Party. The demarcation of the GDR from the corrupting influences of the FRG was key to the concerted effort to foster a sense of East German national identity, distinctive from that of the Federal Republic, and demonstrate that the GDR was its own nation, not just a separate state. Alongside this demarcation was a massive increase in consumer spending. The glorious future was replaced by the acceptable present, and culture became a matter of lifestyle rather than artistic aspiration. This arrangement began to break down in the 1980s. Western culture was still policed, but it increasingly flooded into the GDR, often with the coordination of state agencies who used it to generate much-needed revenue. At the same time, subcultures were proliferating beyond the capacity of the state to organize them within the existing associational structures that had allowed for the controlled adoption of international trends in earlier generations. Finally, there was the rise of a counterculture, which officials rejected as corrupt and illegitimate, that deliberately sought to separate itself from the mainstream. The hegemony of traditional state socialist culture was under strain from all directions.

As the utopian future of communism receded in the 1980s, the SED turned to the glorious past to legitimize itself. Martin Luther, the father of the Reformation, had always been vilified in East German historiography for his betrayal of peasant revolutionaries (seen as early ancestors of the communist movement), but for the five-hundredth anniversary of his birth in 1983, he was suddenly transformed into a national hero.[26] Celebrations were held in the two cities most crucial to his personal history—Eisenach and Wittenberg, both of which were located in the GDR. DEFA turned his life into an inspirational biopic. Ideology chief Kurt Hager told the Politburo that this turnaround was not in ignorance of Luther's politics, but a "question of how we can make this heritage productive for our time and our society."[27] The history of Prussia was similarly rehabilitated, and the monument to Friedrich the Great that had been taken down in 1950 was restored to its former position of prominence in East Berlin in 1980. The massive commemorations for the seven-hundred-and-fiftieth anniversary of Berlin in 1987 brought with it a further re-evaluation and celebration of the progressive contributions of Prussia to German history.[28]

As public history was becoming less explicitly socialist, so too was East German culture. The capacity of the SED's cultural apparatus to carefully modify international trends into acceptable socialist culture was in decline. Instead of adapting Western culture, it was imported wholesale. Cultural controls were liberalized (though not abolished) as more Western media entered the country for financial reasons— audiences were willing to pay for Western culture, and the SED followed the money. For example, American blockbusters drew large crowds to the cinema, and the revenue from those screenings became an essential source of funding for the domestic film industry, as both direct state subsidies dried up and cultural production was expected to become financially self-sufficient. In the late 1980s, the biggest films of the year in the GDR were *Beverly Hills Cop*, *E.T. the Extra-Terrestrial*, and *Dirty Dancing* (which sold five million tickets, in a country of seventeen million).[29] East German artists increasingly lost their role in envisioning the path to a better socialism. The SED began to allow artists to sell their work in the West, and musicians to go on tour (with the state taking a generous cut of the proceeds). This generated revenue for the state, but put artists beyond the control of East German censors who wielded their power through domestic album production, venue booking, and exhibition organization rather than outright bans.[30] The cultural erasure of the division between East and West was also apparent in consumer production. In the

The German Democratic Republic

1950s and 1960s, the need for a new kind of socialist consumerism had driven the development of a unique material culture that emerged from East German state enterprises seeking to serve their domestic market. The plastic goods of the late 1950s and 1960s, for example, became iconic representations of East German culture.[31] From the 1970s onwards, however, the focus on selling abroad to generate hard currency undermined the distinctive character of this work: "In order to establish itself and survive in an international market, the East German production aesthetic converged with western ones," to create a kind of joint aesthetic of "conservative modernism."[32]

Although Western bands like ABBA had been able to perform songs on GDR TV programs like the variety show "Ein Kessel Buntes" (Cauldron of Color), over the course of the 1980s, big musical acts from the West were increasingly allowed to perform live in the GDR. First it was West German Udo Lindenberg—who had a hit song "Sonderzug nach Pankow" (special train to Pankow, the East Berlin neighborhood where many of the SED elite lived), in which he imagined Erich Honecker putting on a leather jacket and locking himself into the bathroom to listen to rock music on the radio—who was allowed to give a concert at the Palace of the Republic in 1983. In front of a crowd of specifically selected members of the Free German Youth (FDJ), he performed as part of a music festival dedicated to world peace, though his set did not include the song everyone wanted to hear.[33] While a follow-up tour was not allowed in large part because Lindenberg used the concert as an opportunity to denounce nuclear missile deployments in West Germany *and* the GDR, other major performers followed. West German rockstar Peter Maffay and American soul singer Solomon Burke sang at the 750th anniversary festival in East Berlin in 1987. That same year, American folk singer Bob Dylan performed at Treptower Park in East Berlin in front of an audience of 100,000. Carlos Santana, Joe Cocker, and Bryan Adams all held major rock concerts. The largest rock concert in the history of the GDR came in 1988, when the FDJ booked Bruce Springsteen to play at an event officially dedicated to solidarity with Nicaragua. 160,000 fans turned up in Berlin-Weißensee, with many waving American flags in

Stagnation, Collapse, and Reunification

tribute to Springsteen, who told the audience in German that he was singing in "the hope that one day all barriers will be torn down."[34]

While Western imports were now far more tolerated, there were some trends that proved indigestible even in a time of cultural convergence. The 1984 American film *Beat Street* created a youth craze for hip-hop music and breakdancing. African American culture was at times racistly dismissed as inferior, but also often viewed as innately more politically progressive, due to its associations with the American Civil Rights Movement. The FDJ created hip-hop clubs, and soon young East Germans in home-made Adidas sweatsuits were popping and locking.[35] New Wave came to the GDR in the form of bands like Silly, which actually produced their first album in the West after the East German music label Amiga proved uninterested. Led by singer Tamara Danz, it would become one of the most popular bands of the 1980s.[36] Electronic music took off after a performance by Tangerine Dream at the Palace of the Republic. The main impediment to its spread was the importation of expensive equipment, not state censors or the Stasi. Musicians often worked with contacts in the Church who could help source electronic instruments from colleagues in the West.[37] At this time, the East German jazz scene also continued to evolve from its traditionalist roots to become a major center of free jazz experimentation, which had previously been denounced as unsocialist.[38]

Other genres, conversely, proved more problematic. State officials were concerned by the rapid growth of a heavy metal subculture, with its focus on emotional displays of aggression that were difficult to reconcile with officially sanctioned forms of public culture.[39] Even more threatening to the state were punks, who were seen as deviant antisocials and consequently faced harsh state repression. The SED understood punk culture as a product of the hopelessness of capitalism, so its appearance in the GDR was seen as an alien import from the West. A crackdown in 1984 resulted in many in the punk scene being arrested, sent into military service, or deported to West Germany.[40] Punks took refuge in the Church—just as political dissidents did—to find a space that was safe from the wrath of the

Stasi. But even within more traditional art forms, the SED was losing control. Cultural events and venues meant to transmit ideological messages to the population were increasingly being used to send messages to the state instead.[41] Artists began to demand space for public dialogue or moved into open dissent; others moved out of the mainstream to embrace experimental and avant-garde art.[42]

In the world of sports, the GDR appeared to be incredibly successful at this time. From 1972 onward, the GDR was never ranked less than third in the medal count at the Olympics and came in first at the 1984 Winter Games in Sarajevo. Some of the swimming and track and field records set by East German athletes took decades to be broken; both the women and men's world record for the discus throw are still held by East German athletes today. Even as rumors swirled that East German athletic success was underpinned by widespread doping (which was true and imposed on many athletes without their consent), there was a concerted effort to use these international sporting achievements to rally patriotic feelings at home and raise prestige abroad.[43] That being said, the GDR sporting landscape was so overtly corrupt that it generated its own negative cultural impact at home. The East German football league was dominated by a Stasi-sponsored team, BFC (Berlin Football Club) Dynamo. With the personal patronage of Stasi chief Erich Mielke, it had the best players and was granted favorable rulings by referees. The team became widely hated, and some football clubs, such as East Berlin's FC Union, became a breeding ground for discontent and dissent. By identifying with one club so closely, matches against BFC Dynamo became an opportunity to express one's distaste for the Stasi by proxy.[44]

Other subcultures that the SED had sought to keep hidden away were also emerging from private spaces. Since the decriminalization of homosexuality, the SED had told gay East Germans that they should be satisfied with being tolerated by the state—so long as they kept out of the public eye. In the 1970s, East German gays and lesbians began to demand the right to exist publicly by forming activist organizations such as the Homosexual Interest Group Berlin (*Homosexuelle Interessengemeinschaft Berlin*, HIB) and nurturing a nascent queer cultural scene, including the cross-dressing cabaret group Hibaré.[45] By the 1980s, they were able to gain greater public acceptance, including the establishment of officially recognized gay youth groups.[46] In the final years of the GDR, homosexuality was slowly moving into the mainstream. The first East German film focused on homosexuality, Heiner Carow's *Coming Out*, premiered to the public on November 9, 1989—the same day the Berlin Wall opened.[47]

The darker side of this increasing pluralism from below was the rise of a neo-Nazi subculture. Skinheads had emerged in the early 1980s and proliferated mostly in connection with football hooligan culture. Many were connected to BFC Dynamo, which the club tolerated, as they were useful in conflicts with "rowdys" from opposing clubs. In 1987, the growing problem of young neo-Nazis came to public prominence when a group of thirty skinheads attacked a concert at East Berlin's Zion Church, attended mostly by punks and members of various dissident church groups.[48] The next year, skinheads defaced a historic Jewish cemetery on East Berlin's Schönhauser Allee. Beyond East Berlin, neo-Nazis established contact with the West German far-right, which laid the groundwork for their collaboration across Germany after reunification.[49]

The Return of the Emigration Crisis

The Berlin Wall had effectively ended the wave of emigration that destabilized the GDR in the early 1960s, but this did not eliminate the desire for East Germans to leave the country. The normalization of relations with the West in the 1970s was a boon to the SED in terms of its legitimacy, but it also raised hopes for many East Germans that the draconian border regime would be relaxed. The Berlin Wall had always been justified as a defensive measure to prevent the supposedly militaristic fascists in Bonn from staging an invasion of the GDR and destroying the socialist project. Improved relations with West Germany due to Détente and the Helsinki Accords in 1975 undercut the apocalyptic visions of the early Cold War that undergirded the ideological basis for lethal measures at the East German border.

It was possible to make a formal application to travel to the West or to emigrate from the GDR: anyone who wanted to leave permanently had to apply to the Ministry of the Interior asking to be relieved of their East German citizenship. The application then had to be processed, interviews with applicants arranged so officials could evaluate motivations, and a decision on the further course of action made. The SED was happy to see retirees emigrate, as the Federal Republic would then have to cover their pensions. But it was loath to let younger, productive workers and especially professionals leave the country for any reason. The SED did not recognize emigration as a right, and all applications inconsistent with "the social interests of the GDR" were rejected.[50] Applying to leave the country brought scrutiny from the Stasi, with most facing—at a minimum—intense pressure to withdraw their request if they were at all desirable as citizens. Pressure was brought to bear on applicants in a variety of ways, including losing jobs or access to education, the harassment of family members, and in some cases imprisonment. Relatives and acquaintances were in turn pressured to cut off contact so that applicants would be socially isolated.[51]

Demand to leave the GDR nonetheless steadily grew over the course of the 1970s. East Germans had a range of motives for wanting to exit. While the economic situation in East Germany did improve for average citizens under Honecker due to increased spending on consumer goods, this was also the era in which social mobility completely flatlined. The early years of the GDR offered many avenues for advancement, especially for workers and farmers. Entire professions were remade almost from scratch due to the mass purge of Nazis after the Second World War and the emigration of so many skilled workers. The legal system in particular was remade with prewar communists, rapidly trained layman and graduates from the recently founded Academy for State and Legal Science in Babelsberg. The early land reforms that redistributed land expropriated from the aristocracy also provided new opportunities. Yet by the 1960s, most of these avenues for social advancement were closing, and by the 1970s, the GDR had become a rigidly stratified society once more with the Party elite holding almost all positions of social status and power.[52]

There were periodic spikes in the number of applications to exit throughout the 1970s associated with each act of diplomatic normalization with the West. The signing of the Transit Agreement (1971), the Basic Treaty (1972), and East Germany's entry into the United Nations (1973) were all used as a pretext for East Germans to apply to exit.[53] The 1975 Helsinki Accords in particular sparked a wave of emigration attempts. Even before the terms of the treaty had been published, many were already submitting applications on the assumption that such a major agreement must mean that travel rules had been relaxed. After the text of Accords was published in *Neues Deutschland*, many latched onto the language about human rights and free movement to justify their requests. In that year, the total number of applications to leave jumped by 40 percent to 13,000; in 1976, that number rose to 20,000.[54] Almost all were rejected.

More concerning for the SED was the explosion in the late 1970s in public demands to leave made via Western nongovernmental organizations and not by the standard application procedure. While the West German government preferred to quietly pay the SED for the migration of specific East Germans rather than engage in direct confrontation about the SED's human rights record, private organizations—including Amnesty International or the Frankfurt am Main-based International League for Human Rights—launched public campaigns for the release of East Germans trying to leave.[55] This caused the Stasi to pay even more negative attention to petitioners, but also allowed more citizens to eventually leave faster—their applications approved rapidly simply to make the problem go away. In one famous case, a doctor in the town of Riesa who had previously petitioned to emigrate drafted a public letter denouncing the SED and demanding to exit based on his rights in the Helsinki Accords. He posted this letter in his office, where it was signed by others; he also sent copies to Western NGOs who printed it in the media. Many of the signatories were arrested but subsequently allowed to emigrate.

The 1970s saw a massive expansion of the Stasi to deal with the increased international traffic to the GDR and the pressure from those seeking to emigrate. There had been around 100,000 IMs (*inoffizielle Mitarbeiter*, unofficial informants) in 1968. In the late

1970s, the numbers of IMs reached more than 180,000 in a country of seventeen million.[56] The Stasi turned to a strategy of *Zersetzung*—a tactic of psychological pressure directed first at intellectual dissidents, cultural nonconformists, citizens seeking to exit the country and, eventually, the emerging peace and human rights movements. It included not only heavy-handed surveillance (so that subjects knew they were always being followed and watched) but also a diverse collection of destabilizing psychological tactics, from rearranging furniture in people's homes while they were out to having agents try to instigate an affair with someone's spouse to destroy their family life.[57] The Stasi saw the increase in applications to exit the country as a sign of a coordinated attack on the GDR by Western intelligence agencies seeking to create an underground political opposition within East Germany. In 1976, the Zentrale Koordinierungsgruppe zur Bekämpfung von Flucht und Übersiedlung (ZKG, Central Coordination Group for Flight and Emigration) was created to lead the fight against Western NGOs making contact with GDR citizens, which was deemed a form of espionage.

While the SED was previously able to point to the migration of cultural notables to the GDR as a sign of its superiority, the emigration of many prominent East German artists—including actors such as Manfred Krug (the lead in *Traces of Stones*), Angelica Domröse (the lead in *The Legend of Paul and Paula*), and Armin Müller-Stahl, who had played a Stasi equivalent to James Bond in a popular East German TV series—in the 1970s was a major embarrassment. For many of these émigrés, the denationalization of Wolf Biermann was a major turning point. A popular singer who had been born in Hamburg and migrated to the GDR, Biermann was a friend of dissident Robert Havemann and had become increasingly critical of the SED in the 1970s. While on tour in West Germany in 1976, he was summarily stripped of his citizenship and barred from returning to the GDR. A group of East German intellectuals and cultural figures including internationally renowned authors such as Christa Wolf and Stefan Heym wrote an open letter of protest to the SED, citing Biermann's loyalty to socialism: "Wolf Biermann was and is an uncomfortable poet—he shares that quality with many poets of the past. Bearing in mind Marx's *Eighteenth Brumaire*, according to which the proletarian revolution is constantly self-critical, our socialist state should, in contrast to anachronistic social forms, be able to tolerate such discomfort in a calm contemplative way."[58] All the signatories were professionally punished and placed under state surveillance. The long-standing SED critic Robert Havemann, who had already been fired from his position as a professor at Humboldt University in 1962, was now placed under house arrest from 1976–9 as punishment for his agitation on Biermann's behalf and smuggling texts to the West for publication.

After a brief lull, major shortages of meat, coffee, and other consumer goods set off another wave of applications to exit beginning in 1984. In that year, the SED, faced with a barrage of repeat applicants, decided that it would be more efficient to allow the most determined to leave—that way, they could no longer cause problems, and their dissatisfaction would no longer affect social relations at home. Around 37,000 people, described as "enemies, criminal elements, and incorrigibles," were allowed to depart. This mass exit, however, did not have the intended effect: Seeing so many receive permission to leave only encouraged those who had previously thought it was impossible, causing the number of first-time applicants to rise by 400 percent to more than 57,000. The number of exit applications would rise every year from 1984 until 1989, when the Berlin Wall finally opened.[59]

Dissent: Environmentalism, Peace, and Human Rights

The fracturing of a state socialist culture paralleled the fissures that emerged in the political life of the GDR in the 1970s. Under state socialism, there could be no loyal opposition outside of the system; accordingly, so believed the SED, these groups had to be disrupted and suppressed. As one Stasi officer later recounted, "in a developed socialist society, there could not exist such a thing as a genuine opposition. All there was, was a so-called opposition, which was in reality an anti-socialist political underground, inspired and directed by the class enemy."[60] As a result, the steady proliferation of small independent groups that sought change within East Germany could logically only be part of a sinister Western plot to destroy socialism.[61] As a result, the increasing turn to dissent, especially among the younger educated elements of the population, was treated as a sign of enemy infiltration and not as a signal that reforms were urgently needed.

In the early decades of the GDR, the SED had made great efforts to create the appearance of engagement with the population through regular mass consultations on issues like the reform to family law or the adoption of the socialist constitution. After a national mass consultation regarding the overhaul of civil law in 1975, Honecker abandoned such events. Although this final consultation had proceeded without incident, the increase in dissent in the years following made such opportunities for spontaneous mass expressions of dissatisfaction and criticism too risky. This left only petitions as the only official channel for citizens to constructively engage with state policy; dissidents took advantage of this neglect by demanding increased dialogue between the people and the party. Crucially, they called for the renewal of socialist democracy, rather than the abolishing of SED rule and free elections, which had been demanded by protestors during the 1953 Uprising (see Chapter 1).

In contrast to the rise of critical civil society organizations in different parts of Eastern Europe (such as the human rights group Charter 77 in Czechoslovakia or the independent trade union Solidarność in Poland), dissident activism in the GDR was confined to small circles under the protection of the Church, which insisted that the groups they sheltered did not seek to air their grievances to the wider public (see Chapter 2).[62] They were thus only allowed to produce mimeographed newsletters stamped with "only for inner-church circulation," which made connecting to like-minded individuals in different parts of the country difficult. From within these church-based circles, opposition to the Cold War arms race manifested itself in a growing peace movement, while the increasingly devastating impact of East German industrial policy and brown coal pollution led to the rise of grassroots environmental activist groups. Similarly, even though East Germany had not seen the emergence of a human rights movement (as had happened in the late 1970s in the USSR, Czechoslovakia, and Poland), the first human rights initiative independent of the church was founded in East Berlin at the end of 1985 and demanded increased political pluralism and freedom of expression.

Far more than in other Eastern European states, the intelligentsia of the GDR was still committed to socialism, even if many began to waver in their support for the SED itself.[63] Since the GDR had a capitalist counterpoint next door, German cultural and intellectual elites had gone through a process of self-sorting in the early years as socialists migrated East out of ideological conviction. By the 1970s, Western European Communist Parties distanced themselves from Moscow and embraced pluralistic democratic collaboration in parliaments. Emblematic of this ideological shift of these so-called "Eurocommunist" parties was the historic compromise between the Italian Communist and Christian Democratic Parties and the participation of Spanish Communists in the democratization process following the death of General Francisco Franco. Conversely, East German intellectuals took a different path by searching for a purer version of the socialist project to counteract their increasing disillusionment with "actually existing socialism"—the official term for socialism as it had been realized in the Eastern Bloc, rather than any kind of utopian version imagined by intellectuals. Former SED functionary-turned-dissident Rudolf Bahro, for example, critiqued the bureaucratism of the SED on ecological grounds, but had no interest in adopting Western liberal democracy in its place. Instead, he outlined a vision for an eco-utopian socialism in his manifesto *Die Alternative* (The Alternative in Eastern Europe).[64] After his work was smuggled to the West, where it was published and then re-imported to the GDR, Bahro was first imprisoned, kicked out of the SED, and then deported to the Federal Republic.

In addition to Bahro, rampant environmental degradation encouraged a number of alternative ecology activists, many of whom found safety in the Protestant Church, to speak out about the environmental damage innate to bureaucratized state socialism—albeit in forums with limited reach in the GDR. East Germany was one of the first countries to mention the protection of the environment in its constitution in 1968, and Erich Honecker made it part of the standard SED rhetoric.[65] Yet air and water quality continued to decline as East German agriculture and heavy industry prioritized output over ecology.[66] The official promotion of outdoor activities as a means of connecting to the socialist homeland began to clash with complaints from citizens that state policy was poisoning that very same space. The SED stopped publishing statistics on pollution in 1982, but this only led to increased demands from grassroots groups for more data.

Environmental issues during this period also highlighted the international interconnections that continued despite the Berlin Wall: the cross-border impact of East German air and water pollution meant that the SED had to negotiate with West Germany over compensation for transnational economic damages. Similarly, the SED also had to deal with transnational environmental dissent as activists in the GDR connected to groups in West Germany, as well as Poland and Czechoslovakia. The 1986 Chernobyl nuclear accident only increased the appeal of environmental issues as a cause for grassroots activism, as it cut through traditional political and national divisions.[67]

SED rhetoric had always emphasized the importance of peace through the specific lens of antifascism, which demanded armed resistance against the forces of war, namely the capitalist and imperialist West. This stance had long put the SED at odds with the pacifism of the Churches, which had successfully lobbied for the option to conscientiously object to military service. When compulsory military education was nonetheless introduced beginning in the eighth grade in 1978, it sparked a new round of conflict between Christians and the SED. Two years earlier, a pastor, Oskar Brüsewitz, had self-immolated in protest of the ideological indoctrination in schools, so this further militarization of the educational system hit a nerve. From within the Church, an independent peace movement arose to challenge militarism in everyday life, including the regular parades of the armed forces and the mostly voluntary paramilitary training in youth groups. Thousands began to wear a "Swords into Plowshares" patch sewn onto their clothing. Produced by church groups, these patches sported the image of a sculpture, on display at the United Nations, by Soviet artist Yevgeny Vuchetich showing a blacksmith beating a sword into a plow blade with a hammer. Shortly before his death in 1982, Robert Havemann, along with the pastor Rainer Eppelmann, released a manifesto: the *Berliner Appell* (Berlin Appeal), which called on the GDR and others to "make peace without weapons" (which was a refutation of the SED position that peace could only be achieved in Europe through military readiness). The painter Bärbel Bohley, along with Havemann's widow Katja, Ulrike Poppe, and others, protested against a reform of the military draft laws that included the option to mobilize women during wartime by founding the GDR chapter of Women for Peace, an international organization with a large following in West Germany and Northern Ireland.[68] The Concrete Peace network was also formed during this period, linking church groups and numerous grassroots circles around the country through annual seminars.[69]

Ulrike Poppe

Born 1953, Rostock, GDR

Ulrike Poppe was one of the many activists in the GDR who was crucial to the creation of a dissident movement, but did not personally seek political power once the SED collapsed. She was placed under Stasi surveillance beginning in 1976 under the Operational Case name Compass II and her Stasi file grew to more than forty volumes of documentation.

Ulrike Wick was born to a family of academics and raised in a small town just north of West Berlin in Brandenburg. After a degree in history at Humboldt University, she worked as an assistant at the Museum for German History (today, the German Historical Museum). In 1979, she married Gerd Poppe, who would also become one of the leading figures in the *Bürgerrechtsbewegung* (citizens' rights movement). Her own career as a rights activist began in 1980 when she helped open an independent daycare in the Prenzlauer Berg neighborhood of East Berlin, and escalated in 1982 when she and artist Bärbel Bohley founded the activist group Women for Peace. She was briefly imprisoned by the Stasi on suspicion of having communicated treasonous information to a foreigner after meeting with a New Zealand peace activist in 1983, but was released in part due to international solidarity campaigns for her freedom. In 1985, she was one of the founders of the first independent human rights activist group in the GDR, the Initiative for Peace and Human Rights, and soon became one of the leading figures in the Concrete Peace (Frieden Konkret) activist network. In the late 1980s, she was repeatedly arrested and detained for her activism. In 1989, she cofounded Demokratie Jetzt, a left-wing church-based citizens' rights group, and was one of the first signatories to the "For Our Country" Manifesto, which rejected reunification and called for the GDR to remain an independent democratic socialist country. She represented Demokratie Jetzt at the Central Round Table alongside her husband Gerd, who represented the Initiative for Peace and Human Rights. In the 1990 Volkskammer elections, she worked on the campaign of the left-leaning Bündnis 90 coalition.

Since reunification, Poppe has not played a role in electoral politics and never ran for office. She has been highly active in a range of civic and state initiatives to engage with GDR history and to expose the activities of the Stasi. She retired in 2017.

The members of the peace and environmental movements that had formed under Church protection initially saw "spiritual-cultural activity, social engagement, and a lifestyle grounded in solidarity," as the solutions to these problems—the goal was not to challenge SED rule.[70] The Stasi, however, disagreed that this made them harmlessly apolitical. Activist organizations were put under surveillance, small public demonstrations were met with violent suppression and key figures—such as Bärbel Bohley and Ulrike Poppe—were arrested and imprisoned. After peace activists infiltrated a Free German

Youth rally in Jena with their own critical signs, more than thirty had their citizenship revoked and were forcibly deported to West Germany. Among them was Roland Jahn (who decades later would become director of the Stasi archives), who was handcuffed to the bathroom of a train heading to West Germany.[71] By 1985, such shows of force by the Stasi made it clear to activists that the solution was not to be exclusively found in a better socialism but *also* in political change. The SED's stranglehold on the public sphere had to be loosened—and pluralism in the GDR secured—before its citizens were able to mobilize for purely moral causes like peace.[72] Rather than focus on a righteous lifestyle, activists turned to the idea of human rights activism.

The creation of a human rights movement outside of the protection of the Church proved difficult. Efforts were not only disrupted by Stasi informants and provocateurs among the ranks of the activist scene, but there was also resistance from socialist elements of the dissident movement who still believed in a real socialist revolution and saw human rights as a retreat into liberal democracy. However, at the end of 1985, a small group of activists founded the Initiative Frieden und Menschenrechte (IFM, Initiative for Peace and Human Rights) in East Berlin—around half of its members were Stasi informants. This group sought to bring together the various disaffected activist causes in the GDR, from those fighting unchecked pollution to draft resistors, in order to demand political and civil rights. Rejecting anticommunism as a basis for their activism, the IFM positioned itself as seeking only the highest goals of socialism. As citizens, they were claiming their constitutional and human rights to take part in political and civic affairs and to fight for the goals of international peace outside of the strictures of both the Church and Party organizations. As with the environmental movement, many members of the IFM were also plugged into wider networks; Wolfgang Templin, a former Stasi informant turned dissident, for example, had spent several years in Poland and had taken part in the Polish workers' rights organization KOR. He viewed KOR's commitment to public action over private activism, and pluralism over ideological purity, as a model for East Germany.[73]

By the end of the decade, these disparate groups began to merge and cooperate in different ways. Most dissident groups initially saw the people trying to emigrate as weakening the cause of reform in East Germany and refused to cooperate with them.[74] By 1987, however, members of the IFM began to reach out to groups trying to organize for the right to emigrate. Rather than trying to keep people in the GDR to maintain pressure on the state, they believed that all rights needed to be fought for equally and that the departure of so many citizens would force the SED to see the need to reform and create a system where everyone could feel that their voice counted. In that vein, a group of dissidents founded the Umwelt-Bibliothek (Environmental Library) in East Berlin, which soon became a hub for ecology, peace, and third world solidarity activism. In 1987, the Stasi raided the library and destroyed its printing press, which the IFM used to publish its newsletter *Grenzfall* (a play on words that meant "borderline case" but also "the fall of the border").[75] Most of the Protestant church leadership was still trying to keep dissenters from broadcasting their message to the wider community to avoid the wrath of the Stasi, but there were some, like Erfurt Provost Heino Falcke, who supported them. In 1988, he organized the Ecumenical Assembly for Justice, Peace, and the Integrity of Creation, which created a forum for thousands of Christians to constructively discuss social problems. This series of events blurred the line between religious practice, inner-church dissent, and open political activism.[76]

By 1988, dissidents were breaking out of their niches and into the public eye through public spectacle. In that year, several human rights groups decided to crash the annual Luxemburg-Liebknecht rally, which commemorated the founding leaders of the German Communist Party assassinated in 1919. Dissidents brought their own banners to the rally, including one with a quotation from Rosa Luxemburg that read, "Freedom is always and exclusively freedom for the one who thinks differently."[77] The human rights dissidents presented themselves as the true representatives of the spirit of socialism, not as its enemies. Despite this appeal to socialist values, the protestors were arrested and some, like Wolfgang Templin and Bärbel Bohley, deported from the GDR. This crackdown set back the emerging East Berlin dissident scene; the center of events in 1989 would consequently move to East Germany's second largest city: Leipzig.

Reform Communism and the Decline of the Cold War

As a country, the GDR was a product of the Cold War; for the SED, the rivalry with the West, and its alliance with the Soviet Union formed the basic structure of East German politics. In the 1980s, the rise of reform communism from within the Eastern Bloc and the decline of the Cold War as an organizing principle of global affairs began to erode these fundamental aspects of SED rule. The primary disruption in the socialist status quo came from the very top of the Soviet Union through the ascension of General Secretary Mikhail Gorbachev in 1985. After the stagnation of the Brezhnev years and two short-lived successors who were unable to get a handle on the dysfunction of the Soviet economy or the quagmire of the Afghanistan occupation, Gorbachev's rise to power signaled the shift toward a younger generation after years of geriatric rule. By this time, the Soviet economy was in shambles, and Gorbachev believed that only radical structural changes could save the USSR.[78] He introduced two reform programs: *glasnost* (openness), which aimed to increase freedom of speech and the media to encourage more democratic engagement, and *perestroika* (restructuring), which aimed to decentralize the Soviet economy, increase the role of market forces and shift economic decision-making from state officials to workers' councils.

In the GDR, Gorbachev's reforms were an inspiration to many dissidents who saw the possibility for reform and democratization of socialism from within. To the SED leadership, however, Gorbachev's reforms were a threat rather than a serious plan to tackle stagnation and popular disaffection. Although the official slogan of the party was "to learn from the Soviets is to learn how to win," it now appeared that Moscow itself was becoming a liability, and Erich Honecker rejected reform communism entirely as a menace to the socialist project. Tito's Yugoslavia had broken with the USSR in the late 1940s, and already in the late 1960s, Romania had distanced itself from Moscow to pursue an even more authoritarian system centered on the personal rule of Nicolae Ceaușescu. But now the rest of the Eastern Bloc was beginning to fall apart: Poland had been put under martial law (1981–3) to suppress the rise of the independent trade union Solidarność, and it continued to be rocked by protests and unrest. In Hungary, the ruling elite saw a path out of economic decline by joining the International Monetary Fund to gain access to foreign loans and integrate the country into the globalizing economy.[79] Although the Czechoslovak leadership shared the SED's distrust of Gorbachev's reforms, the binary political logic of the Cold War was breaking down, and the GDR was increasingly economically reliant on Western financial partners rather than socialist allies. As the ideological blocs became less coherent, the lines of conflict blurred.

East German solidarity with revolutionary Third World movements continued in the 1980s, but the GDR's financial crisis meant that funding for various initiatives was scaled back drastically. Nonetheless, when it came to anti-apartheid activism, the GDR remained far more active than the rest of the Eastern Bloc. Nearly 500 children of SWAPO activists from South West Africa (today: Namibia) were evacuated to the GDR for education and refuge.[80] This was, however, undercut by the GDR's increasing trade with South Africa—both legal transactions and the illicit arms trade.[81] Honecker maintained close ties to Ethiopian leader Haile Mengistu Mariam, and the ongoing arms for coffee trade with the GDR helped to deal with multiple insurgency movements that challenged the Derg, the Marxist-Leninist military junta that ruled in Addis Ababa. The victory of the Sandinista movement in Nicaragua created a new socialist state in Latin America, and many East Germans who found themselves jaded about the day-to-day realities of socialism in the GDR were enthusiastic about the chance to help a young revolutionary state through a solidarity program to establish widespread medical care.[82] At the same time, however, university programs were no longer free to foreign students. From 1982 onward, sending countries had to pay the GDR for spots in its universities as international education became a commercial enterprise rather than a form of solidarity.[83] The contract worker program hit upon problems as well: Algerians were recalled in 1984 over political tensions between the two countries, and

Mozambican contract workers were swindled out of much of their pay on the promise that they would be paid when they got home. Rather than send money to Mozambique directly to pay the deferred salaries, the GDR reduced the debt owed by the Mozambican government over trade deals. The returning workers were then paid nothing.[84]

Even before Gorbachev's reform program, Honecker had started a campaign of personal diplomacy with the wider world. Whereas Walter Ulbricht had set out to tour the Middle East in search of diplomatic recognition in the 1950s, Honecker sought to build connections to the nonsocialist world and to erstwhile socialist allies. Building upon the economic cooperation of the 1970s, Honecker made his first official state visit to a non-socialist nation by traveling to neutral Austria in 1980 and to US-allied Japan to personally meet with Emperor Hirohito in 1981. Since the transfer of power in China from Mao Zedong to Deng Xiaoping in 1976, the GDR had been trying to re-establish relations that had essentially broken off in the 1960s due to the Sino-Soviet split. These efforts were finally rewarded in 1986, when Honecker became the first Eastern Bloc leader invited to Beijing for a state visit since the break between Moscow and Beijing two decades earlier.[85] All this international travel culminated in 1987: Honecker visited West Germany. Having ascended to the leadership of the SED when East Germany was still unrecognized by most of the world and its legitimacy as a separate state was categorically denied by the Federal Republic, it was a symbolic triumph for Honecker to be received by Chancellor Helmut Kohl as an equal.

As East and West Germany moved toward more cordial relations, an open split emerged between leaders in Moscow and East Berlin. With Gorbachev's pursuit of reconciliation with the West through disarmament talks with US President Ronald Reagan, financially and politically supporting the GDR at all costs no longer made sense. The increasingly revisionist understanding of state socialism coming from Moscow drove Honecker and other hardliners in the Politburo to openly reject the Soviet reforms as a model for the GDR. East German ideology chief Kurt Hager summed up the position of SED elite in an interview saying, "Would you, by the way, feel obligated to redo the wallpaper in your apartment just because your neighbor redid his?"[86] Invoking the rhetoric of the KPD in 1945, he asserted that East Germany should not be forced onto the Soviet path of development. In the immediate postwar, that message had signaled an openness to cooperation with a broad alliance of antifascist forces, but now it meant a total refusal to deviate from the status quo. The SED was not devoid of reformers, but they were consistently marginalized. The most prominent was Hans Modrow, who was made party chief in the city of Dresden to keep him sufficiently far away from the center of power in East Berlin.[87]

For those East Germans trying to work within the system and follow the party line, the idea that the Soviets were now also a threat to the socialist project seemed outlandish. In one particularly controversial incident from 1988, the SED removed the German-language Soviet press digest *Sputnik* from the list of officially permitted publications—essentially banning it from circulation. East German officials had taken offense to an article that criticized the KPD's failure to work with Social Democrats during the Weimar Republic to prevent Hitler's rise to power in 1933. For many loyal East Germans, *Sputnik* had been a valuable source of information on the state of political affairs in both the GDR and the communist world writ large. Many looked to it to help them navigate the increasingly murky ideological waters in an era of uncertain reform and shifting alliances. As a result, the ban on *Sputnik* caused what the Stasi described as a "massive wave of critical opinion," particularly from SED members.[88] Teachers wrote petitions to complain that they felt helpless and clueless in the face of such arbitrary action by the state bureaucracy. While it was clear to almost everyone that the country was slipping into a state of crisis, the leadership of the SED refused to change course. Anyone who sought to tackle the overwhelming challenges facing the GDR was, with little hesitation, deemed an enemy of the state.

1989 and the Fall of the Berlin Wall

By 1989, there was a pervasive sense of decline and crisis in the GDR. Erich Honecker and other key figures in the SED leadership refused to enact significant political, economic, or social reforms to tackle the problems of mass emigration and ballooning foreign debt. The ideological fracturing of the Eastern Bloc meant that the lower tier officials and functionaries who actually enacted party policy were confused and demoralized. Any sense of socialist cultural cohesion that had been fostered over the decades was likewise rapidly breaking down as dissident groups proliferated—a sign of the coming mass demonstrations against SED rule. East Germans also continued to risk death by escaping across the Berlin Wall—early in the morning of February 6, 1989, Chris Gueffroy became the last person to be shot to death while trying to emigrate from the GDR. The twenty-year-old waiter decided to leave East Germany on the cusp of being conscripted into the National People's Army. With his friend Christian Gaudian, Gueffroy hoped to cross the Britz Canal to the West Berlin district of Neukölln—they erroneously believed that the order to use deadly force at the border had been suspended because of a diplomatic visit from the West. Border guards opened fire on the pair as they scaled the final layer of border fencing. Gaudian made it across, but Gueffroy was hit twice in the chest and died instantly. The last person to die crossing the border came a little over a month later: Winfried Freudenberg's makeshift balloon failed while he was flying over the border, and he fatally crashed in the West Berlin suburb of Zehlendorf. The public outcry over these deaths led Honecker to alter the standing orders on border security in April 1989, restricting the use of deadly force to situations where the guards were themselves threatened with violence.

By the close of the year, however, the Berlin Wall would be relegated to history. The SED rapidly lost control in 1989 due to the intersection of long-term trends that had eroded domestic stability with the immediate crisis of renewed mass emigration resulting from the collapse of authority elsewhere in the Eastern Bloc. The split between hardliners and reformers that had opened up since Gorbachev implemented glasnost and perestroika in the Soviet Union reached a breaking point: Hungary and Poland turned to elite-driven reform and liberalization, while the leaders of East Germany, Czechoslovakia, and Romania all steadfastly refused.[89] Moving even faster than the Soviets, old-guard elements in Hungary came together with reformist factions to form a Round Table to negotiate the transition to a pluralistic and competitive political system in early 1989. In Poland, General Wojciech Jaruzelski held elections in which Solidarność was allowed to run candidates against the Communist Party in a limited number of seats—they won almost every competitive vote.[90] While Poland was holding its first semi-free elections, China provided a terrifying counterexample. In the face of mass demonstrations in the heart of Beijing at Tiananmen Square, the leaders of the Chinese Communist Party chose to send in tanks and suppress protests with lethal force, leaving thousands dead.

In the GDR, even the pro forma nods to socialist democracy were being openly flouted by the SED. In May 1989, municipal and district elections were held across the country. Unlike in Poland, voting would take place according to the electoral system in place since 1950, with citizens affirming the political status quo by submitting ballots prefilled with the members of the National Front. As a gesture to reform, the SED had decided to allow resident foreigners to vote in local elections. Facing calls for a voting boycott from dissident groups and the threat that many citizens could choose, for the first time, to openly vote against the party list, SED officials decided to cheat. Election results for the National Front had always been greater than 99 percent in favor, and the national election in 1986 had been no exception with 99.7 percent voting for the list. This time, SED officials were willing to accept a slight drop, but nothing significant. Official results published in *Neues Deutschland* the next day claimed 98.85 percent voted in favor of the National Front candidates, which most understood to be an obvious lie. The voting system, which demanded a public display of voting against the National Front by depositing ballots in a separate urn, had backfired completely as people waiting in line to vote had seen with their own eyes just how many citizens had refused to play along. Denied even the chance at a symbolic protest, East Germans held demonstrations in major cities. These were met by the full force of the Volkspolizei and the Stasi, who broke up the protests through brutality and mass arrests. These public displays of state violence only caused more dissent and set off a near-unstoppable cycle of escalating protest. The leaders of the SED refused to accept that the discontent was genuine and continued to blindly attribute the protests and demonstrations both at home and in other parts of the socialist world to Western interference and networks of "hostile-negative" forces. As *Neues Deutschland* editor Joachim Hermann told the Politburo in June 1989, the GDR was subject to "political, economic and ideological pressure [...] to adopt capitalist structures and concepts of society, bourgeois pluralism, and bourgeois ideology," under the banner of "renewing socialism."[91]

Criticism of the SED was understood only in terms of a plot to destroy socialism; reform was out of the question. While the SED's reaction to the Polish election was muted, it publicly congratulated the government in Beijing on restoring order. Among the population, fears spread that mass dissent could be met with a "Chinese Solution" of violent mass repression unseen since the 1953 Uprising.[92] The Stasi had informants in almost all dissident groups, but it was impossible to round up every disgruntled East German for imprisonment or deportation. The emigration wave that had begun in 1984 continued to grow as more than 150,000 people petitioned to emigrate to the West in 1989. In August, a gap opened in the Iron Curtain separating East and West at the Pan-European Picnic. The event was held in Sopron, Hungary, to call for peace and European unity, but it turned into a mass exodus of visiting East Germans as hundreds ran to the nearby border with Austria and pushed through the lightly guarded barbed-wire fence.[93]

In September 1989, the crisis of emigration turned into a crisis of political stability. On September 4, the first Monday demonstration took place in Leipzig. Organized out of the Nikolai Church, the first march started small, but grew larger every consecutive week. Word of the demo moved through the many small dissident circles and started to attract citizens who had never previously been involved in any kind of protest. On September 9, a group of active dissidents from various social backgrounds met in East Berlin to found Neues Forum (New Forum), to act as a national umbrella organization linking together the dozens of grassroots groups that had formed in recent years. Their manifesto framed the problems of the GDR as a failure of basic democracy and called for a dialogue to address the problems of rule of law, the economy, and culture. On September 11, Hungary announced that it was opening its border with neutral Austria. Within three days, more than 15,000 East Germans had departed via this route to the West. Six thousand more took refuge in the West German embassy in Prague, camping in the villa's gardens, while the demonstrations in Leipzig grew by the thousands each week. Mass emigration was recreating the widespread sense of crisis and collapse that had preceded the building of the Berlin Wall in 1961.

On a state visit to East Berlin to celebrate the fortieth anniversary of the founding of the GDR on October 7, Gorbachev informed Honecker that the Soviet Union would not militarily intervene if the SED lost its grip on power. The Stasi issued warnings to Party leaders that groups like the New Forum now had the support of many in the working class—and even the rank and file of the SED. In the streets, the crowds adopted the slogan "we are the people" (*Wir sind das Volk*). The demonstrations asserted the legitimacy of the protests to speak for the "people" over the Party that allegedly represented their objective class interests. For his part, Honecker stubbornly refused to accept that the unrest could be anything other than Western-instigated sabotage. While the CIA had been active in supporting underground resistance groups in the early years of the GDR, anticommunist covert action in the 1980s was concentrated on Third World hotspots like Nicaragua and Angola; in Eastern Europe, it was almost exclusively interested in aiding Solidarność in Poland.[94] Although Reagan had famously given a speech at the Brandenburg Gate in 1987 calling on Gorbachev to "tear down this wall," his administration had little interest in effecting regime change in East Berlin. Moreover, most East Germans had *always* been able to receive critical Western radio or television news reports about the SED, and there had not been a significant change in access to outside information in the late 1980s. Honecker, however, simply could not believe that the protests were authentic or homegrown. As one colleague later said, that "Honecker always remained the Saarland Communist Youth functionary of 1932. […] The highest that could be achieved was that everyone had enough to eat at cheap prices, that everyone had work, and that everyone had a good and cheap apartment [...] He thought that everyone was happy [since] everyone had cheap bread, a cheap apartment, and work."[95] While the top leaders of the SED remained intransigent, local party officials began to try and engage in a dialogue with protestors to somehow defuse the situation before it boiled over.

On October 9, the country hit a breaking point. Leipzig braced for another Monday demonstration, and Stasi Chief Erich Mielke vowed that the security services would make clear who was in charge by decisively stopping the protests. Special Stasi units backed up by the People's Police, the Combat Groups of the Working Class, and the National People's Army were deployed to Leipzig in an enormous public show of force. While many in the Combat Groups, the militia composed of older working-class civilians, refused to muster or claimed to be ill, it was still possible to raise 8,000 security personnel. That day, the conductor of the Leipzig orchestra, Kurt Masur, put out a call for nonviolence and organized public talks between dissident cultural figures and SED officials in an attempt to prevent—what felt like inevitable—bloodshed.[96] However, at least 80,000 demonstrators (likely as many as 130,000) took to the streets that evening chanting "we are the people" and "no violence," with the knowledge that the SED could be ready to choose a "Chinese Solution."[97] In the end, neither Honecker nor Mielke was willing to explicitly order the use of lethal force to break up the demonstration that night. There was no certainty that security services would obey orders to conduct a massacre; to give such an order risked sparking a mutiny instead. The military officers on the ground similarly chose to retreat from the mass of protestors and allow the crowds to take over the streets rather than engage in indiscriminate killing without explicit orders to fire on protestors.[98]

The loss of control in Leipzig signaled the end of Erich Honecker's rule. Within the SED, Party members at all levels lost all confidence that their leaders had any capacity to deal with the problems facing the GDR. At a meeting in Moscow, Gorbachev was happy to endorse a plan by the SED inner circle to remove Honecker from power, just as Brezhnev had been pleased to see Honecker displace Walter Ulbricht back in 1971. Abandoned by even his close allies (including

Secretary of the Economy Günter Mittag and Stasi chief Erich Mielke), Honecker was formally removed from power by the SED Politburo on October 18. In justifying the decision, it was noted that debt had climbed from two billion to forty billion marks under Honecker. To maintain the principle of a united Party leadership, Honecker voted *for* his own ouster so that the decision remained unanimous.[99] The Politburo selected Egon Krenz as the new general secretary and chair of the Council of State. As with the transition to Mikhail Gorbachev in the Soviet Union, this represented a shift to a younger generation (Krenz had been a child during the Second World War). Previously the head of the FDJ, like his mentor, Krenz had served as Honecker's deputy and heir apparent for several years. Two previous heirs apparent to Honecker had already died—first Werner Lamberz in a helicopter crash in Libya during a diplomatic mission in 1978, and then Paul Verner of old age in 1986. Krenz presented himself as a national savior and a reformer, even though only months earlier he had been the public face of the fraudulent local elections and the SED's public support for the Chinese government after the Tiananmen Square massacre.

Speaking directly to East Germans in a televised address, Krenz promised a turn—*die Wende*—that would include open dialogue between the Party and the people about the problems of socialism, in addition to competitive elections, economic reform, and more travel to the West. These reforms would entail a liberalization of the current system, but not a transition to bourgeois democracy. Krenz assumed the SED would still be able to garner at least 70–80 percent of the vote, although he did not envision any elections taking place until 1991 at the earliest.[100] The brief era of reform from above was marked by a massive demonstration on November 4 at Alexanderplatz, East Berlin's main square, where half a million people gathered to hear speeches from prominent intellectual and cultural dissidents like Bärbel Bohley and Christa Wolf, but also SED reformers like Berlin Party chief Günter Schabowski and the recently retired Markus Wolf (see bio on page 73).

While Krenz initially believed that he had enough time to implement his turnaround through incremental changes, he also

Stagnation, Collapse, and Reunification

Figure 4.1 More than 500,000 East Germans take part in the demonstration at Alexanderplatz in East Berlin on November 4, 1989. Hubert Link, ADN.

Figure 4.2 Nearly 500,000 East Germans take part in the demonstration during a rainstorm in Leipzig on November 6, 1989. Liebe, Bundesbildstelle.

quickly lost control. In the weeks after October 7, millions of East Germans participated in hundreds of protests. The SED scrambled to find some kind of policy that would placate the crowds but maintain control over the border to prevent uncontrolled mass emigration. The dire economic situation also accelerated the crisis. Gerhard Schürer, head of the State Planning Commission, informed the Politburo that "capping the debt alone would require a 25–30 percent reduction in the living standard in 1990, and would make the GDR ungovernable."[101] The unexpected spark that opened the wall on November 9 came from a press conference held by the head of the East Berlin SED Günter Schabowski, who had been tasked with explaining new travel regulations that included easier access to travel visas. Poorly briefed and operating on little sleep, Schabowski seemed confused about the details and when asked when the policy would take effect, he shuffled his papers and replied "immediately, without delay." The press conference was broadcast on the 8:00 p.m. news, and Western radio began reporting that the SED had already opened the border. Thousands of East Berliners began to gather at border checkpoints demanding to cross without a visa. As with the October 7 demonstrations, border guards were faced with the option to use lethal force to stem the tide or to stand by. They chose to refrain from violence. The first opening in the wall was at the Bornholmer Straße checkpoint between Prenzlauer Berg in East Berlin and Gesundbrunnen in West Berlin at 9:20 p.m. Guards initially stamped passports as invalid so that people were unable to return, but by 11:00 p.m. they had abandoned even this futile gesture to their own authority and simply let the jubilant crowd pass. After twenty-eight years and at least 140 deaths, the Berlin Wall was open.[102]

The opening of the wall not only brought down the short-lived era of General Secretary Egon Krenz, who was almost instantly sidelined as the Party lost functional control over the country, but it also marked the collapse of SED one-party rule and the demise of the anti-reform bloc in Eastern Europe. What little power was left within the SED was transferred to the reformist Hans Modrow, brought back from exile in

Dresden and named Prime Minister after Willi Stoph and his cabinet had resigned in response to the Alexanderplatz demonstration. Events in the GDR were moving so quickly that Stoph's resignation was based on an event (the Alexanderplatz demo) that was superseded by much greater events (the fall of the Wall) before his resignation had even taken effect on November 13. On December 1, the SED abolished its claim to lead the GDR in an effort to remake itself as a democratic party; Krenz, along with the remainder of the Politburo and the Central Committee of the SED, would not resign until December 3. The State Council (Staatsrat der DDR), created in 1960 by Walter Ulbricht to consolidate his power as leader of the SED, became toothless and was formally abolished a few months later.

Meanwhile, mass demonstrations in Prague, akin to those that had taken place in Leipzig, led to the peaceful collapse of communist rule in Czechoslovakia by the end of November. In Romania, Nicolae Ceaușescu took a different path, and the military fired on protestors in Timișoara on December 17. Revolution spread across the country and, after attempting to flee, Ceaușescu was deposed. After a very brief military trial, Ceaușescu and wife Elena were executed by firing squad on Christmas Day. While Bulgaria had seen little organized dissent, its leaders saw the writing on the wall and implemented Round Table talks with the few opposition leaders they could find on the path to free elections. Across the Eastern Bloc, the political elite had run out of ideas on how to tackle the problems facing their societies, and many lost faith in their right to rule on the basis of the historical correctness of socialism.[103] But in the case of the GDR in particular, the resistance to reform at the top—from a party elite that arrived too late and thought that they still had time to implement cosmetic, incremental changes to placate the population—created a bulwark to change that was only overcome through mass demonstrations by a significant minority of the country. Ultimately, the mass demonstrations in East Germany forced the end of dictatorship in the GDR, which subsequently played a vital role in bringing down the last holdouts of state socialist dictatorship across Eastern Europe.[104]

The German Democratic Republic

The End of the GDR

The opening of the Berlin Wall effectively destroyed the political system of the GDR as it had operated since its founding. The top echelons of the SED had lost the loyalty of the armed forces, which had first surrendered control of the streets to the demonstrators and then abandoned control of the border. The moribund parliamentary institutions of the GDR, which had existed for decades as decoration, suddenly came to life and began to chart a new course. The SED membership tried to take control of the party and put it onto a path toward reform communism and democratization; in the Volkskammer, the National Front fell apart as the bloc parties asserted their independence from the SED. The bloc parties evicted their leaders and rapidly became actual political parties that contested existing SED policy. In Moscow, Gorbachev effectively abandoned the Soviet veto over liberalization in Eastern Europe and made no effort to intervene and rescue the SED. Yet the existence of a democratically vibrant and independent GDR was short-lived. The seismic political changes that took place in the fall of 1989 did not alter East Germany's fundamental economic problems, nor did it stem the tide of emigration that the Berlin Wall was designed to stop. Less than a year after the opening of the Wall, the GDR would no longer exist.

Laying out an agenda for reform a week after November 9, the new SED Prime Minister Hans Modrow stated, "we need an advance on trust from anyone willing to give it to us. I know that's a lot to ask." He promised a package of reforms to overhaul the political system and foster more avenues for democratic accountability by providing "self-determination to the people." He vowed that his program "gives new strength to the GDR's legitimacy as a socialist state, as a sovereign German state," and "will serve to clearly reject unrealistic and dangerous speculations about reunification."[105] But the population was unwilling to let up the pressure on the SED, and the Monday demonstrations continued.

The collapse of one-party SED rule opened up the question of what comes next—reform or reunification. For many in the cultural and intellectual elite as well as reformers within the SED, this was a unique opportunity to realize a program of renewal and create the "better Germany" that for many had existed only as a distant ideal. A joint letter by leading dissidents and cultural figures entitled "Für unser Land" (For our Country) was published on November 26. It appealed to East Germans to salvage the true ideals of the GDR from the wreckage of the SED state: "We still have the chance to build a socialist alternative to West Germany, in equitable neighborliness with the states of Europe. We have not forgotten the anti-fascist and humanist ideals with which we began."[106] The initial signatures included famous cultural figures like writer Christa Wolf and rock signer Tamara Danz, dissidents like Ulrike Poppe and Sebastian Pflugbeil, and representatives of the Church like Pastor Friedrich Schorlemmer. The manifesto garnered 200,000 signatures in two weeks.

But in West Germany, Chancellor Kohl put forward an alternative agenda in the Bundestag (the West German Parliament) two days later, on November 28: the Zehn-Punkte-Plan für die deutsche Einheit (Ten-Point Plan for German Unity). Kohl called for the democratization of the GDR's political system and the liberalization of its economy as steps toward eventual German reunification under the auspices of the European Community and the Helsinki Accords.[107] Kohl had so hastily drafted the plan after the fall of the Wall that he had not even stopped to consult his Foreign Minister Hans-Dietrich Genscher of the FDP. Although many were enthusiastic about Kohl's plans for rapid reunification, he had purposefully omitted the recognition of the current GDR-Poland border, in order to use the issue as leverage to settle all outstanding business between the FRG and Poland. For many in the Bundestag, this raised the specter of territorial revanchism.[108] These fears were enhanced by West German politicians with connections to the expellee lobby—such as CSU Finance Minister Theo Waigel—who still openly spoke about restoring Germany's 1937 borders, including the lands annexed to Poland and the USSR in 1945.[109] Among West Germany's intellectuals, the prospect of reunification was also unpopular, as it was viewed as the pet project of militaristic nationalists who could undo all of the postwar work of democratization and integration of the Federal Republic into Western Europe. Some denounced the idea of a unified Germany as morally untenable: The renowned novelist (and future Nobel Prize winner) Günther Grass published an op-ed in *The New York Times* with the title "Don't Reunify Germany," stating that "there can be no demand for a new version of a unified nation that in the course of barely 75 years, though under several managements, filled the history books, ours and theirs, with suffering, rubble, defeat, millions of refugees, millions of dead and the burden of crimes that can never be undone."[110]

Hans Modrow thought that the enthusiasm of the "For Our Country" manifesto indicated popular support for democratic socialism in the GDR, and thus resisted calls to dilute his little remaining power by initiating Round Table talks between the remnants of the government and the opposition. Like his predecessor, he sought to emulate Gorbachev's revolution from above and maintain the authority of the party via renewal. On December 1, the Volkskammer voted almost unanimously to abolish the SED's constitutionally mandated leading role in the political system of the GDR. The country was shaken by details of Party corruption coming

Figure 4.3 Graffiti in Jena mocks demands from nationalists for the return of territory from Poland: "We demand: Germany in the borders of 1254! Naples belongs to us! Recognize the Western border of Poland!" (photographed in January 1990). Jan Peter Kasper, ADN.

to light through the now liberalized media; public outcry led to the creation of various commissions.[111] On December 3, the SED expelled former General Secretary Erich Honecker, former Prime Minister Willi Stoph, and former Stasi Chief Erich Mielke from the Party (they had all already resigned from their posts in government). Economic chief Günther Mittag was arrested, and KoKo head Alexander Schalck-Golodkowski fled to West Berlin to claim asylum, fearing he would be killed. Internal party critics from past decades like Wolfgang Harich and Rudolph Bahro were rehabilitated. The new leaders of the Party were reform communist insiders like the newly chosen Chairman Gregor Gysi, an attorney who had defended dissident Rudolf Bahro (and would remain a fixture of the German political landscape for more than three decades following reunification), who was also the son of Klaus Gysi, retired SED Minister of Culture and State Secretary of Church Affairs. The new Party leadership vowed to implement a program of de-Stalinization and clear out the old guard on the path to democratization. The SED was rebranded as the SED-PDS (Partei des Demokratischen Sozialismus, Party of Democratic Socialism); within weeks, the "SED" was discarded entirely, and the party simply became the PDS.[112]

But these measures did not placate the protestors, nor did it cut the flow of emigrants to the West. After Mielke's removal, the Stasi rebranded itself as the Office of National Security (with the unfortunate abbreviation in German of NaSi—Amt für Nationale Sicherheit). Its new leaders tried to make the case that they were a necessary defense against the rising tide of neo-Nazi activity and the boom in cross-border drug trafficking.[113] Few outside the security apparatus accepted this rationale. When it appeared in December as though Stasi officials were burning files, crowds stormed branch offices in Erfurt and Leipzig to prevent the destruction of evidence. The Monday demonstrations continued; demonstrators began taking on a more nationalistic tone: the chant "we are *the* people" (*Wir sind das Volk*) shifted to "we are *one* people" (*Wir sind ein Volk*). The East German flag was flown with its hammer and compass crest cut out of the center, so it looked like the West German tricolor.[114] Modrow finally relented and held the first meeting of the Zentraler Runder Tisch (Central Round Table)

The German Democratic Republic

talks with the opposition in early December 1989. Of the thirty-odd members (the numbers fluctuated over the coming months), half came from the SED, the bloc parties, and the mass organizations that had been represented in the Volkskammer, and the other half from various dissident groups and church-oriented organizations. On the streets, protestors were becoming more militant and less interested in heeding the advice of prominent dissidents to seek solutions through dialogue. On January 15, 1990, crowds ignored pleas from members of the New Forum to disperse, and stormed Stasi headquarters in East Berlin. Protestors looted the building and took photos of themselves playing in the wreckage.

While the crowds in the street were creating facts on the ground, the question of the GDR's fate also rested in the hands of the Allied powers. The United Kingdom, France, the United States, and the Soviet Union still retained occupation rights over Berlin and had large

Figure 4.4 View from inside the Stasi headquarters in Leipzig shortly before it was stormed by protestors on December 4, 1989. Interfoto/Alamy Stock Photo.

armies stationed in both East and West.[115] French President François Mitterrand and British Prime Minister Margaret Thatcher were both skeptical of German unification and urged caution. Not only did both have lingering concerns about a revival of German nationalism, but also the impact an enlarged Germany would have on the balance of power within Europe. American President George H. W. Bush, in office since January 1989, however, welcomed Kohl's plans for rapid reunification, and lobbied his fellow leaders to follow suit. In Moscow, Gorbachev believed that the collapse of SED rule was not an impediment to his proposed idea of a "common European home" in which East and West would work cooperatively toward a joint future of security and prosperity. The Soviet Union was undergoing its own painful reforms and did not have the funds to underwrite continued SED rule, and he believed that the basic socialist structure of East Germany would be preserved as part of a gradual process of confederation with the West.[116] At the Central Round Table, reform communists and dissidents worked diligently together to write a new constitution for a democratic GDR. Plans were floated for a "modern socialism" that would tackle the chronic economic crisis of East Germany by gradually abolishing central planning and allowing firms to become functionally independent to improve productivity and profitability.[117]

But the idea of a democratic socialist GDR was slipping away rapidly. The economy continued to deteriorate precipitously. Not only was trade with the West in a tailspin from a lack of credit, the collapse of the CMEA trading system eliminated the captive market of socialist Eastern Europe. After decades of underinvestment, most goods produced in the GDR were not competitive on the international market—not always for reasons of quality, but because they were too cost-inefficient to produce. In a last-ditch effort, Hans Modrow requested 15 billion DM (approximately 7.7 million euros) as a "solidarity payment" from West Germany to stabilize the country. Although Kohl at first considered it, he ultimately refused.[118] One of the points in his Ten-Point Plan for German Unity was the need for the GDR to transition to a market economy; further aid, his thinking went, would merely postpone necessary reforms. Kohl was under increasing pressure to fix the problem of East Germany—quickly. While the elderly may have still viewed East Germany as an innate part of the Federal Republic, younger generations who had always known division saw it as a foreign country: As the GDR disintegrated, a xenophobic backlash was fomented in the FRG against the rapid influx of so many GDR citizens emigrating to the West after the fall of the Berlin Wall. Social Democrats like Oskar Lafontaine warned that migration from the GDR (and the rest of the Eastern Bloc) could destroy the social welfare system of the Federal Republic.[119]

With pressure on the Round Table mounting, the first (and last) free Volkskammer elections were scheduled for March 18, 1990. A huge number of new parties joined the democratized bloc parties and the reformed PDS (formerly SED, briefly SED-PDS). A Social Democratic Party was reformed alongside dozens of smaller parties that mostly emerged from existing dissident and church groups. Several dissident organizations, including the IFM, Demokratie Jetzt (Democracy Now), and the New Forum, came together to run under the banner of Bündnis 90 (Alliance 1990), while a hastily organized umbrella group founded by pastors Rainer Eppelmann and Friedrich Schorlemmer, among others, coalesced under the banner of Demokratischer Aufbruch (DA, Democratic Awakening) to encompass a large number of activist church groups. The DA then joined forces with the Deutsche Soziale Union (DSU, German Social Union) and the CDU to form the Allianz für Deutschland (Alliance for Germany). At the more marginal end of the spectrum, there were, among others, also a new Communist Party of Germany, the Trotskyite Socialist Equality Party, and the German Beer Drinker's Union.

The spectrum of party positions largely fanned out on the question of independence or reunification. The PDS ran on a platform of reform communism, promising democratic freedoms and the preservation of the "accomplishments of socialism." The dissidents of Bündnis 90 called for a new kind of direct democratic engagement within the GDR and a confederation with the FRG. The Social Democrats supported reunification, but warned that it would be a long and difficult process. The Alliance for Germany, however,

Stagnation, Collapse, and Reunification

ran under the slogan "never again socialism" and promised the importation of West German prosperity to the East through rapid reunification.

Western parties arrived in the East ready to share their experience in running democratic elections to help their GDR compatriots on the campaign trail—Helmut Kohl appeared at events for the Alliance for Germany to back the Christian Democrats, and the Bavarian CSU financially supported the right-wing DSU, while ex-West German Chancellor Willy Brandt greeted crowds for the Social Democrats. As Jens Reich, a member of the IFM, put it, "The Bonn hippopotamus arrived with such a massive weight, that one was simply helpless. The entire electoral apparatus was transferred from West to East. We were completely unprepared to withstand it. These were West German elections exported into the GDR."[120] Beyond the sheer weight of the money and media influence from the West, practically no one in East Germany had any experience in everyday democratic organizing for elections (that had not been fixed in advance) or in the basics of performing in television campaign ads.[121] Long-standing membership in the bloc parties provided little help in actual democratic party management, voter outreach, or electioneering since these parties had always functioned more as a means of distributing the favors of the state than as organizations designed to contest power via the masses. Most dissidents were young, and, in addition to their age, their political activities—in small underground circles of like-minded individuals, afraid of Stasi infiltration—had prevented most from gaining the necessary experience to advocate for their ideas in open discussions of public policy. The mass demonstrations in the fall of 1989 against SED rule did not provide any proficiency in selling a positive agenda to a national audience. The prominence of so many former Protestant church officials in the ranks of the new political actors in the East can thus partially be explained by the fact that they were among the few people in the dissident movement who had experience in running meetings that often required larger-scale consensus and coalition building.

In a surprise upset, the conservative Alliance for Germany won an almost absolute majority on March 18 with more than 48 percent of the vote. The Social Democrats came in at less than 22 percent, and the PDS managed little more than 16 percent—ironically, about what the SED had garnered in the first postwar Berlin elections of 1946. The dissidents of Bündnis 90 received less than 3 percent. Many of the participants at the Central Round Table who had taken on the mantle of speaking for the people of East Germany had been eclipsed by the electoral formations that had emerged since the start of the year, and talk of a new kind of East German democracy was displaced by plans to abolish the GDR entirely. While many had expected the Social Democrats to do well, more than 55 percent of GDR workers voted

Figure 4.5 Bündnis 90 campaign sticker from the March 1990 elections found in Berlin-Buch in 2017. Julia Sittmann.

for the Alliance for Germany. As one historian has noted, "perhaps the irony of the story is that the 'workers and peasants' state, the SED dictatorship, received the democratically legitimated death blow from just those in whose name the societal experiment was enforced for decades."[122] Christian Democratic leader Lothar de Maizière became the first freely elected Prime Minister of the GDR at the head of a unity government comprised of the Alliance for Germany, the Social Democrats, and a handful of liberals. The Central Round Table's draft of a new democratized GDR constitution was voted down by the newly elected Volkskammer; most of the intellectual and cultural dissidents, as well as the reform communists who had sought to create a better and genuinely democratic GDR, were sidelined. Rather than merging the two states and creating a new joint constitution, the GDR was to be dissolved and integrated into the Federal Republic as five new federal states according to Article 23 of the (West German) Basic Law. The very provisions of the West German constitution that had anticipated reunification at its founding in 1949 were now being used to end the existence of East Germany through its accession into the Federal Republic.[123]

The Informants

Ibrahim Böhme
Born 1944, Bad Dürrenberg, Nazi Germany
Died 1999, Neustrelitz, FRG

Wolfgang Schnur
Born 1944, Stettin, Nazi Germany (today Szczecin, Poland)
Died 2016, Vienna, Austria

Lothar de Maizière
Born 1940, Nordhausen, Nazi Germany

The first open elections in the GDR in 1990 coincided with the seizure of the files of the Ministry for State Security by activists and the public revelation of the widespread network of "unofficial collaborators" (IMs). Three of the most prominent political figures of the early democratization of the GDR were uncovered as Stasi informers: Wolfgang Schnur of Democratic Awakening, the Social Democrat Ibrahim Böhme, and Lothar de Maizière of the CDU—the first democratically elected prime minister of the GDR.

Wolfgang Schnur was a prominent lawyer who worked with dissidents and peace activists and was also a leader within the Protestant church, becoming one of the founders of the church-oriented Democratic Awakening in October 1989. He had also been a Stasi informer since 1965 under the cover name IM Torsten. In 1990, he appointed future-Chancellor Angela Merkel to the post of the press secretary of the Democratic Awakening; he himself was nominated to be its leading candidate in the March 1990 Volkskammer elections.

In October 1989, Ibrahim Böhme took part in the illegal founding of the Sozialdemokratische Partei der DDR (SDP), and by November he was part of the official visit by former SPD Chancellor Willy Brandt in East Berlin. Böhme went on to represent the SDP at the Central Round Table talks in December 1989. Böhme had joined the SED in 1962, but had repeated run-ins with authorities and began to inform to the Stasi under the cover names IM Paul Bonkarz, IM Rohloff, and, later, IM Maximilian. In the 1970s, he used his position with the Kulturbund to befriend young intellectuals whom he reported on to the secret police. In the mid-1980s, he moved into the dissident scene in Mecklenburg and East Berlin, becoming close to Ulrike and Gerd Poppe and others in the Initiative for Peace and Human Rights to report on their activities to the Stasi. By February 1990, he had been named the lead candidate for the East German Social Democrats in the Volkskammer elections.

Lothar de Maizière was the face of the renewal of the GDR's Christian Democratic bloc party. He was the first leader of any bloc party to announce its withdrawal from the SED-led National Front in November 1989. A viola player and lawyer, de Maizière came from a prominent French Huguenot family. In the 1990 elections, he became the leader of the Alliance for Germany—the coalition of conservative parties, including Democratic Awakening.

The first revelations hit Wolfgang Schnur two weeks before the election. While he denied the reports, shortly before voting began, he resigned from his positions within Democratic Awakening and was expelled from the party the following day. Schnur never worked in politics again, and his license to practice law was revoked on the basis that, as a lawyer in the GDR, he had violated his clients' privacy by leaking information to the Stasi. He died impoverished in 2016.

Shortly after the March 1990 election, the newsmagazine *Der Spiegel* published reports that Ibrahim Böhme had also worked for the Stasi. He denied all accusations. At the end of the year, the writer Reiner Kunze, upon whom Böhme had spied in the 1970s, published definitive proof of his collaboration with the Stasi. He was formally expelled from the SPD in 1992 and died in 1999.

After serving as the GDR's last Prime Minister and overseeing reunification, Lothar de Maizière continued as a representative to the Bundestag as a member of the now-unified CDU and as a Minister without portfolio in Helmut Kohl's cabinet. Rumors that he had been an IM had surfaced after the election, but de Maizière denied them. In December 1990, after the first unified German Bundestag election, *Der Spiegel* put out a report identifying de Maizière as IM Czerni. Although he again denied the accusations, he stepped down from his ministerial position, only to return the following year with the backing of his party; in September 1991, he finally resigned from all positions. In 1992, he was formally identified as IM Czerni, but the contents of his Stasi file were lost to the wave of destruction carried out in 1989/90 before the archives had been secured.

The German Democratic Republic

With the Wall open and the East German economy still in terminal decline, emigration continued apace: At the ongoing Monday demonstrations, protestors vowed that if the Deutsche mark did not come to the GDR, then they would go West for it.[124] The first step toward unification was thus the passage of the Monetary, Economic, and Social Union between East and West in May 1990, which would end the existence of a separate GDR currency on July 1. It was hoped that this preliminary step toward unification, which put the economy on a path toward a West German-style social market economy—including the legal right to strike—would help stem further mass migration.

In parallel to negotiations over the terms of unification, there were also discussions among the Allies over the end of the formal occupation of Germany. The so-called 4+2 talks began in January 1990 between the leaders of the United Kingdom, France, the United States, and the USSR, along with West Germany and initially Hans Modrow representing what was left of the East German government, followed by Lothar de Maizière after the March elections. Consequently, the Allies renounced all claims over Germany and permitted it to become a fully sovereign country once again. The treaty recognized the Oder-Neisse Line as the German-Polish border and affirmed the 1945 annexation of territories east of that line by Poland and the Soviet Union. United Germany was to shrink its armed forces to no more than 370,000 members, and the entirety of the Soviet occupation force would leave Eastern Germany by 1994.[125] Although de Maizière's unity government began to collapse over a number of social and financial issues, at the end of August 1990, the Volkskammer voted to approve the accession of the GDR into the Federal Republic of Germany with 294 votes in favor, 62 against, and 7 abstentions.[126] On October 3, 1990, four days short of its forty-first birthday, the German Democratic Republic ceased to exist.

Stagnation, Collapse, and Reunification

Although the GDR was marked by a notable stability for much of its existence and faced far less open resistance than other Eastern

Stagnation, Collapse, and Reunification

Bloc countries, its collapse was swift once crisis took hold in 1989. Disillusionment with the status quo went so deep that the safeguards in place to secure the SED all failed simultaneously: In the USSR, Gorbachev had lost interest in maintaining a Soviet sphere of influence in Eastern Europe; in the GDR, the security apparatus found it difficult to mobilize the very militia units designed to crush such uprisings. Fearful of the consequences of mass violence, the leadership of the SED was too paralyzed to save itself by force. On the ground, the police, soldiers, and border guards who confronted the opposition chose to step aside, rather than kill to keep the SED in power. Across the rapid succession of East German leaders in 1989 and 1990, it became clear that no one was able to solve the chronic problems of the East German economy or the proliferation of dissent. Although the demonstrations in the fall of 1989 had been directed toward dialogue and democratization, the opening of the Berlin Wall summarily shifted the debate from how the GDR could be reformed to how it could best be abolished.

CONCLUSION: A COLD WAR GERMANY

The history of the German Democratic Republic was inexorably tied to the Cold War. It was created in the wake of a collapsing wartime alliance between the United States and the Soviet Union and the inability of the victorious powers to find a common solution to how to deal with the defeated Third Reich. The political priorities of the SED were always oriented around maintaining the strategic alliance with the Soviet Union, integration into the Eastern Bloc, and the competition for legitimacy with the Federal Republic over which German state represented the "better" Germany. East German society was continually shaped by the pressure to provide the material well-being that was on offer in West Germany, and its culture was perpetually in the process of ideologically assimilating innovations from the West. Fears of Western saboteurs and infiltrators defined the rise and proliferation of the East German security state as epitomized by the Stasi (and, ultimately, the GDR's downfall as well). The foreign relations of the GDR were always filtered through the lens of Cold War competition—at first the denial of its existence through the West German diplomatic blockade, and then by the search for ideological allies with whom long-term strategic trade agreements could be made. As the Cold War began to wind down in the 1980s, so too did the domestic and international logics of the socialist dictatorship. The ideological and economic disintegration of the Eastern Bloc generated intense pressure for political reforms that the SED could not accommodate without collapsing entirely. International conflicts could no longer as easily be divided between clear friends and clear enemies. The end of the Cold War also marked the end of the German Democratic Republic as an independent socialist state.

While the GDR was only viable in a Cold War world, it was not merely a proxy of the competition between East and West, nor a simple copy of the Soviet Union. The GDR was also defined by its place in the longer history of Germany itself. The GDR as a state had to contend with the same problems that defined all German states since the founding of the Empire in 1871: the balance between centralized political authority and demands for popular democracy, the tension between forces of modernization and tradition, the drive to be part of the world alongside the difficulties in finding a global role. Creating a system of state socialism in the GDR also meant grappling with the long-standing German traditions of organized labor and the radical left (and not just importing systems from the USSR wholesale). The early SED had to wrestle with the dashed hopes of an older generation of communists who had dreamed of greater emancipation and the realization of promises made by the Weimar-era KPD, such as free access to abortion.

In addition, the trauma of the Nazi past loomed large over East German society: SED claims to power were rooted in the correctness of Marxism-Leninsim, but also ideological antifascism, which centered on the victory of Soviet-led socialism over Nazism during the Second World War. The choice of where communists spent their exile to escape Nazi persecution proved decisive in postwar power arrangements, as those with close ties to the Soviets displaced those who fled elsewhere. While former Nazis had to reinvent themselves to survive in a radically new system and society, surviving victims of the Third Reich were often less resistant to the SED's installation of a dictatorship due to fears of resurgent Nazism. Memories of the violence, chaos, and deprivation of the Weimar and Nazi eras informed popular enthusiasm for material security and social stability. Here too, while the founding of the GDR was built upon its recent past, as memory of these horrors faded, so too did the popular acceptance of both SED rule and state socialism; the following generation, without direct experiences of the war, became even less likely to accept the SED's self-legitimization.

Which brings us to the many paradoxes of East German history. The GDR was remarkably stable for several decades and then rapidly fell apart over the course of 1989. East Germany only existed for forty years, but that was longer than the Weimar Republic's fifteen and the Nazi era's twelve years. Although the SED was able to construct

Conclusion

a political, economic, and social system that was subject to fewer periods of mass unrest than in the rest of the Eastern Bloc, it was always contested from below by the population, and increasingly reliant on the security services and mass surveillance as time went on. While in the early years of the GDR under Walter Ulbricht, the SED framed its demands upon East Germans around the prospect of a glorious future, the expectations of a better tomorrow faded over time, leaving only the status quo of "actually existing socialism." By the 1970s under Erich Honecker, the Party sought to maintain control by increasing consumerism at the cost of ever-increasing loans from the West. The SED's reliance on declining Soviet aid and then later Western loans to compensate for the GDR's structural inability to meet the demands of the public led to a loss of control over state finances and a growing dependence on West German financial and political actors. As one dissident ruefully noted in 2024, "How undignified was all this! Precisely those people that drove everything into the mud, that sank socialism, then opened the wall. If I had wanted to go to a capitalist country, I would have applied for an exit visa. But suddenly that capitalist country came to me instead."[1]

The political structures that created stability—namely the "democratic centralism" of the SED, which placed immense power at the top of the Party pyramid—also proved brittle in the face of systemic crisis and upheaval. From the 1950s onward, the SED chose to suppress, imprison, or exile critics from within the Party rather than seek pluralistic dialogue within its ranks. There was no possibility of a loyal opposition, and the space for constructive criticism was severely curtailed and ritualized in the form of citizens' petitions. Even at the top levels, Party officials found it difficult to openly discuss the problems facing the GDR, in particular its chronic economic struggles. By the 1980s, as the Soviet Union and much of the socialist world in Eastern Europe and beyond looked to economic and political reform, the leadership of the SED remained one of the most hardline forces resisting calls for change and sticking instead with the crumbling status quo. Instead of bending to popular demands for more pluralism or adapting to the economic problems it faced, the political structures of the GDR simply broke down.

The German Democratic Republic

Another paradox of the GDR were the official claims to equality within a system dominated by rigid hierarchies. Political power was wielded by a select group with no real institutional limits. Elections and referenda, the parliamentary system of the Volkskammer, and the National Front with its many bloc parties and mass organizations—all provided an elaborate façade of democracy, but one that generated no popular control over the Party. Although officially a state of "workers and farmers," class differences remained. The intelligentsia and managerial classes had more privileges than workers, and the workers themselves were economically stratified by type of work. Farmers and rural East Germans were very aware that their communities had less access to resources and consumer goods than those in the cities. There may have been less social and economic inequality than in the West, but resentments grew due to a sense of unfairness, hypocrisy, and the pressures of the shortage economy, which made even small differences appear subjectively greater. There was also the problem of minority groups—be they religious, ethnic, sexual, or racial—that faced formal and informal discrimination and prejudices in everyday life. Even mild forms of non-conformity could be met with not only social disapproval but also the loss of work and social benefits—and surveillance by the Stasi.

For the citizens of the GDR, the demands of the state on their time and their labor were also contradictory and led to regular conflict. Participation was mandatory, and enthusiasm expected. In the workplace, heroic acts of overproduction were celebrated and encouraged. Outside of work, society was structured around a vast array of mass organizations, professional associations, and interest-based groups all under the umbrella of the state. The social, economic, and political structures of GDR society created a system of incentives for East Germans to join and actively participate in these organizations to demonstrate their commitment to the socialist ideal, but also a range of punishments for noncompliance or nonparticipation. Workplaces and membership in these groups gave citizens access to education, housing, childcare, professional opportunities, and leisure activities. Failing to participate sufficiently in organizational life could bring about the attention of the Stasi, and refusing to work (or working in illicit trades such as prostitution) marked citizens as "asocials" who faced persecution and imprisonment. Emblematic of this tension was the position of the intellectual and cultural elite, who were expected to both interpret and disseminate state socialist ideology for the masses, but continuously generated problems for the SED when they pursued their convictions on behalf of the socialist project. Citizens seeking to realize the socialist project often came into conflict with the everyday political needs of the SED as an authoritarian ruling party. The sense of national identity that the SED sought to instill in the population was so closely tied to the legitimation of its own power that disillusion and disaffection with the ruling Party also brought with it alienation from the GDR as a whole.

Looking at the GDR in a global perspective reveals further contradictions. The SED positioned East Germany as a global leader of the socialist world and in the struggle against imperialism—its solidarity support for anti-colonial forces and national liberation movements represented a significant expenditure for a country with endemic economic shortages. But this connection to the world was also contrasted by an isolationism epitomized by the Berlin Wall and the East German border regime. Foreigners were always viewed as potential threats to the political and social order and subject to intense surveillance within the GDR. Increases in tourists and international visitors to East Germany in the 1970s came alongside a massive increase in the capacities of the Stasi. The output of the GDR economy was also unable to match the global aspirations of the SED and found customers primarily among fellow socialist states in the Eastern Bloc. Ambitions to remake the GDR into a high-tech export economy floundered, while the dodgy business of arms exports flourished.

The events of 1989 represent the final resolution of many of these points of conflict and enduring tensions. The de facto one-party system led by the SED was unable to cope with the combined crisis of a declining economy, renewed emigration, and mass protest. Even if some in the SED were theoretically prepared to give the order to use mass violence to quell unrest, it is unlikely that there were many left by then—in the People's Police, the Combat Group militias, the National People's Army and the Stasi—who would have obeyed such an order and unleashed lethal force against demonstrators (as had recently occurred at Tiananmen Square in China), all to sustain either state socialism or SED rule. With Mikhail Gorbachev driving a program of liberalization in the USSR and abandoning the strategic priority of maintaining state socialism in Eastern Europe by force, Soviet occupation forces also stayed in their barracks. Unable to pivot to a plausible program of liberalization to allow the Party to retain power but also satisfy the demands of demonstrators, SED rule crumbled internally—even without an organized force on the outside to actively displace it from power. Although there were those who sought to salvage an independent GDR after the end of SED rule, none had a good answer to the economic obstacles that had plagued the Honecker era, nor did anyone have a workable plan for how to deal with the massive drive toward out-migration that had plagued East Germany since its founding in 1949. The collapse of SED rule rapidly translated into the end of the GDR as Volkskammer elections in 1990 produced a near-absolute majority for parties running on a slogan of "never again socialism" and a promise of rapid reunification with West Germany. After four decades of division, the GDR was absorbed into the Federal Republic of Germany as its population voted to abolish its existence as an independent state.

EPILOGUE: THE GDR AFTER THE END OF THE GDR

The end of the German Democratic Republic brought forth the question of where it belongs in the history of Germany writ large. For some, the GDR was an unfortunate detour. While in the Federal Republic, the wrongs of history were righted, and the dictatorial past of the Nazis was corrected by its choice to follow the path of liberal democracy and market economics, East Germany represents a mere repetition of the same mistakes of the past. The year 1990 thus marked the end of a delayed learning process as those Germans who happened to be in the GDR arrived at the correct modernity that was awaiting them in the Federal Republic. The eminent West German historian Hans-Ulrich Wehler famously claimed the GDR was "only 'a footnote of world history'" (quoting writer Stefan Heym) and that only the inherent resilience and viability of the FRG allowed it to overcome the Nazi past and erase East Germany from history.[1] Like the Lenin Monument of East Berlin, which had been removed and replaced by a square now centered on a nondescript fountain dedicated to the most unobjectionable of institutions (the United Nations) instead of the leader of the Russian Bolsheviks, the GDR had been unceremoniously swept away.

Yet the history of the GDR has continued to reverberate long after it ceased to exist. Reunification was a hugely dislocating event for most East Germans. Social, cultural, and economic life radically changed in the fall of 1989 as the dominance of the Socialist Unity Party (SED) collapsed and the vast array of organizations and associations that had ordered life in East Germany disappeared or quickly evolved into something very new. Many older East Germans could not reinvent themselves to meet the new reality of life in the Federal Republic; for younger people, it was a shock to have to navigate a new society in which and for which one had not been raised. The rapid transition after 1990 produced many new opportunities, and those who were able to adapt quickly reaped the benefits, while others were left behind. Reunification was not a single event but a series of processes, some of which began before the collapse of the GDR and some which continue into the present.[2]

The accession of East Germany into the Federal Republic did not actually solve all the chronic problems that afflicted the GDR under SED rule. Emigration, for example, continued despite reunification. After October 3, 1990, more than 3.6 million people left the former GDR—nearly one-quarter of the population. Not only Germans departed but also more than 50,000 contract workers returned to Vietnam, Mozambique, Angola, and elsewhere as the closure of their workplaces meant that their visas were suddenly null and void. Although the number of departures initially settled down after reunification, the recession of the late 1990s sparked another wave of people—especially young women—leaving the East as economic prospects dimmed again. Only in 2017 did the number of people migrating from West to East outnumber those moving in the other direction (largely due to the popularity of reunified Berlin).[3]

Reunification was also unable to rescue much of the East German economy. West German Chancellor Helmut Kohl had promised that "no one will be worse off than before—and many will be better off," but the radical restructuring of the economy resulted in many losing their livelihoods and having to reimagine their working lives entirely. Instead of a gradual transition to the market, West German experts opted for shock therapy. The massive East German *Kombinate* composed of dozens of subcompanies of varying economic profitability were broken up and triaged by the Treuhandanstalt (trust agency) entrusted with the restructuring and privatization of the economy. Elements deemed profitable were sold off, mostly to West German and European companies. While some businesses were able to adapt to new conditions, even those had to shed jobs to remain competitive, since the mandate to maintain high levels of employment was now irrelevant. The long-standing lack of investment in mechanization and automation meant that state enterprises picked up by Western companies were often unsalvageable because the equipment was so old as to be useless. Eastern Germany was also hit with the same shocks to industrial manufacturing sectors that had hit the West over the course of the 1970s and 1980s—but all at once. Just as had happened in the West, coal mines were shuttered and steel mills closed down because they were not competitive in the global marketplace. As a result, 2.5 million East German lost their jobs—this represented one in four workers pushed into early retirement or unemployment. Many others had hours cut or their positions made more precarious. The closures prompted protests from workers who believed their workplaces could still be saved, and in some cases claimed that state-owned enterprises (VEBs) were being purposely closed down by Western companies to kill competition. While the Treuhand was expected to turn a profit, putting up so many companies for sale at once created a fire-sale atmosphere and revenue generated from privatization fell short of expectations. In addition, the cumulative debts were massive. By the time the Treuhand was absorbed into the Berlin Republic's state bureaucracy in 1995, it posted a total loss of over 200 billion DM (over 102 billion euros)—more than six times the foreign debt of the GDR in 1989.[4] To avoid keeping the faltering GDR economy alive through subsidies, the German state was now on the hook for huge transfers to the new Eastern federal states to cover the cost of unemployment benefits for hundreds of thousands of workers who had been gainfully employed until 1990.[5]

The economic restructuring of society also had a massive social impact. East Germans had to adapt to entirely new forms of consumption, employment, and property rights.[6] The closures of workplaces were not only an economic but also a social issue, because state enterprises were such crucial vectors for the welfare state in the GDR. In addition to the corrosive effects of mass unemployment, the mass closures of workplaces directly undermined women's hard-earned independence and bodily autonomy. By the 1980s, it was understood as completely normal for women to have career ambitions and for the state to support them through the provision of childcare and other social mechanisms. Gender norms between the two German states had diverged greatly by 1990, with East German women much more likely to view a career in addition to motherhood as a basic element of life. The gender equality of SED propaganda had never been fully realized on the ground, but the end of the GDR deprived hundreds of thousands of women of their economic independence due to the loss of both jobs and the services that enabled full-time work. In addition, there was the rollback of access to abortion: while East German women had witnessed the liberalization of abortion in 1972, in the Federal Republic, the Constitutional Court had ruled against similar legislation, and under Paragraph 218 of the criminal code it remained (and remains today) a crime outside of specific medical and social exemptions that have to be certified by a panel of experts. For many women, there was a sense that while their political rights had increased, their economic rights and their right to bodily autonomy had suffered in return.

Within the legal realm, there was also the question of what to do with the old regime. The purges and prosecutions of former SED leaders forced out in the fall of 1989 had already begun by the close of the year. This expanded greatly with reunification. Most professors were removed from their posts—the few who were allowed to remain had to be cleared by review panels that evaluated whether their work had academic merit outside of its service to East German state ideology. Much of the state bureaucracy was replaced by civil servants imported from the West. The institutions of administration and justice were extended from the Federal Republic into the five new federal states (Länder) that once made up the GDR. Although some argued that the surveillance files of the Ministry for State Security should be destroyed, they were instead preserved and used to vet people on the basis of their collaboration with the security services. Activists had occupied Stasi headquarters in 1989 first to prevent the destruction of documents and then to demand the right of the public to review what material had been gathered on them. Placed under the control of a state agency led first by GDR pastor (and later German President) Joachim Gauck, the files of collaborators and informants were exposed to public scrutiny, while those who were subjected to surveillance were (and still are) allowed to see their Stasi file at their own discretion. The Stasi Archive quickly came to serve as a source of judgment on whether one had been a victim or a perpetrator in the old regime. Several prominent East Germans who had led political parties into the March 1990 elections were quickly drummed out of political life when their status as Stasi informants was revealed (see Chapter 4). Others were confronted with the fact that their trusted coworkers, friends, or even family members had acted (or been forced to act) as informants against them.[7]

While revelations about the Stasi rippled through the former GDR, major trials were also held to judge individual border guards and the leaders of the SED and the Stasi. Around 75,000 investigations into GDR-era crimes were conducted after reunification, leading to approximately 1,000 trials.[8] Erich and Margot Honecker initially fled to Moscow, but after the Soviet Union collapsed and their Soviet allies all disappeared from power, he sought refuge in the Chilean embassy, living there for nearly a year as German and Chilean authorities negotiated; Chile had offered Honecker asylum in gratitude for East Germany's role in protecting so many Chilean refugees during the military junta of Augusto Pinochet. Honecker was subsequently deported back to Germany to face charges of complicity in murders at the GDR border. Margot (see bio on page 133), despite facing her own charges, was allowed to fly directly to Santiago de Chile. Erich Honecker was charged alongside former Prime Minister Willi Stoph, Stasi chief Erich Mielke, Defense Minister Heinz Keßler, and other members of the National Defense Council. Border guards who had received medals for their efforts to stop "flight from the Republic" with deadly force were now put on trial as murderers.[9] Conversely, Stasi foreign intelligence chief Markus Wolf was charged with treason against the Federal Republic.

As per the Unification Treaty, prosecutions were conducted according to both East and West German law. The GDR was not treated legally as an "Unrechtsstaat"—a state of total injustice—on par with that of the Third Reich. The legal system was deemed to have been unevenly and politically applied, but it did substantially exist and could be used to prosecute the leaders of the SED and others. Honecker and his colleagues were charged with violating GDR law as interpreted through the lens of the SED's accession to the Helsinki Accords and its provisions on the protection of human rights. Nonetheless,

The German Democratic Republic

Honecker was in such poor health that the charges were ultimately dropped, and he was allowed to claim asylum in Santiago, where he died soon thereafter, surrounded by his family. Wolf (see bio on page 73) was initially convicted, but that decision was overturned on the grounds that as an East German he could not commit treason against West Germany, a foreign state; Mielke was eventually convicted, but on charges of murder for his part in the killing of two policemen in Weimar Berlin in 1931. While some SED leaders—including Egon Krenz and Günther Schabowski—and several border guards were successfully convicted for their role in the border killings, there was no mass incarceration on the basis of criminal prosecutions.[10] Krenz served nearly four years in prison (with the rest of his 6.5-year sentence on parole); Schabowski was convicted to three years and pardoned after one, on the grounds that he had admitted his own guilt and denounced the GDR; Mielke was sentenced to six years in prison and released after five. By that point, he was very ill and, at eighty-seven, Germany's oldest prison inmate.

The GDR trials were part of a larger effort to determine an official history and memory of East Germany in reunified Germany. Just as Nazi Germany had stood as the negative example for those in both East and West attempting to fashion a new national identity in the aftermath of the Second World War, the GDR stood as the totalitarian other to the democratic Berlin Republic. Two major parliamentary inquiries (Enquete-Kommissionen) were conducted by the Bundestag in 1992 and 1995 to uncover the nature of the SED dictatorship, producing thirty-two volumes of material.[11] Yet, the creation of an official record has done little to settle popular debates around the memory of the GDR: the Enquete Commission's writing of the official history, in short, did not relegate the GDR to history.

The relationship of the Berlin Republic to sites of GDR memory has been ambivalent. Memorials commemorating the Berlin Wall have served as ongoing sites of conflict over the meaning of the East German state and how it should be remembered.[12] The East German past has become a tourist draw, including the creation of numerous museums dedicated to the Stasi and the prison system of the former GDR.[13] At the same time, there have been major acts of erasure,

Epilogue

Figure E.1 The demolition of the Palace of the Republic in 2006. The bilingual signage at the site stated in English: A Democratic Decision: A National Debate—A Collective Conclusion. The German text "Eine demokratische Entscheidung/Ein Land diskutiert—und findet den Weg" literally translates as "A country debates—and finds the path forward." Julia Sittmann.

such as the demolition of the Palace of the Republic, replaced by a recreation of the Prussian-era City Palace. Less spectacular markers of East German history, like the ubiquitous GDR-produced public art on buildings and in public squares, have been steadily disappearing, with some viewing it as a by-product of ideological indoctrination and others seeking to preserve it as part of Germany's cultural heritage.[14] Other remnants of the GDR have been largely stripped of their historical origins. Berlin's TV Tower was meant to serve as a symbol of socialist engineering capabilities and the scientific capacities of the GDR. Schoolchildren had to memorize the exact height of the tower, touted as one of the great accomplishments of socialism that needed to be appreciated by the youth. Unlike the Palace of the Republic, there were practically no efforts to remove it after 1990 in spite of its

Figure E.2 The Berlin TV Tower made to look like a magenta football as part of a Deutsche Telekom sponsorship in connection with the FIFA World Cup in Summer 2006. Julia Sittmann.

dominating position in the Berlin skyline. Its political and ideological importance faded rapidly, becoming a general symbol of Berlin and Germany as a whole. While there were competing stop-motion animated children's shows featuring the figure of the Sandmännchen in both East and West, the GDR version was more popular on both sides of the Wall, and the Western version was discontinued. Similarly, the Ampelmännchen (the jaunty traffic signal figure of the GDR, with his little straw hat) was supposed to be replaced by a figure from the West. After a successful grassroots campaign to save him, the tides shifted, and he was derided as Ostalgie kitsch, before finally gaining widespread acceptance and adorning traffic lights throughout Berlin

Epilogue

and beyond the former East, in part because the larger surface area increases visibility. He has become a beloved souvenir staple, fully depoliticized from his past as a symbol of a fallen dictatorship.

More than three decades after the fall of the Berlin Wall, the subject of GDR history remains contentious, as does the question of who has the right to write its history.[15] Within academic scholarship, such questions have become less partisan, and perspectives on the GDR past have become more differentiated among newer generations of historians.[16] Yet the meaning of the GDR remains a hot-button issue in German politics. The election of the Linke—the present-day successor party of the SED and the PDS—at the head of a coalition in the Federal State of Thuringia in 2014 was denounced by opponents as the return to power of a party implicated in dictatorship and mass human rights violations. The Linke responded by noting that the Christian Democrats in Thuringia were also the successor of a party that had been in the National Front led by the SED.[17] The following

Figure E.3 The Sandmännchen on set at the Babelsberg film studios in Potsdam, 2009. Invented by Gerhard Behrendt, the Sandmännchen debuted in 1959 as an evening broadcast to encourage children to go to bed. Sean Gallup/Getty Images.

year, the xenophobic and Islamophobic movement PEGIDA (Patriotic Europeans against the Islamization of the Occident) took up the slogan of the 1989 protestors—"We are the People"—when it held mass demonstrations in 2015. While PEGIDA disappeared during the Covid-19 pandemic (absorbed by other far-right streams, including the anti-vaccination Querdenker movement), the populist right-wing party Alternative for Germany (AfD, Alternative für Deutschland) now claims to represent the true spirit of 1989. In regional elections in Eastern Germany, the AfD has promised to avenge the wrongs done to the East through the privatization process of the 1990s and to "complete the turn" referring to Egon Krenz's reform slogan of "die Wende," which became a shorthand for the events that led to the fall of the Berlin Wall.[18] On a lighter note, when Angela Merkel retired in December 2021 after nearly sixteen years in office as Chancellor— the only woman and former GDR citizen to hold the position—and over thirty years in public office (beginning as a spokesperson for Democratic Awakening in 1990), a military band played the still beloved East German pop song "You Forgot the Colour Film" (Du hast den Farbfilm vergessen) by Nina Hagen (step-daughter of Wolf Biermann) as part of her formal sendoff.

The ongoing political relevance of the GDR reflects the reality that reunification did not bring together one indivisible nation that had been separated only by an artificial border. The process of creating a unified social, cultural, and economic life in Germany is still ongoing.[19] Although the East German cultural identity promoted by the SED failed to save the GDR, there remains a sense among some of a separate East Germany identity.[20] This sense of a continued East German identity is tied in some cases to a nostalgia for the GDR—*Ostalgie*—which can mean anything from a longing for an authoritarian past to a set of grievances against the Federal Republic over the inequalities between East and West in the Berlin Republic or a more benign means of processing social displacement and the loss of the material world of the GDR.[21] A sense of separate East German existence has more current material causes as well: due to the differential social policies of the two states, there continue to be more daycare facilities for working parents in the East, and significantly higher female participation in

Epilogue

the labor force.[22] At the same time, pensions for those working in the former GDR were only equalized with those in the West in 2023.[23] Differing understandings of what democracy is and how it should function also continue to mark a divide between East and West.[24] All that to say: the end of the GDR as a state in 1990 was not the end of the history of the German Democratic Republic. Its existence, including its demise, has continued to echo through the history of the reunified Germany until today.

NOTES

Introduction

1. Mirjana Ristic, "Post-Fallism: The Afterlife of the Lenin Monument in Berlin," *City* 24, no. 3 (2020): 656–67.
2. Andrew Port, "Introduction: The Banalities of East German Historiography," in *Becoming East German: Socialist Structures and Sensibilities after Hitler*, ed. Andrew Port and Mary Fulbrook (New York: Berghahn, 2013).
3. Konrad Jarausch, ed., *Dictatorship as Experience: Towards a Socio-Cultural History of the GDR* (New York: Berghahn, 1999); Corey Ross, *The East German Dictatorship: Problems and Perspectives in the Interpretation of the GDR* (London: Arnold, 2002); Mary Fulbrook, *The People's State* (New Haven, CT: Yale University Press, 2008).
4. Thomas Lindenberger, *Herrschaft und Eigen-Sinn in der Diktatur: Studien zur Gesellschaftsgeschichte der DDR* (Cologne: Böhlau, 1999); Mary Fulbrook, "The Concept of 'Normalisation' and the GDR in Comparative Perspective," in *Power and Society in the GDR, 1961–1979*, ed. Mary Fulbrook (New York: Berghahn, 2009), 1–30.
5. Jens Gieseke, "After the Battles: The History of East German Society and Its Sources," *German History* 36, no. 4 (2018): 599.
6. Daniel Siemens, ed., "What's Next? Historical Research on the GDR Three Decades after German Unification," *German History*, 41, no. 2 (2023): 279–96.
7. Ilko-Sascha Kowalczuk, "Es gab viele Mauern in der DDR," *Deutschland Archiv Online* (1/2012).
8. Kati Marton, "Review of Katja Hoyer's Beyond the Wall: Life during Cold Wartime in East Berlin," Book Section, *The New York Times* (September 5, 2023).
9. Norbert Pötzl, "Eine ganz kommode Diktatur," Das Politische Buch, *Süddeutsche Zeitung* (May 4, 2023).
10. Franziska Kuschel, "Katja Hoyers »Diesseits der Mauer«: Dieses DDR-Buch ist ein Ärgernis—einseitig, grotesk verkürzt, faktische Fehler," Geschichte, *Spiegel Online* (May 12, 2023).

Notes

Chapter 1

1. Manfred Wilke, *The Path to the Berlin Wall: Critical Stages in the History of Divided Germany* (New York: Berghahn, 2014), 25.
2. Nicole Eaton, *German Blood, Slavic Soil: How Nazi Königsberg Became Soviet Kaliningrad* (Ithaca, NY: Cornell University Press, 2023).
3. R.M. Douglas, *Orderly and Humane: The Expulsion of the Germans after the Second World War* (New Haven, CT: Yale University Press, 2012).
4. Norman Naimark, *The Russians in Germany: A History of the Soviet Zone of Occupation, 1945–1949* (Cambridge, MA: Harvard University Press, 1995), chapter 1.
5. Ilko-Sascha Kowalczuk, *Walter Ulbricht: Der deutsche Kommunist* (Munich: C.H. Beck, 2023).
6. Naimark, *The Russians in Germany*, chapter 6.
7. Dirk Spilker, *The East German Leadership and the Division of Germany: Patriotism and Propaganda 1945–1953* (Oxford: Oxford University Press, 2006).
8. Proclamation by the Central Committee of the German Communist Party (June 11, 1945), *German History in Documents and Images* (online).
9. Mario Keßler and Thomas Klein, "Repression and Tolerance as Methods of Rule in Communist Societies," in *Dictatorship as Experience: Towards a Socio-Cultural History of the GDR*, ed. Konrad Jarausch (New York: Berghahn, 1999), 112.
10. Francine Hirsch, *Soviet Judgment at Nuremberg: A New History of the International Military Tribunal after World War II* (Oxford: Oxford University Press, 2020).
11. Bettina Greiner, *Suppressed Terror: History and Perception of Soviet Special Camps in Germany* (Lanham, MD: Lexington, 2014), 2.
12. Devin Pendas, *Democracy, Nazi Trials, and Transitional Justice in Germany, 1945–1950* (Cambridge: Cambridge University Press, 2020), 63.
13. Andrew Beattie, *Allied Internment Camps in Occupied Germany: Extrajudicial Detention in the Name of Denazification, 1945–1950* (Cambridge: Cambridge University Press, 2020).
14. Gareth Pritchard, *Niemandsland: A History of Unoccupied Germany, 1944–45* (Cambridge: Cambridge University Press, 2012), 193.
15. Timothy Vogt, *Denazification in Soviet-Occupied Germany: Brandenburg, 1945–1948* (Cambridge: Harvard University Press, 2000).

Notes

16. Dietmar Remy and Axel Salheiser, "Integration or Exclusion: Former National Socialists in the GDR," *Historical Social Research* 35, no. 3 (2010): 10.

17. Enquete-Kommission, "Aufarbeitung von Geschichte und Folgen der SED-Diktatur in Deutschland" (1992–1994), Band III/1, 141.

18. André Steiner, *The Plans That Failed: An Economic History of East Germany, 1945–1989* (New York: Berghahn, 2010), 19.

19. Douglas O'Reagan, *Taking Nazi Technology: Allied Exploitation of German Science after the Second World War* (Baltimore, MD: Johns Hopkins University Press, 2021), 104.

20. Asif Siddiqi, "Germans in Russia: Cold War, Technology Transfer, and National Identity," *Osiris* 24, no. 1 (2009): 120–43.

21. Mark Jones, *Founding Weimar: Violence and the German Revolution of 1918–1919* (Cambridge: Cambridge University Press, 2016).

22. Norman Laporte and Ralf Hoffrogge, *Weimar Communism as Mass Movement: 1918–1933* (London: Lawrence & Wishart, 2017).

23. Catherine Epstein, *The Last Revolutionaries: German Communists and Their Century* (Cambridge, MA: Harvard University Press, 2009), chapter 2; Eric Weitz, *Creating German Communism, 1890–1990: From Popular Protests to Socialist State* (Princeton, NJ: Princeton University Press, 2021), chapter 8.

24. J.H. Brinks, "Political Anti-Fascism in the German Democratic Republic," *Journal of Contemporary History* 32, no. 2 (1997): 207–17.

25. Josie McLellan, *Antifascism and Memory in East Germany: Remembering the International Brigades 1945–1989* (Oxford: Clarendon, 2004); Russel Lemmons, *Hitler's Rival: Ernst Thälmann in Myth and Memory* (Lexington, KY: University Press of Kentucky, 2013).

26. Jon Berndt Olsen, *Tailoring Truth: Politicizing the Past and Negotiating Memory in East Germany, 1945–1990* (New York: Berghahn, 2017).

27. Alexander Walther, "Keine Erinnerung, nirgends? Die *Shoah* und die DDR," *Deutschland-Archiv* (July 15, 2019).

28. Anton Ackermann, The "German Path to Socialism" (February 1946), *German History in Documents and Images* (online).

29. Miriam Gebhardt, *Crimes Unspoken: The Rape of German Women at the End of the Second World War* (New York: John Wiley & Sons, 2016).

30. Gareth Pritchard, *The Making of the GDR, 1945–53: From Antifascism to Stalinism* (Manchester: St. Martin's Press, 2000), chapter 7.

31. Wolfgang Leonhard, *Die Revolution entlässt ihre Kinder* (Cologne: Kiepenheuer & Witsch, 2017), 440.

32. Spilker, *The East German Leadership*, 5.
33. Maria Mitchell, *The Origins of Christian Democracy: Politics and Confession in Modern Germany* (Ann Arbor: University of Michigan Press, 2012), 140.
34. Erich Gniffke, *Jahre mit Ulbricht* (Cologne: Wissenschaft und Politik, 1966).
35. Mark Fenemore, *Dismembered Policing in Postwar Berlin: The Limits of Four-Power Government* (London: Bloomsbury, 2023).
36. Peter Quint, *The Imperfect Union: Constitutional Structures of German Unification* (Princeton, NJ: Princeton University Press, 2012).
37. Sebastian Gehrig, "Cold War Identities: Citizenship, Constitutional Reform, and International Law between East and West Germany, 1967–75," *Journal of Contemporary History* 49, no. 4 (2014): 795.
38. Matthias Lienert, *Zwischen Widerstand und Repression: Studenten der TU Dresden, 1946–1989* (Cologne: Böhlau, 2011), 40.
39. Wolfgang Buschfort, *Parteien im Kalten Krieg: die Ostbüros von SPD, CDU und FDP* (Berlin: Ch. Links, 2000), 28; *Wer war wer in der DDR?* (Berlin: Ch. Links, 2009).
40. Robert Goeckel, *The Lutheran Church and the East German State: Political Conflict and Change under Ulbricht and Honecker* (Ithaca, NY: Cornell University Press, 1990), 198.
41. Hedwig Richter, "Mass Obedience: Practices and Functions of Elections in the German Democratic Republic," in *Voting for Hitler and Stalin: Elections under 20th Century Dictatorships*, ed. Ralph Jessen and Hedwig Richter (Chicago, IL: University of Chicago Press, 2011).
42. Dominic Boyer, "Censorship as a Vocation: The Institutions, Practices, and Cultural Logic of Media Control in the German Democratic Republic," *Comparative Studies in Society and History* 45, no. 3 (2003): 511–45.
43. Nicholas Schlosser, *Cold War on the Airwaves: The Radio Propaganda War against East Germany* (Urbana, IL: University of Illinois Press, 2015); Franziska Kuschel, *Schwarzhörer, Schwarzseher und heimliche Leser: Die DDR und die Westmedien* (Göttingen: Wallstein, 2016).
44. Heather Gumbert, *Envisioning Socialism: Television and the Cold War in the German Democratic Republic* (Ann Arbor: University of Michigan Press, 2014).
45. Anke Fiedler and Michael Meyen, *Fiktionen für das Volk: DDR-Zeitungen als PR-Instrument: Fallstudien zu den Zentralorganen Neues Deutschland, Junge Welt, Neue Zeit und Der Morgen* (Münster: LIT, 2011).

Notes

46. Lorn Hillaker, "Representing a 'Better Germany': Competing Images of State and Society in the Early Cultural Diplomacy of the FRG and GDR," *Central European History* 53, no. 2 (2020): 372–92.

47. Stefan Berger and Norman Laporte, *Friendly Enemies: Britain and the GDR, 1949–1990* (New York: Berghahn, 2010), 65.

48. Peter Ruggenthaler, "The 1952 Stalin Note on German Unification: The Ongoing Debate," *Journal of Cold War Studies* 13, no. 4 (2011): 172–212.

49. Weitz, *Creating German Communism*, 355–6.

50. Alan McDougall, *Youth Politics in East Germany: The Free German Youth Movement, 1946–1968* (Oxford: Oxford University Press, 2004), 28.

51. Andrew Port, "When Workers Rumbled: The Wismut Upheaval of August 1951 in East Germany," *Social History* 22, no. 2 (1997): 145–73.

52. Wayne Geerling, Gary Magee, and Russell Smyth, "Occupation, Reparations, and Rebellion: The Soviets and the East German Uprising of 1953," *The Journal of Interdisciplinary History* 52, no. 2 (2021): 225–50.

53. Jens Schöne, *Jenseits der Städte: der Volksaufstand vom Juni 1953 in der DDR* (Erfurt: Landeszentrale für politische Bildung Thüringen, 2023).

54. Christian Ostermann, *Uprising in East Germany, 1953: The Cold War, the German Question, and the First Major Upheaval behind the Iron Curtain* (Budapest: Central European University Press, 2001).

55. Sandrine Kott, *Communism Day-to-Day: State Enterprises in East German Society* (Ann Arbor: University of Michigan Press, 2014), 26.

56. Gary Bruce, *Resistance with the People Repression and Resistance in Eastern Germany, 1945–1955* (Lanham, MD: Rowman and Littlefield, 2003).

57. McDougall, *Youth Politics in East Germany*, chapter 1.

58. Edda Ahrberg, Tobias Hollitzer and Hans-Hermann Hertle, "Der Aufstand—Die Toten des Volksaufstandes," *Bundeszentrale für politische Bildung* (May 17, 2013), (online).

59. Marianne Brentzel, *Die Machtfrau: Hilde Benjamin, 1902–1989* (Berlin: Ch. Links, 1997).

60. Falco Werkentin, *Politische Strafjustiz in der Ära Ulbricht: vom bekennenden Terror zur verdeckten Repression* (Berlin: Ch. Links, 1997), 150.

61. Christian Ostermann, *Between Containment and Rollback: The United States and the Cold War in Germany* (Stanford, CA: Stanford University Press, 2021), chapter 5.

Notes

62. Victor Klemperer, *The Lesser Evil: The Diaries of Victor Klemperer 1945-1959* (London: Orion, 2003), 419.

63. Richard Millington, *State, Society and Memories of the Uprising of 17 June 1953 in the GDR* (Basingstoke: Palgrave, 2014).

64. Roger Engelmann and Karl Wilhelm Fricke, *Konzentrierte Schläge: Staatssicherheitsaktionen und politische Prozesse in der DDR 1953-1956* (Berlin: Ch. Links, 2006).

65. Molly Pucci, *Security Empire: The Secret Police in Communist Eastern Europe* (New Haven, CT: Yale University Press, 2020), Chapters 3 & 6.

66. Tilmann Siebeneichner, *Proletarischer Mythos und realer Sozialismus: die Kampfgruppen der Arbeiterklasse in der DDR* (Cologne: Böhlau, 2014).

67. Hope Harrison, *Driving the Soviets up the Wall: Soviet-East German Relations, 1953-1961* (Princeton, NJ: Princeton University Press, 2011), chapter 1.

68. Jeffrey Herf, "East German Communists and the Jewish Question: The Case of Paul Merker," *Journal of Contemporary History* 29, no. 4 (1994): 627-61.

69. Alexey Tikhomirov, *The Stalin Cult in East Germany and the Making of the Postwar Soviet Empire, 1945-1961* (Lanham, MD: Rowman & Littlefield, 2022), 270.

70. Jens Gieseke, *The History of the Stasi: East Germany's Secret Police, 1945-1990* (New York: Berghahn, 2014), 47.

71. Epstein, *The Last Revolutionaries*, 78.

72. Henrik Bispinck and Damian van Melis, *"Republikflucht": Flucht und Abwanderung aus der SBZ/DDR 1945 bis 1961* (Berlin: De Gruyter, 2015).

73. Keith Allen, *Interrogation Nation: Refugees and Spies in Cold War Germany* (Lanham, MD: Rowman & Littlefield, 2017).

74. Bernd Stöver, *Zuflucht DDR: Spione und andere Übersiedler* (Munich: C.H. Beck, 2009).

75. Albrecht Ritschl and Tamás Vonyó, "The Roots of Economic Failure: What Explains East Germany's Falling behind between 1945 and 1950?," *European Review of Economic History* 18, no. 2 (2014): 166-84.

76. Steiner, *The Plans That Failed*, 90-2.

77. Barry Eichengreen and Albrecht Ritschl, "Understanding West German Economic Growth in the 1950s," *Cliometrica, Journal of Historical Economics and Econometric History* 3 (2009): 191-219.

78. Lorenz Lüthi, *Cold Wars: Asia, the Middle East, Europe* (Cambridge: Cambridge University Press, 2020), 422.

Notes

79. Vladislav Zubok, *A Failed Empire: The Soviet Union in the Cold War from Stalin to Gorbachev* (Chapel Hill: University of North Carolina Press, 2009), 132–7.
80. Steiner, *The Plans That Failed*, 96–7.
81. Patrick Major, *Behind the Berlin Wall: East Germany and the Frontiers of Power* (Oxford: Oxford University Press, 2010), 57.
82. Harrison, *Driving the Soviets Up the Wall*.
83. Julia Sonnevend, *Stories without Borders: The Berlin Wall and the Making of a Global Iconic Event* (Oxford: Oxford University Press, 2016), 44.
84. Major, *Behind the Berlin Wall*, chapter 5.
85. Corey Ross, "East Germans and the Berlin Wall: Popular Opinion and Social Change before and after the Border Closure of August 1961," *Journal of Contemporary History* 39, no. 1 (2004): 25–43.
86. Ned Richardson-Little, *The Human Rights Dictatorship: Socialism, Global Solidarity and Revolution in East Germany* (Cambridge: Cambridge University Press, 2020), 68.
87. Hans-Hermann Hertle and Maria Nooke, *Die Todesopfer an der Berliner Mauer 1961–1989. Ergebnisse eines Forschungsprojektes des ZZF Potsdam und der Stiftung Berliner Mauer*, Version 4.0 (August 2020), Potsdam/Berlin (online).
88. Hans-Hermann Hertle, "Grenzverletzer sind festzunehmen oder zu vernichten," *Aus Politik und Zeitgeschichte* 61, no. 31/34 (2011): 22–8.
89. Pertti Ahonen, *Death at the Berlin Wall* (Oxford: Oxford University Press, 2010), chapter 2.
90. Hans-Hermann Hertle and Maria Nooke, eds., *Die Todesopfer an der Berliner Mauer 1961–1989: Ein biographisches Handbuch* (Berlin: Ch. Links Verlag, 2019), 370–7; Kate Brady, "50 years later, German Stasi agent is convicted of murder, gets 10 years," *Washington Post* (14 October 2024).
91. Ahonen, *Death at the Berlin Wall*, chapter 3.
92. Hope Harrison, *After the Berlin Wall: Memory and the Making of the New Germany, 1989 to the Present* (Cambridge: Cambridge University Press, 2019), 181.
93. W.R. Smyser, *Kennedy and the Berlin Wall: "A Hell of a Lot Better than a War"* (Lanham, MD: Rowman & Littlefield, 2009).
94. Stefanie Eisenhuth and Scott Krause, "Inventing the 'Outpost of Freedom.' Transatlantic Narratives and the Historical Actors Crafting West Berlin's Postwar Political Culture," *Zeithistorische Forschungen* 11, no. 2 (2014): 188–211.

Notes

Chapter 2

1. Jens Gieseke, "Soziale Ungleichheit im Staatssozialismus. Eine Skizze," *Zeithistorische Forschungen* 10, no. 2 (2013): 171–98.
2. Jutta Braun, *Politische Medizin: Das Ministerium für Gesundheitswesen der DDR 1950 bis 1970* (Göttingen: Wallstein, 2023), chapter IV.1.2.
3. Jürgen Danyel and Elke Kimmel, *Waldsiedlung Wandlitz: eine Landschaft der Macht* (Berlin: Ch. Links, 2016).
4. Michel Christian, Jens Gieseke, and Florian Peters, *Die SED als Mitgliederpartei: Dokumentation und Analyse* (Berlin: Ch. Links, 2019); Rüdiger Bergien, *Inside Party Headquarters: Organizational Culture and Practice of Rule in the Socialist Unity Party of Germany* (New York: Berghahn, 2023).
5. Siegfried Suckut, *Blockparteien und Blockpolitik in der SBZ/DDR 1945–1990* (Leipzig: Leipziger Universitätsverlag, 2018).
6. Barbara Koelges, *Der Demokratische Frauenbund: Von der DDR-Massenorganisation zum modernen politischen Frauenverband* (Wiesbaden: Westdeutscher Verlag, 2013); Andreas Zimmer, *Der Kulturbund in der SBZ und in der DDR: Eine ostdeutsche Kulturvereinigung im Wandel der Zeit zwischen 1945 und 1990* (Wiesbaden: Springer, 2018).
7. Thomas Goldstein, *Writing in Red: The East German Writers Union and the Role of Literary Intellectuals* (Rochester, NY: Boydell & Brewer, 2017).
8. Dorothee Wierling, "Work, Workers, and Politics in the German Democratic Republic," *International Labor and Working-Class History* 50 (1996): 44–63.
9. Katharina Lenski, "The Stigma of 'Asociality' in the GDR," in *After Auschwitz: The Difficult Legacies of the GDR*, ed. Enrico Heitzer, Anetta Kahane, Martin Jander, and Patrice Poutrus (New York: Berghahn, 2021).
10. Uta Falck, *VEB Bordell: Geschichte der Prostitution in der DDR* (Berlin: Ch. Links, 2012); Steffi Brüning, *Prostitution in der DDR: Eine Untersuchung am Beispiel von Rostock, Berlin und Leipzig, 1968 bis 1989* (Berlin: BeBra Wissenschaft, 2020).
11. Gieseke, "Soziale Ungleichheit im Staatssozialismus. Eine Skizze."
12. Christoph Klessmann, *Arbeiter im "Arbeiterstaat" DDR: deutsche Traditionen, sowjetisches Modell, westdeutsches Magnetfeld (1945–1971)* (Berlin: Dietz, 2007).

Notes

13. Sandrine Kott, *Communism Day-to-Day: State Enterprises in East German Society* (Ann Arbor: University of Michigan Press, 2014), 94–101.
14. Ned Richardson-Little, *The Human Rights Dictatorship: Socialism, Global Solidarity and Revolution in East Germany* (Cambridge: Cambridge University Press, 2020), 65–6.
15. Kott, *Communism Day-to-Day*, 47.
16. Peter Hübner, *Konsens, Konflikt und Kompromiss: Soziale Arbeiterinteressen und Sozialpolitik in der SBZ/DDR 1945–1970* (Berlin: De Gruyter, 1995), chapter 1.
17. Kott, *Communism Day-to-Day*, 88–94.
18. Gregory Witkowski, *The Campaign State: Communist Mobilizations for the East German Countryside, 1945–1990* (Ithaca, NY: Cornell University Press, 2017), 230.
19. Kott, *Communism Day-to-Day*, 236–8.
20. Alan McDougall, *The People's Game: Football, State and Society in East Germany* (Cambridge: Cambridge University Press, 2014), 248.
21. George Bodie, "'It Is a Shame We Are Not Neighbours': GDR Tourist Cruises to Cuba, 1961–89," *Journal of Contemporary History* 55, no. 2 (2020): 411–34.
22. Kott, *Communism Day-to-Day*, 35.
23. Andrew Port, *Conflict and Stability in the German Democratic Republic* (Cambridge: Cambridge University Press, 2007), chapter 4.
24. Donna Harsch, "Between State Policy and Private Sphere: Women in the GDR in the 1960s and 1970s," *Clio: Women Gender History* 41 (2015): 89–91.
25. Annemette Sørensen and Heike Trappe, "The Persistence of Gender Inequality in Earnings in the German Democratic Republic," *American Sociological Review* 60, no. 3 (1995): 398–406. Dagmar Langenhan and Sabine Roß, "The Socialist Glass Ceiling: Limits to Female Careers," in *Dictatorship as Experience: Towards a Socio-Cultural History of the GDR*, ed. Konrad Jarausch (New York: Berghahn, 1999).
26. Henrike Voigtländer, *Sexismus im Betrieb: Geschlecht und Herrschaft in der DDR-Industrie* (Berlin: Ch. Links, 2023).
27. Alexandria Ruble, *Entangled Emancipation: Women's Rights in Cold War Germany* (Toronto: University of Toronto Press, 2023), chapter 2.
28. Alexandria Ruble, "Creating Postfascist Families: Reforming Family Law and Gender Roles in Postwar East and West Germany," *Central European History* 53, no. 2 (June 2020): 423.

Notes

29. Jennifer Lynn, *Contested Femininities: Representations of Modern Women in the German Illustrated Press, 1920–1960* (New York: Berghahn, 2024), 226.
30. Josie McLellan, *Love in the Time of Communism: Intimacy and Sexuality in the GDR* (Cambridge: Cambridge University Press, 2011), 72.
31. Donna Harsch, *Revenge of the Domestic: Women, the Family, and Communism in the German Democratic Republic* (New Haven, NJ: Princeton University Press, 2007), 112–15.
32. Jane Freeland, *Feminist Transformations and Domestic Violence Activism in Divided Berlin, 1968–2002* (Oxford: Oxford University Press, 2022), chapter 4.
33. Maxie Wander, *Guten Morgen, du Schöne: Frauen in der DDR* (Berlin: Der Morgen, 1977); Jennifer Creech, *Mothers, Comrades, and Outcasts in East German Women's Films* (Bloomington, IN: Indiana University Press, 2016).
34. Norman Naimark, *The Russians in Germany: A History of the Soviet Zone of Occupation, 1945–1949* (Cambridge, MA: Harvard University Press, 1995), 123; Jessica Bock, *Kontrollierte Selbstbestimmung: Schwangerschaftsabbruch in Sachsen 1945–1990* (Dresden: Weiterdenken—Heinrich Böll Stiftung Sachsen, 2023), chapter 1.
35. Donna Harsch, "Society, the State, and Abortion in East Germany, 1950–1972," *The American Historical Review* 102, no. 1 (1997): 67.
36. Jennifer Evans, "The Moral State: Men, Mining, and Masculinity in the Early GDR," *German History* 23, no. 3 (2005): 355–70.
37. Dagmar Herzog, "East Germany's Sexual Evolution," in *Socialist Modern: East German Everyday Culture and Politics*, ed. Katherine Pence and Paul Betts (Ann Arbor: University of Michigan Press, 2008), 74.
38. Andrea Rottmann, *Queer Lives across the Wall: Desire and Danger in Divided Berlin, 1945–1970* (Toronto: University of Toronto Press, 2023), 70.
39. Samuel Huneke, *States of Liberation: Gay Men between Dictatorship and Democracy in Cold War Germany* (Toronto: University of Toronto Press, 2022), 150–3.
40. McLellan, *Love in the Time of Communism*, 11.
41. Josie McLellan, "State Socialist Bodies: East German Nudism from Ban to Boom," *The Journal of Modern History* 79, no. 1 (2007): 48–79.
42. Eva Sudholt, "Malweib – Brigitte Fugmann," *Die Zeit* nr. 06 (2024).
43. Gerd Gemünden, "Between Karl May and Karl Marx: The DEFA Indianerfilme (1965–1983)," *Film History* 10, no. 3 (1998): 399–407.

Notes

44. Andreas Agocs, *Antifascist Humanism and the Politics of Cultural Renewal in Germany* (Cambridge: Cambridge University Press, 2019).
45. Sean Forner, "Reconsidering the 'Unpolitical German': Democratic Renewal and the Politics of Culture in Occupied Germany," *German History* 32, no. 1 (2014): 53–78.
46. Stephen Brockman, "Resurrected from the Ruins: The Emergence of GDR Culture," in *Rereading East Germany: The Literature and Film of the GDR*, ed. Karen Leeder (Cambridge: Cambridge University Press, 2015), 42.
47. April Eisman, *Bernhard Heisig and the Fight for Modern Art in East Germany* (Rochester, NY: Camden House, 2018), 43.
48. Eisman, *Bernhard Heisig*, 25.
49. William Waltz, *Of Writers and Workers: The Movement of Writing Workers in East Germany* (Oxford: Peter Lang, 2018).
50. Gunnar Decker, *1965: Der kurze Sommer der DDR* (Munich: Carl Hanser, 2015).
51. Kira Thurman, *Singing Like Germans: Black Musicians in the Land of Bach, Beethoven, and Brahms* (Ithaca, NY: Cornell University Press, 2021).
52. Gerd Dietrich, *Kulturgeschichte der DDR* (Göttingen: Vandenhoeck & Ruprecht, 2019), 358–78.
53. Edward Larkey, "Contested Spaces: GDR Rock between Western Influence and Party Control," in *A Sound Legacy: Music and Politics in East Germany* (Washington, DC: American Institute for Contemporary German Studies, 2000).
54. Mark Fenemore, *Sex, Thugs and Rock 'n' Roll: Teenage Rebels in Cold-War East Germany* (New York: Berghahn, 2007), 147.
55. Michael Rauhut, *Beat in der Grauzone: DDR-Rock 1964 bis 1972, Politik und Alltag* (Berlin: BasisDruck, 1993), 262.
56. Uta Poiger, *Jazz, Rock, and Rebels: Cold War Politics and American Culture in a Divided Germany* (Berkeley, CA: University of California Press, 2000), 150–3.
57. Helma Kaldewey, *A People's Music: Jazz in East Germany, 1945–1990* (Cambridge: Cambridge University Press, 2020), 173.
58. Caroline Moine, *Screened Encounters: The Leipzig Documentary Film Festival, 1955–1990* (New York: Berghahn Books, 2018).
59. Elke Neumann, "The Biennale der Ostseeländer: The GDR's Main International Arts Exhibition," in *Art beyond Borders: Artistic Exchange in Communist Europe (1945–1989)*, ed. Jérôme Bazin et al. (Budapest: Central European University Press, 2016).

60. Michael Scholz, "East Germany's North European Policy Prior to International Recognition of the German Democratic Republic," *Contemporary European History* 15, no. 4 (2006): 553–71.

61. Holly Case, "Blind Spot: On Christa Wolf," *The Nation* (May 16, 2012).

62. Seán Allan, "DEFA's Antifascist Myths and the Construction of National Identity in East German Cinema," in *Rereading East Germany: The Literature and Film of the GDR*, ed. Karen Leeder (Cambridge: Cambridge University Press, 2016).

63. *Ernst Thälmann—Sohn seiner Klasse* (Son of his Class) released in 1954, followed by the 1955 sequel, *Ernst Thälmann—Führer seiner Klasse* (Leader of his Class); *Das Kaninchen bin ich*, directed by Kurt Maetzig (1965).

64. *Spur der Steine* (1966), *Nackt unter Wölfen* (1963), both directed by Frank Beyer. Elizabeth Ward, *East German Film and the Holocaust* (New York: Berghahn, 2021).

65. April Eisman, "East German Art and the Permeability of the Berlin Wall," *German Studies Review* 38, no. 3 (2015): 601.

66. *Die Legende von Paul und Paula*, directed by Heiner Carow (1973).

67. Richard Millington, "'Crime Has No Chance': The Discourse of Everyday Criminality in the East German Press, 1961–1989," *Central European History* 50, no. 1 (2017): 59–85.

68. David Crew, "Consuming Germany in the Cold War: Consumption and National Identity in East and West Germany, 1949–1989," in *Consuming Germany in the Cold War* (London: Bloomsbury, 2003).

69. Ina Merkel, "Alternative Rationalities, Strange Dream, Absurd Utopias: On Socialist Advertising and Market Research," in *Socialist Modern: East German Everyday Culture and Politics*, ed. Katherine Pence and Paul Betts (Ann Arbor: University of Michigan Press, 2008), 328.

70. Corey Ross, "East Germans and the Berlin Wall: Popular Opinion and Social Change before and after the Border Closure of August 1961," *Journal of Contemporary History* 39, no. 1 (2004): 27.

71. Katherine Pence, "Grounds for Discontent? Coffee from the Black Market to the Kaffeeklatsch in the GDR," in *Communism Unwrapped: Consumption in Cold War Eastern Europe*, ed. Paulina Bren and Mary Neuburger (Oxford: Oxford University Press, 2012).

72. Annette Kaminsky, "Ungleichheit in der SBZ/DDR am Beispiel des Konsums: Versandhandel, Intershop und Delikat," in *Soziale Ungleichheit in der DDR: zu einem tabuisierten Strukturmerkmal der SED-Diktatur*, ed. Lothar Mertens (Berlin: Duncker & Humblot, 2002).

Notes

73. Alice Weinreb, *Modern Hungers: Food and Power in Twentieth-Century Germany* (Oxford: Oxford University Press, 2017), 128–9.
74. Eli Rubin, *Synthetic Socialism: Plastics and Dictatorship in the German Democratic Republic* (Chapel Hill: University of North Carolina Press, 2012), chapter 2.
75. Ina Merkel, " … in Hoyerswerda leben jedenfalls keine so kleinen viereckigen Menschen." Briefe an das Fernsehen der DDR," in *Akten, Eingaben, Schaufenster: die DDR und ihre Texte: Erkundungen zu Herrschaft und Alltag*, ed. Peter Becker and Alf Lüdtke (Berlin: Akademie, 1997).
76. Judd Stitziel, "Shopping, Sewing, Networking, Complaining: Consumer Culture and the Relationship between State and Society in the GDR," in *Socialist Modern: East German Everyday Culture and Politics*, ed. Katherine Pence and Paul Betts (Ann Arbor: University of Michigan Press, 2008).
77. André Steiner, *The Plans That Failed: An Economic History of the GDR* (New York: Berghahn, 2013), 130.
78. Andrew Kloiber, *Brewing Socialism: Coffee, East Germans, and Twentieth-Century Globalization* (New York: Berghahn, 2022).
79. Patrice G. Poutrus, *Die Erfindung des Goldbroilers: über den Zusammenhang zwischen Herrschaftssicherung und Konsumentwicklung in der DDR* (Cologne: Böhlau, 2002).
80. Lewis Siegelbaum, ed., *The Socialist Car: Automobility in the Eastern Bloc* (Ithaca, NY: Cornell University Press, 2013), chapters 7 & 9.
81. Rubin, *Synthetic Socialism*, 9.
82. Paul Betts, "The Twilight of the Idols: East German Memory and Material Culture," *The Journal of Modern History* 72, no. 3 (2000): 753.
83. Robbie Aitken and Eve Rosenhaft, *Black Germany: The Making and Unmaking of a Diaspora Community, 1884–1960* (Cambridge: Cambridge University Press, 2013); Kim Christian Priemel, *Transit: Politik und Praxis der Einwanderung in die DDR 1945–1990* (Berlin: BeBra Wissenschaft, 2011).
84. Hedwig Richter, *Pietismus im Sozialismus: die Herrnhuter Brüdergemeine in der DDR* (Göttingen: Vandenhoeck & Ruprecht, 2009).
85. Colleen Anderson, "Youth Space Education and the Future of the GDR," *Central European History* 53, no. 1 (2020): 159.
86. Paul Betts, *Within Walls: Private Life in the German Democratic Republic* (Oxford: Oxford University Press, 2012), chapter 2.

Notes

87. Marcus Colla, "Memory, Heritage and the Demolition of the Potsdam Garnisonkirche, 1968," *German History* 38, no. 2 (2020): 290–310; Andrew Demshuk, *Demolition on Karl Marx Square: Cultural Barbarism and the People's State in 1968* (Oxford: Oxford University Press, 2017).
88. Donna Harsch, "Society, the State, and Abortion in East Germany."
89. Bernd Schäfer, *The East German State and the Catholic Church, 1945–1989* (New York: Berghahn, 2010).
90. John Burgess, *The East German Church and the End of Communism* (Oxford: Oxford University Press, 1997).
91. Angelika Timm, "The Burdened Relationship Between the GDR and the State of Israel," *Israel Studies* 2 (1997) 1: 22–49.
92. Jeffrey Herf, "East German Communists and the Jewish Question: The Case of Paul Merker," *Journal of Contemporary History* 29, no. 4 (1994): 627–61.
93. Karin Hartewig, *Zurückgekehrt. Die Geschichte der jüdischen Kommunisten in der DDR* (Cologne: Böhlau 2000).
94. Alexander Walther, "Keine Erinnerung, nirgends? Die Shoah und die DDR," *Deutschland Archiv* (July 15, 2019).
95. Mario Keßler, "Anti-Semitism in East Germany, 1952–1953," in *Unlikely History: The Changing German-Jewish Symbiosis, 1945–2000*, ed. Leslie Morris and Jack Zipes (New York: Palgrave, 2002).
96. Cora Granata, "The Ethnic 'Straight Jacket': Bilingual Education and Grassroots Agency in the Soviet Occupied Zone and German Democratic Republic, 1945–1964," *German Studies Review* 29, no. 2 (2006): 331–46.
97. Special Issue "DDR postkolonial" *PERIPHERIE* 41, no. 1 (2021); Zoé Samudzi, "Socialist Statecraft and 'Decolonizing' Genocide Denial" (forthcoming).
98. Quinn Slobodian, "Socialist Chromatism: Race, Racism, and the Racial Rainbow in East Germany," in *Comrades of Color: East Germany in a Cold War World* (New York: Berghahn, 2015).
99. Jamele Watkins, "One Million Roses for Angela Davis. Drama and the Archive: Solidarity Campaigns in Europe," *Goethe Institut USA* (online).
100. Priscilla Layne, "East Germany's Anti-Racist Politics and Black Abjection in Documentary Film," in *Documenting Socialism: East German Documentary Cinema*, ed. Seán Allan and Sebastian Heiduschke (New York: Berghahn Books, 2024).

Notes

101. Patrice G. Poutrus and Katharina Warda, "Ostdeutsche of Color—Schwarze Geschichte(n) der DDR und Erfahrungen nach der deutschen Einheit," *Aus Politik und Zeitgeschichte* 72 (2022), 12: 19–25.

102. *Verliebt, verlobt, verloren,* directed by Sung-Hyung Cho (2015); Esther Felden, "Loved, Engaged, Lost" *dw.com* (June 26, 2015).

103. Peggy Piesche, "Making African Diasporic Pasts Possible: A Retrospective View of the GDR and Its Black (Step-)Children," in *Remapping Black Germany: New Perspectives on Afro-German History, Politics, and Culture,* ed. Sara Lennox (Amherst: University of Massachusetts Press, 2017); *Becoming Black,* directed by Ines Johnson-Spain (2019).

104. Ulrike Winkler, *Mit dem Rollstuhl in die Tatra-Bahn: Menschen mit Behinderungen in der DDR: Lebensbedingungen und materielle Barrieren* (Halle: Mitteldeutscher Verlag, 2023).

105. Anja Werner, "Building an Organization According to Our Own Wishes: Deaf Agency in East Germany, 1945 to 1960," *German Studies Review* 45, no. 3 (2022).

106. James Chappel, "'On the Border of Old Age': An Entangled History of Eldercare in East Germany," *Central European History* 53, no. 2 (2020): 353–71.

107. Enrico Heitzer, *Die Kampfgruppe gegen Unmenschlichkeit (KgU): Widerstand und Spionage im Kalten Krieg 1948–1959* (Cologne: Böhlau, 2015).

108. Susanne Muhle, *Auftrag: Menschenraub: Entführungen von Westberlinern und Bundesbürgern durch das Ministerium für Staatssicherheit der DDR* (Göttingen: Vandenhoeck & Ruprecht, 2015), 136–41.

109. Daniel Siemens, "Elusive Security in the GDR: Remigrants from the West at the Faculty of Journalism in Leipzig, 1945–61," *Central Europe* 11, no. 1 (2013): 24–45.

110. Sean Forner, *German Intellectuals and the Challenge of Democratic Renewal: Culture and Politics after 1945* (Cambridge: Cambridge University Press, 2017), chapter 6.

111. Peter Caldwell, *Dictatorship, State Planning, and Social Theory in the German Democratic Republic* (Cambridge: Cambridge University Press, 2003).

112. Alexander Amberger, *Bahro—Harich—Havemann: Marxistische Systemkritik und politische Utopie in der DDR* (Paderborn: Ferdinand Schöningh, 2014).

113. Betts, *Within Walls*, chapter 6.
114. Jeremy Straughn, "'Taking the State at Its Word': The Arts of Consentful Contention in the German Democratic Republic," *American Journal of Sociology* 110, no. 6 (2005): 1598–650.
115. Siegfried Suckut, *Volkes Stimmen: »Ehrlich, aber deutlich«— Privatbriefe an die DDR-Regierung* (Munich: DTV, 2016).
116. Jonathan Zatlin, *The Currency of Socialism: Money and Political Culture in East Germany* (Cambridge: Cambridge University Press, 2007), chapter 7.
117. Harsch, *Revenge of the Domestic*, 205.
118. Bernd Eisenfeld and Peter Schicketanz, *Bausoldaten in der DDR: die" Zusammenführung feindlich-negativer Kräfte" in der NVA* (Berlin: Ch. Links, 2011).
119. Mark Allinson, *Politics and Popular Opinion in East Germany, 1945–68* (Manchester: Manchester University Press, 2000), chapter 9; Richardson-Little, *The Human Rights Dictatorship*, 140–52.
120. Betts, *Within Walls*, 23.
121. Jens Gieseke, *The History of the Stasi: East Germany's Secret Police, 1945–1990* (New York: Berghahn, 2014), 75–6.
122. Molly Pucci, *Security Empire: The Secret Police in Communist Eastern Europe* (New Haven, CT: Yale University Press, 2020), 148.
123. Jeffrey Herf, *Divided Memory: The Nazi Past in the Two Germanys* (Cambridge, MA: Harvard University Press, 1997), 245.
124. Catherine Epstein, *The Last Revolutionaries: German Communists and Their Century* (Cambridge, MA: Harvard University Press, 2009), 154.
125. Inga Markovits, *Justice in Lüritz: Experiencing Socialist Law in East Germany* (Princeton, NJ: Princeton University Press, 2010), 107.
126. Scott Moranda, *The People's Own Landscape: Nature, Tourism, and Dictatorship in East Germany* (Ann Arbor: University of Michigan Press, 2014), chapter 3.
127. Betts, *Within Walls*, 28–9.
128. Gieseke, *The History of the Stasi*, 81.
129. Alison Lewis, *A State of Secrecy: Stasi Informers and the Culture of Surveillance* (Lincoln: University of Nebraska Press, 2021).
130. Bettina Bock, *"Blindes" Schreiben im Dienste der DDR-Staatssicherheit: eine text- und diskurslinguistische Untersuchung von Texten der inoffiziellen Mitarbeiter* (Bremen: Hempen, 2013).

Notes

131. Katrin Passens, *MfS-Untersuchungshaft: Funktionen und Entwicklung von 1971 bis 1989* (Berlin: Lukas, 2012). Sarah Colvin, *Shadowland: The Story of Germany Told by Its Prisoners* (London: Reaktion, 2022).
132. Christian Sachse, *Das System der Zwangsarbeit in der SED-Diktatur: die wirtschaftliche und politische Dimension* (Leipzig: Leipziger Universitätsverlag, 2014).
133. Marie-Luise Warnecke, *Zwangsadoptionen in der DDR* (Berlin: BWV, 2009).
134. Emmanuel Droit, *Vorwärts zum neuen Menschen? Die sozialistische Erziehung in der DDR (1949–1989)* (Cologne: Böhlau, 2014).
135. Dorothee Wierling, "Youth as Internal Enemy: Conflicts in The Education Dictatorship of the 1960s," in *Socialist Modern: East German Everyday Culture and Politics*, ed. Katherine Pence and Paul Betts (Ann Arbor: University of Michigan Press, 2008).
136. Poiger, *Jazz, Rock, and Rebels*, 48–51.
137. Fenemore, *Sex, Thugs and Rock 'n' Roll*, 190–3.
138. Jens Giesecke, "The Stasi and East German Society. Some Remarks on Current Research," *GHI Bulletin Supplement* 9 (2014): 62.

Chapter 3

1. Sebastian Gehrig, *Legal Entanglements: Law, Rights and the Battle for Legitimacy in Divided Germany, 1945–1989* (New York: Berghahn, 2021).
2. Andreas Förster, *Zielobjekt Rechts: Wie die Stasi die westdeutsche Neonaziszene unterwanderte* (Berlin: Ch. Links, 2018).
3. Frank Bösch, ed., *A History Shared and Divided: East and West Germany since the 1970s* (New York: Berghahn, 2018); Petra Weber, *Getrennt und doch vereint: deutsch-deutsche Geschichte 1945–1989/90* (Berlin: Metropol, 2020).
4. Frank Wolff, *Die Mauergesellschaft: Kalter Krieg, Menschenrechte und die deutsch-deutsche Migration 1961–1989* (Berlin: Suhrkamp, 2019).
5. Edith Sheffer, Burned Bridge: How East and West Germans Made the Iron Curtain (Oxford: Oxford University Press, 2014); Sagi Schaefer, States of Division: Border and Boundary Formation in Cold War Rural Germany (Oxford: Oxford University Press, 2014); Jason Johnson,

Divided Village: The Cold War in the German Borderlands (New York: Routledge, 2017).

6. Thomas Henseler and Susanne Buddenberg, *Tunnel 57: A True Escape-Story* (Berlin: Ch. Links, 2013).

7. Sophie Lange, *Deutsch-deutsche Umweltpolitik 1970–1990: Eine Verflechtungsgeschichte im internationalen und gesellschaftlichen Kontext des Kalten Krieges* (Berlin: De Gruyter, 2023).

8. Katrin Schreiter, *Designing One Nation: The Politics of Economic Culture and Trade in Divided Germany* (Oxford: Oxford University Press, 2020), 89–91.

9. Gilles Grin, *Battle of Single European Market* (London: Routledge, 2012), 145.

10. Patrick Major, *The Death of the KPD: Communism and Anti-Communism in West Germany, 1945–1956* (Oxford: Oxford University Press, 1998); Dominik Rigoll, *Staatsschutz in Westdeutschland: Von der Entnazifizierung zur Extremistenabwehr* (Göttingen: Wallstein, 2013).

11. Sandrine Kott, *Communism Day-to-Day: State Enterprises in East German Society* (Ann Arbor: University of Michigan Press, 2014), 239–41.

12. "Jasmin Werner: Palast der Republik Burj Khalifa," accessed July 10, 2024, www.goethe.de/ins/ae/en/kul/sup/jwe.html.

13. Michael Lemke, *Einheit oder Sozialismus? Die Deutschlandpolitik der SED 1949–1961* (Cologne: Böhlau, 2001), 435.

14. Ned Richardson-Little, *The Human Rights Dictatorship: Socialism, Global Solidarity and Revolution in East Germany* (Cambridge: Cambridge University Press, 2020), 69.

15. Dietrich Orlow, "Between 'Unity of Action' and 'Lackeys of Imperialism': The Contradictory Attitudes of the East German Communists toward the West German Social Democrats, 1959–1989," *German Studies Review* 36, no. 2 (2013): 307–25.

16. Gehrig, *Legal Entanglements*, chapter 4.

17. Kathrin Bower, "Learning to Live with the Other Germany in the Post-Wall Federal Republic," in *Migration, Memory, and Diversity*, ed. Cornelia Wilhelm (New York: Berghahn, 2017), 260.

18. The Communist Case for "Demarcation" from the West (February 10, 1971), *German History in Documents and Images* (online).

19. Dietrich Orlow, "The GDR's Failed Search for a National Identity, 1945–1989," *German Studies Review* 29, no. 3 (2006): 537–58.

Notes

20. Jan Palmowski, *Inventing a Socialist Nation: Heimat and the Politics of Everyday Life in the GDR, 1945–90* (Cambridge: Cambridge University Press, 2013).
21. Hermann Wentker, *Außenpolitik in engen Grenzen: Die DDR im Internationalen System 1949–1989* (Munich: Oldenbourg, 2007).
22. Silke Satjukow, *Besatzer: "Die Russen" in Deutschland 1945–1994* (Göttingen: Vandenhoeck & Ruprecht, 2008).
23. Dierk Hoffmann and Andreas Malycha, *Erdöl, Mais und Devisen: Die ostdeutsch-sowjetischen Wirtschaftsbeziehungen 1951–1967. Eine Dokumentation* (Berlin: De Gruyter, 2016).
24. Dominik Trutkowski, *Der geteilte Ostblock: die Grenzen der SBZ/DDR zu Polen und der Tschechoslowakei* (Cologne: Böhlau, 2011).
25. Sheldon Anderson, *A Cold War in The Soviet Bloc: Polish-East German Relations, 1945–1962* (London: Routledge, 2018); Michael Skalski, "Building a Socialist Neighborhood: Efforts at Integration among Poland, East Germany, and Czechoslovakia, 1969–1989" (PhD Dissertation, University of North Carolina at Chapel Hill, 2021), 70–1.
26. Andrew Tompkins, "Caught in the Net: Fish, Ships, and Oil in the GDR-Poland Territorial Waters Dispute, 1949–1989," *Central European History* 56, no. 2 (2023): 173–95.
27. Ondřej Klípa, "Disenchanting Socialist Internationalism: Polish Workers in Czechoslovakia and East Germany, 1962–91," *Journal of Contemporary History* 57, no. 2 (2022): 455–78.
28. Colleen Anderson, "The First German in Space: Sigmund Jähn and East Germany," *German Studies Review* 47, no. 3 (2024): 475–95.
29. Jonathan Zatlin, "Scarcity and Resentment: Economic Sources of Xenophobia in the GDR, 1971–1989," *Central European History* 40, no. 4 (2007): 683–720; Daniel Logemann, *Das polnische Fenster: deutsch-polnische Kontakte im staatssozialistischen Alltag Leipzigs, 1972–1989* (Munich: Oldenbourg, 2012).
30. Kyrill Kunakhovich, "Ties That Bind, Ties That Divide: Second World Cultural Exchange at the Grassroots," in *Socialist Internationalism in the Cold War*, ed. Patryk Babiracki and Austin Jersild (Cham: Springer, 2016).
31. James Koranyi, "Voyages of Socialist Discovery: German-German Exchanges between the GDR and Romania," *The Slavonic and East European Review* 92, no. 3 (2014): 479–506.
32. José Luis Aguilar López-Barajas, "'The Black Sea Is Our Mallorca': The Making of the Tourist Experience in the German Democratic Republic," *German History* 40, no. 3 (2022): 405–24.

33. George Bodie, "'It Is a Shame We Are Not Neighbours': GDR Tourist Cruises to Cuba, 1961–89," *Journal of Contemporary History* 55, no. 2 (2020): 411–34.

34. Rüdiger Wenzke, *Die NVA und der Prager Frühling 1968: die Rolle Ulbrichts und der DDR-Streitkräfte bei der Niederschlagung der tschechoslowakischen Reformbewegung* (Berlin: Ch. Links, 1995).

35. Jan Zofka, "The China Market: East German and Bulgarian Industrial Facility Export to the PRC in the 1950s," *European Review of History* 30, no. 3 (2023): 452–72.

36. Jennifer Altehenger, "Industrial and Chinese: Exhibiting Mao's China at the Leipzig Trade Fairs," *Journal of Contemporary History* 55, no. 4 (2020): 845–70.

37. Tao Chen, "The Dilemma of Socialist Solidarity: East German Specialists in Mao's China, 1952–64," *Journal of Contemporary History* 58, no. 3 (2023): 488–508.

38. Quinn Slobodian, "The Maoist Enemy: China's Challenge in 1960s East Germany," *Journal of Contemporary History* 51, no. 3 (2016): 635–59.

39. Lorenz Lüthi, *Cold Wars: Asia, the Middle East, Europe* (Cambridge: Cambridge University Press, 2020).

40. William Glenn Gray, *Germany's Cold War: The Global Campaign to Isolate East Germany, 1949–1969* (Chapel Hill: University of North Carolina Press, 2003).

41. Hubertus Büschel, *Hilfe zur Selbsthilfe: Deutsche Entwicklungsarbeit in Afrika 1960–1975* (Frankfurt am Main: Campus, 2014).

42. Lorena de Vita, *Israelpolitik: German-Israeli Relations, 1949–69* (Manchester: Manchester University Press, 2022).

43. Angelika Timm, "Ideology and Realpolitik: East German Attitudes towards Zionism and Israel," *Journal of Israeli History* 25, no. 1 (2006): 203–22.

44. Katherine Pence, "Showcasing Cold War Germany in Cairo: 1954 and 1957 Industrial Exhibitions and the Competition for Arab Partners," *Journal of Contemporary History* 47, no. 1 (2012): 69–95.

45. Gray, *Germany's Cold War*, 100–2.

46. Eric Burton, "Diverging Visions in Revolutionary Spaces: East German Advisers and Revolution from above in Zanzibar, 1964–1970," in *Between East and South: Spaces of Interaction in the Globalizing Economy of the Cold War*, ed. Anna Calori, Jan Zofka, Anne-Kristin Hartmetz, James Mark, and Bence Kocsev (Berlin: De Gruyter, 2019).

Notes

47. George Roberts, *Dilemmas of Non-Alignment: Tanzania and the German Cold War* (Cambridge: Cambridge University Press, 2021), chapter 3.
48. Mathias Stein, *Der Konflikt um Alleinvertretung und Anerkennung in der UNO: Die deutsch-deutschen Beziehungen zu den Vereinten Nationen von 1949 bis 1973* (Göttingen: V&R Unipress, 2011), 126.
49. Richardson-Little, *The Human Rights Dictatorship*, chapter 3.
50. Frank Bösch, Caroline Moine, and Stefanie Senger, *Internationale Solidarität: globales Engagement in der Bundesrepublik und der DDR* (Göttingen: Wallstein, 2018).
51. George Bodie, "Global GDR? Sovereignty, Legitimacy and Decolonization in the German Democratic Republic, 1960–1989" (doctoral thesis, University College London, 2020), 158–73.
52. Young-Sun Hong, *Cold War Germany, the Third World, and the Global Humanitarian Regime* (Cambridge: Cambridge University Press, 2015), chapter 2; Maren Hachmeister, "'Without Solidarity, No People': International Solidarity in the East German People's Solidarity," *International Review of Social History* 69, no. 32 (2024): 117–37.
53. Jessica Dalljo, "'Solidarity Is a Matter of the Heart': Anti-Imperialist Solidarity Donations in GDR Children's Magazines," *International Review of Social History* 69, no. S32 (2024): 159–76.
54. Sebastian Gehrig, "Reaching Out to the Third World: East Germany's Anti-Apartheid and Socialist Human Rights Campaign," *German History* 36, no. 4 (2018): 574–97.
55. Stefan Berger and Norman Laporte, *Friendly Enemies: Britain and the GDR, 1949–1990* (New York: Berghahn, 2010); Teresa Malice, *Transnational Imaginations of Socialism: Town Twinning and Local Government in "Red" Italy and the GDR* (Berlin: De Gruyter, 2022).
56. Katrina Hagen, "Ambivalence and Desire in the East German 'Free Angela Davis' Campaign," in *Comrades of Color: East Germany in the Cold War World*, ed. Quinn Slobodian (New York: Berghahn, 2015); Sophie Lorenz, *"Schwarze Schwester Angela"—die DDR und Angela Davis: Kalter Krieg, Rassismus und Black Power 1965–1975* (Bielefeld: Transcript, 2020).
57. Ned Richardson-Little and Lauren Stokes, "Bordering the GDR: Everyday Transnationalism, Global Entanglements and Regimes of Mobility at the Edges of East Germany," *Central European History* 56, no. 2 (2023): 159–72.
58. Katherine Pence, "'A World in Miniature': The Leipzig Trade Fairs in the 1950s and East German Consumer Citizenship," in *Consuming Germany*

in the Cold War: Consumption and National Identity in East and West Germany, ed. D.F. Crew (Oxford: Bloomsbury, 2003).

59. Katharine White, "East Germany's Red Woodstock: The 1973 Festival between the 'Carnivalesque' and the Everyday," *Central European History* 51, no. 4 (2018): 585–610.

60. Lea Börgerding, "Staging Emancipation and Its Limits: East German Cultural Diplomacy, the German Democratic Women's League, and the 1975 World Congress of Women in East Berlin," *Women's History Review* 34 (2025): 3–28.

61. Stefanie Eisenhuth, "Tourism through the Iron Curtain. Travelling from West to East Germany," *Journal of Tourism History* 15, no. 3 (2023): 309–35.

62. Stefan Zeppenfeld, *Vom Gast zum Gastwirt?: Türkische Arbeitswelten in West-Berlin* (Göttingen: Wallstein, 2021).

63. Nikola Tohma and Julia Reinke, "'Like We Would Help Brothers or Sisters'? Practising Solidarity with Greek Civil War Refugees in Socialist Czechoslovakia and the GDR in the Shadow of World War II," *International Review of Social History* 69, no. S32 (April 2024): 13–41.

64. Patrice G. Poutrus, "Zuflucht im Nachkriegsdeutschland. Politik und Praxis der Flüchtlingsaufnahme in Bundesrepublik und DDR von den späten 1940er bis zu den 1970er Jahren," *Geschichte und Gesellschaft* 35 (2009): 135–75.

65. Victor Grossman, *A Socialist Defector: From Harvard to Karl-Marx-Allee* (New York: New York University Press, 2019); Nadja Klopprogge, "'To Live a Peaceful Life': African American Defectors in the German Democratic Republic," *German History* 42, no. 1 (2024): 101–22.

66. Sebastian Koch, *Zufluchtsort DDR? Chilenische Flüchtlinge und die Ausländerpolitik der SED* (Paderborn: Schöningh, 2016).

67. Bernd Schaefer, "Relationship in the Shadow of Vietnam: The GDR and Cambodia/Kampuchea 1969–1989," *Pamięć i Sprawiedliwość* 41, no. 1 (2023): 166–83.

68. Lutz Maeke, *DDR und PLO: Die Palästinapolitik des SED-Staates* (Berlin: De Gruyter, 2017); Matthias Bengtson-Krallert, *Die DDR und der internationale Terrorismus* (Baden-Baden: Tectum, 2017). Ulrich van der Heyden and Anja Schade, *GDR Solidarity with the ANC of South Africa* (Berlin: De Gruyter, 2019), 77–102.

69. Toni Weis, "The Politics Machine: On the Concept of 'Solidarity' in East German Support for SWAPO," *Journal of Southern African Studies* 37, no. 2 (2011): 351–67.

Notes

70. Jan-Hinrick Pesch, "Die DDR als 'strategisches Hinterland'" *Deutschland Archiv* (10.03.24).
71. Ulrich van der Heyden, *GDR Development Policy in Africa: Doctrine and Strategies between Illusions and Reality 1960–1990. The Example (South) Africa* (Münster: LIT, 2013), 201–2.
72. Mike Dennis and Norman LaPorte, *State and Minorities in Communist East Germany* (New York: Berghahn, 2011), chapter 4.
73. Jadwiga Pieper Mooney, "East Germany: Chilean Exile and the Politics of Solidarity in the Cold War," in *European Solidarity with Chile, 1970s–1980s*, ed. Kim Christiaens, Idesbald Goddeeris, and Magaly Rodríguez García (Frankfurt am Main: Peter Lang, 2014).
74. Deniz Göktürk, David Gramling, and Anton Kaes, *Germany in Transit: Nation and Migration, 1955–2005* (Los Angeles, CA: University of California Press, 2007), 88–9.
75. Marcia Schenck, *Remembering African Labor Migration to the Second World: Socialist Mobilities between Angola, Mozambique, and East Germany* (Basingstoke: Palgrave, 2023), 164–7.
76. Quinn Slobodian, "Socialist Chromatism: Race, Racism, and the Racial Rainbow in East Germany," in *Comrades of Color: East Germany in a Cold War World* (New York: Berghahn, 2015).
77. Christina Schwenkel, "The Things They Carried (and Kept): Revisiting Ostalgie in the Global South," *Comparative Studies in Society and History* 64, no. 2 (2022): 493.
78. Sara Pugach, *African Students in East Germany, 1949–1975* (Ann Arbor: University of Michigan Press, 2022), chapter 5.
79. Kira Thurman, *Singing Like Germans: Black Musicians in the Land of Bach, Beethoven, and Brahms* (Ithaca, NY: Cornell University Press, 2021), 262–6.
80. Patrice G. Poutrus and Katharina Warda, "Die DDR als Migrationsgesellschaft und die rassistische Gewalt der 'Baseballschlägerjahre' in Ostdeutschland: Der Weg in die Berliner Republik," in *Erinnerungskämpfe: Neues deutsches Geschichtsbewusstsein*, ed. Jürgen Zimmerer (Ditzingen: Reclam, 2023), 380.
81. Esther Adaire, "'This Other Germany, the Dark One': Post-Wall Memory Politics Surrounding the Neo-Nazi Riots in Rostock and Hoyerswerda," *German Politics and Society* 37, no. 4 (2019): 43–57.
82. Benedikt Schoenborn, *Reconciliation Road: Willy Brandt, Ostpolitik and the Quest for European Peace* (New York: Berghahn, 2020).
83. Gray, *Germany's Cold War*, 212–19.

Notes

84. William Glenn Gray, "Paradoxes of 'Ostpolitik': Revisiting the Moscow and Warsaw Treaties, 1970," *Central European History* 49, no. 3/4 (2016): 409–40.

85. M.E. Sarotte, *Dealing with the Devil: East Germany, Détente, and Ostpolitik, 1969–1973* (Chapel Hill: University of North Carolina Press, 2003), 120–32.

86. Martin Sabrow, *Erich Honecker: Das Leben davor* (Munich: C.H. Beck, 2016).

87. See "Division and Interconnection Between the Two Germanies" at the beginning of chapter 3.

88. Sarotte, *Dealing with the Devil*, chapter 6.

89. Bower, "Learning to Live with the Other Germany," 260.

90. Sebastian Gehrig, "Dividing the Indivisible: Cold War Sovereignty, National Division, and the German Question at the United Nations," *Central European History* 55, no. 1 (2022): 70–89.

91. Anja Hanisch, *Die DDR im KSZE-Prozess 1972–1985: Zwischen Ostabhängigkeit, Westabgrenzung und Ausreisebewegung* (Munich: Oldenbourg, 2012).

92. Jeremi Suri, "Détente and Human Rights: American and West European Perspectives on International Change," *Cold War History* 8, no. 4 (2008): 527–45; Adam Taylor, "Henry Kissinger: Nobel Peace Laureate, War Criminal?" The Washington Post (November 30, 2023).

93. Richardson-Little, *The Human Rights Dictatorship*, 125–7.

94. André Steiner, *The Plans That Failed: An Economic History of the GDR* (New York: Berghahn, 2013), 109–18.

95. Peter Caldwell, *Dictatorship, State Planning, and Social Theory in the German Democratic Republic* (Cambridge: Cambridge University Press, 2003), 174.

96. Steiner, *The Plans That Failed*, 119–21.

97. Dolores Augustine, *Red Prometheus: Engineering and Dictatorship in East Germany, 1945–1990* (Boston, MA: MIT Press, 2007).

98. Frank Ebbinghaus, *Ausnutzung und Verdrängung: Steuerungsprobleme der SED-Mittelstandspolitik 1955–1972* (Berlin: Duncker & Humblot, 2003).

99. Annemarie Sammartino, "The New Socialist Man in the *Plattenbau*: The East German Housing Program and the Development of the Socialist Way of Life," *Journal of Urban History* 44, no. 1 (2018): 78–94.

Notes

100. Mark Allinson, "More from Less: Ideological Gambling with the Unity of Economic and Social Policy in Honecker's GDR," *Central European History* 45, no. 1 (2012): 102–27.

101. Jeffrey Kopstein, *The Politics of Economic Decline in East Germany, 1945–1989* (Chapel Hill: University of North Carolina Press, 2000), 86–7.

102. Konrad Jarausch, "Care and Coercion: The GDR as Welfare Dictatorship," in *Dictatorship as Experience: Towards a Socio-cultural History of the GDR* (New York: Berghahn, 1999).

103. Jan Philipp Wölbern, *Der Häftlingsfreikauf aus der DDR 1962/63–1989: Zwischen Menschenhandel und humanitären Aktionen* (Göttingen: Vandenhoeck & Ruprecht, 2014).

104. Matthias Judt, *Der Bereich Kommerzielle Koordinierung: Das DDR-Wirtschaftsimperium des Alexander Schalck-Golodkowski—Mythos und Realität* (Berlin: Ch. Links, 2013).

105. Klaus Storkmann, *Geheime Solidarität: Militärbeziehungen und Militärhilfen der DDR in die "Dritte Welt"* (Berlin: Ch. Links, 2012).

106. Ray Stokes, "From Schadenfreude to Going-Out-of-Business Sale: East Germany and the Oil Crises of the 1970s," in *The East German Economy, 1945–2010: Falling Behind or Catching Up?*, ed. Hartmut Berghoff and Uta Andrea Balbier (Cambridge: Cambridge University Press, 2013).

107. Andrew Kloiber, *Brewing Socialism: Coffee, East Germans, and Twentieth-Century Globalization* (New York: Berghahn, 2022).

108. Hans-Joachim Döring, *"Es geht um unsere Existenz": Die Politik der DDR gegenüber der Dritten Welt am Beispiel von Mosambik und Äthiopien* (Berlin: Ch. Links, 2010).

109. Berthold Unfried, "Friendship and Education, Coffee and Weapons: Exchanges between Socialist Ethiopia and the German Democratic Republic," *Northeast African Studies* 16, no. 1 (2016): 15–38.

110. Julia Sittmann, "Illusions of Care: Iraqi Students between the Ba'thist State and the Stasi in Socialist East Germany, 1958–89," *Cold War History* 18, no. 2 (2018): 187–202.

111. Max Hirsh, "Postmodern Architectural Exchanges Between East Germany and Japan," in *Postmodern Architectural Exchanges between East Germany and Japan* (Basel: Birkhäuser, 2016).

Chapter 4

1. Jeffrey Kopstein, "Chipping Away at the State: Workers' Resistance and the Demise of East Germany," *World Politics* 48, no. 3 (1996): 391–423.
2. Susan Colbourn, *Euromissiles: The Nuclear Weapons That Nearly Destroyed NATO* (Ithaca, NY: Cornell University Press, 2022).
3. Andrzej Paczkowski et al., *From Solidarity to Martial Law: The Polish Crisis of 1980–1981: A Documentary History* (Budapest: Central European University Press, 2007).
4. Andrew Kloiber, *Brewing Socialism: Coffee, East Germans, and Twentieth-Century Globalization* (New York: Berghahn, 2022).
5. Dolores Augustine, *Taking on Technocracy: Nuclear Power in Germany, 1945 to the Present* (New York: Berghahn, 2018), 39.
6. Thomas Fleischman, *Communist Pigs: An Animal History of East Germany's Rise and Fall* (Seattle: University of Washington Press, 2020).
7. Olaf Klenke, *Ist die DDR an der Globalisierung gescheitert?: autarke Wirtschaftspolitik versus internationale Weltwirtschaft—das Beispiel Mikroelektronik* (Frankfurt am Main: Peter Lang, 2001).
8. Gareth Dale, *Between State Capitalism and Globalisation: The Collapse of the East German Economy* (Oxford: Peter Lang, 2004), 187–91.
9. Tobias Wunschik, *Knastware für den Klassenfeind: Häftlingsarbeit in der DDR, der Ost-West-Handel und die Staatssicherheit (1970–1989)* (Göttingen: Vandenhoeck & Ruprecht, 2014).
10. Sophie Lange, *Deutsch-deutsche Umweltpolitik 1970–1990: Eine Verflechtungsgeschichte im internationalen und gesellschaftlichen Kontext des Kalten Krieges* (Berlin: De Gruyter, 2023), chapter 4.3.
11. Eric Burton, James Mark, and Steffi Marung, "Development," in *Socialism Goes Global: The Soviet Union and Eastern Europe in the Age of Decolonisation*, coordinated by James Mark and Paul Betts (Oxford: Oxford University Press, 2022), 108.
12. Miriam Müller, *A Spectre Is Haunting Arabia: How the Germans Brought their Communism to Yemen* (Bielefeld: Transcript, 2015), 364.
13. Hennie van Vuuren, *Apartheid Guns and Money: A Tale of Profit* (Oxford: Oxford University Press, 2019), 217–76.
14. Jessica Lindner-Elsner, *Von Wartburg zu Opel: Arbeit und Ungleichheit im Automobilwerk Eisenach 1970–1992* (Göttingen: Wallstein, 2023), 121–6.

Notes

15. Gregory Witkowski, *The Campaign State: Communist Mobilizations for the East German Countryside, 1945–1990* (Ithaca, NY: Cornell University Press, 2017), 231.

16. Eli Rubin, *Amnesiopolis: Modernity, Space, and Memory in East Germany* (Oxford: Oxford University Press, 2016), 133.

17. Sandrine Kott, *Communism Day-to-Day: State Enterprises in East German Society* (Ann Arbor: University of Michigan Press, 2014), 124.

18. Udo Grashoff, *Schwarzwohnen: Die Unterwanderung der staatlichen Wohnraumlenkung in der DDR* (Göttingen: V & R unipress, 2011); Jacob Nuhn, *Alternative Szenen in der (post-)sozialistischen Stadt. Räume und Verortungen in Dresden und Wroclaw vor und nach 1989* (Bielefeld: Transcript, 2024).

19. Jonathan Zatlin, *The Currency of Socialism: Money and Political Culture in East Germany* (Cambridge: Cambridge University Press, 2007), 304.

20. Johanna Folland, "'Not Even the Highest Wall Can Stop AIDS': Expertise and Viral Politics at the German-German Border," *Central European History* 56, no. 2 (2023): 261.

21. Andrew Demshuk, *Bowling for Communism: Urban Ingenuity at the End of East Germany* (Ithaca, NY: Cornell University Press, 2020).

22. Charles Maier, *Dissolution: The Crisis of Communism and the End of East Germany* (Princeton, NJ: Princeton University Press, 1999), 62. Maximilian Graf, "Before Strauß: The East German Struggle to Avoid Bankruptcy during the Debt Crisis Revisited," *The International History Review* 42, no. 4 (2020): 737–54.

23. Dale, *Between State Capitalism and Globalisation*, 228–35.

24. André Steiner, *The Plans That Failed: An Economic History of the GDR* (New York: Berghahn, 2013), 192.

25. Lauren Stokes, "Racial Profiling on the U-Bahn: Policing the Berlin Gap in the Schönefeld Airport Refugee Crisis," *Central European History* 56, no. 2 (2023): 236–54.

26. Stephen Brown, "'Happy Birthday, Comrade Martin!' The 500th Anniversary of Luther's Birth and the Challenge to State Authority in the German Democratic Republic," in *Ecumenical Perspectives Five Hundred Years after Luther's Reformation*, ed. Gerard Mannion, Dennis Doyle, and Theodore Dedon (Cham: Springer, 2021), 45–65.

27. Jon Berndt Olsen, *Tailoring Truth: Politicizing the Past and Negotiating Memory in East Germany, 1945–1990* (New York: Berghahn, 2017), 140.

28. Marcus Colla, *Prussia in the Historical Culture of the German Democratic Republic: Communists and Kings* (Oxford: Oxford University Press, 2023).
29. Gerd Horten, *Don't Need No Thought Control: Western Culture in East Germany and the Fall of the Berlin Wall* (New York: Berghahn, 2020), 80.
30. Kyrill Kunakhovich, *Communism's Public Sphere: Culture as Politics in Cold War Poland and East Germany* (Ithaca, NY: Cornell University Press, 2022), 212–13.
31. Eli Rubin, *Synthetic Socialism: Plastics and Dictatorship in the German Democratic Republic* (Chapel Hill: University of North Carolina Press, 2012).
32. Katrin Schreiter, *Designing One Nation: The Politics of Economic Culture and Trade in Divided Germany* (Oxford: Oxford University Press, 2020), 184.
33. Lorenz Lüthi, "How Udo Wanted to Save the World in 'Erich's Lamp Shop': Lindenberg's Concert in Honecker's East Berlin, the NATO Double-Track Decision and Communist Economic Woes," *Contemporary European History* 24, no. 1 (2015): 83–103.
34. Ilko-Sascha Kowalczuk, *Endspiel: Die Revolution von 1989 in der DDR* (Munich: C.H. Beck, 2011), 165–6.
35. Leonard Schmieding, *"Das ist unsere Party": HipHop in der DDR* (Stuttgart: Steiner, 2014).
36. Edward Larkey, "GDR Rock Goes West: Finding a Voice in the West German Market," *German Politics & Society* 23, no. 4 (Issue 77) (2005): 45–68.
37. Florian Sievers, "An Oral History of Electronic Music in East Germany" (September 9, 2013), *Red Bull Music Academy* (online).
38. Helma Kaldewey, *A People's Music: Jazz in East Germany, 1945–1990* (Cambridge: Cambridge University Press, 2020), chapter 6.
39. Nikolai Okunew, *Red Metal: Die Heavy-Metal-Subkultur der DDR* (Berlin: Ch. Links, 2021).
40. Jeff Hayton, *Culture from the Slums: Punk Rock in East and West Germany* (Oxford: Oxford University Press, 2022), chapter 4.
41. Kunakhovich, *Communism's Public Sphere*, chapter 8.
42. Seth Howes, *Moving Images on the Margins: Experimental Film in Late Socialist East Germany* (Rochester, NY: Camden House, 2019); Sara Blaylock, *Parallel Public: Experimental Art in Late East Germany* (Boston, MA: MIT Press, 2022).

Notes

43. Mike Dennis and Jonathan Grix, *Sport under Communism: Behind the East German "Miracle"* (Basingstoke: Palgrave, 2012).

44. Alan McDougall, *The People's Game: Football, State and Society in East Germany* (Cambridge: Cambridge University Press, 2014), chapter 10.

45. Josie McLellan, "Glad to Be Gay behind the Wall: Gay and Lesbian Activism in 1970s East Germany," *History Workshop Journal* 74, no. 1 (2012): 105–30; Jennifer Evans, *The Queer Art of History: Queer Kinship after Fascism* (Durham, NC: Duke University Press, 2023), 112–13.

46. Josie McLellan, *Love in the Time of Communism: Intimacy and Sexuality in the GDR* (Cambridge: Cambridge University Press, 2011), chapter 5.

47. Samuel Clowes Huneke, *States of Liberation: Gay Men between Dictatorship and Democracy in Cold War Germany* (Toronto: University of Toronto Press, 2022), 209–10.

48. Jeff Hayton, "Krawall in der Zionskirche: Skinhead Violence and Political Legitimacy in the GDR," *European History Quarterly* 45, no. 2 (2015): 336–56.

49. Gideon Botsch, "From Skinhead-Subculture to Radical Right Movement: The Development of a 'National Opposition' in East Germany," *Contemporary European History* 21, no. 4 (2012): 553–73; Patrice G. Poutrus and Katharina Warda, "Die DDR als Migrationsgesellschaft und die rassistische Gewalt der 'Baseballschlägerjahre' in Ostdeutschland: Der Weg in die Berliner Republik," in *Erinnerungskämpfe: Neues deutsches Geschichtsbewusstsein*, ed. Jürgen Zimmerer (Ditzingen: Reclam, 2023).

50. Steven Pfaff, *Exit-Voice Dynamics and the Collapse of East Germany: The Crisis of Leninism and the Revolution of 1989* (Durham, NC: Duke University Press, 2006), 78.

51. Manfred Gehrmann, *Die Überwindung des "Eisernen Vorhangs": Die Abwanderung aus der DDR in die BRD/West-Berlin 1949–1989 als innerdeutsches Migranten-Netzwerk* (Berlin: Ch. Links, 2009), 148–59.

52. Ralf Jessen, "Mobility and Blockage during the 1970s," in *Dictatorship as Experience: Towards a Socio-cultural History of the GDR*, ed. Konrad Jarausch (New York: Berghahn, 1999).

53. Patrick Major, *Behind the Berlin Wall: East Germany and the Frontiers of Power* (Oxford: Oxford University Press, 2010), 200–3.

54. Ned Richardson-Little, *The Human Rights Dictatorship: Socialism, Global Solidarity and Revolution in East Germany* (Cambridge: Cambridge University Press, 2020), 164.

55. Oliver Bange, "'The Greatest Happiness of the Greatest Number … '. The FRG and the GDR and the Belgrade CSCE Conference (1977–78)," in

From Helsinki to Belgrade: The First CSCE Follow-Up Meeting and the Crisis of Détente, ed. Vladimir Bilandžić, Dittmar Dahlmann, and Milan Kosanović (Göttingen: V&R Unipress, 2012); Jan Philipp Wölbern, *Der Häftlingsfreikauf aus der DDR 1962/63–1989: Zwischen Menschenhandel und humanitären Aktionen* (Göttingen: Vandenhoeck & Ruprecht, 2014); Anja Mihr, *Amnesty International in der DDR: der Einsatz für Menschenrechte im Visier der Stasi* (Berlin: Ch. Links, 2002).

56. Jens Gieseke, *The History of the Stasi: East Germany's Secret Police, 1945–1990* (New York: Berghahn, 2014), 81.

57. Gieseke, *The History of the Stasi*, 146–52.

58. Leading GDR Writers Protest the Expatriation of Wolf Biermann (November 17, 1976) *German History in Documents and Images* (online).

59. Major, *Behind the Berlin Wall*, 215.

60. Andreas Glaeser, *Political Epistemics: The Secret Police, the Opposition, and the End of East German Socialism* (Chicago, IL: University of Chicago Press, 2011), 465.

61. Ehrhart Neubert, *Geschichte der Opposition in der DDR 1949–1989* (Berlin: Ch. Links, 1998).

62. Jonathan Bolton, *Worlds of Dissent: Charter 77, The Plastic People of the Universe, and Czech Culture under Communism* (Cambridge, MA: Harvard University Press, 2012); Anna Delius, "Universal Rights or Everyday Necessities?: Translating Human Rights between Local Workers and Transnational Activism in Late 1970s Poland," *East Central Europe* 46, no. 2–3 (2019): 188–211.

63. Axel Fair-Schulz, *Loyal Subversion: East Germany and its Bildungsbürgerlich Marxist Intellectuals* (Berlin: Trafo, 2009).

64. Rudolf Bahro, *The Alternative in Eastern Europe* (London: NLB, 1978).

65. Julia Ault, *Saving Nature under Socialism* (Cambridge: Cambridge University Press, 2021), chapter 2.

66. Tobias Huff, *Natur und Industrie im Sozialismus: Eine Umweltgeschichte der DDR* (Göttingen: Vandenhoeck & Ruprecht, 2015).

67. Ault, *Saving Nature under Socialism*, 165–7.

68. Almut Ilsen and Ruth Leiserowitz, *Seid doch laut!: Die Frauen für den Frieden in Ost-Berlin* (Berlin: Ch. Links, 2019).

69. Steven Pfaff, "The Politics of Peace in the GDR: The Independent Peace Movement, the Church, and the Origins of the East German Opposition," *Peace and Change* 26, no. 3 (2001): 280–300.

70. Karsten Timmer, *Vom Aufbruch zum Umbruch: die Bürgerbewegung in der DDR 1989* (Göttingen: Vandenhoeck & Ruprecht, 2000), 54.

Notes

71. Jenaer Friedensgemeinschaft, Jena (May 19, 1983) *German History in Documents and Images* (online).
72. Thomas Klein, *"Frieden und Gerechtigkeit!": die Politisierung der unabhängigen Friedensbewegung in Ost-Berlin während der 80er Jahre* (Cologne: Böhlau, 2007).
73. Richardson-Little, *The Human Rights Dictatorship*, 204.
74. John Torpey, *Intellectuals, Socialism, and Dissent: The East German Opposition and Its Legacy* (Minneapolis: University of Minnesota Press, 1995), 71–6.
75. Wolfgang Rüddenklau, *Störenfried: DDR-Opposition 1986–1989: mit Texten aus den "Umweltblättern"* (Berlin: BasisDruck, 1992); Maria Magdalena Verburg, *Ostdeutsche Dritte-Welt-Gruppen vor und nach 1989/90* (Göttingen: V&R unipress, 2012).
76. Stephen Brown, *Von der Unzufriedenheit zum Widerspruch: der konziliare Prozess für Gerechtigkeit, Frieden und Bewahrung der Schöpfung als Wegbereiter der friedlichen Revolution in der DDR* (Frankfurt am Main: Lembeck, 2010).
77. Padraic Kenney, *A Carnival of Revolution: Central Europe 1989* (Princeton, NJ: Princeton University Press, 2003), 113.
78. Chris Miller, *The Struggle to Save the Soviet Economy: Mikhail Gorbachev and the Collapse of the USSR* (Chapel Hill: University of North Carolina Press, 2016).
79. André Steiner, "The Globalisation Process and the Eastern Bloc Countries in the 1970s and 1980s," *European Review of History* 21, no. 2 (2014): 175.
80. Uta Rüchel, "Zwischen Paternalismus und Solidarität. Das SWAPO-Kinderheim in Bellin," in *Fremde und Fremd-Sein in der DDR. Zur Einführung*, ed. Jan Behrends, Thomas Lindenberger, and Patrice G. Poutrus (Berlin: Metropol, 2003), 251–69.
81. Ulrich van der Heyden, *Zwischen Solidarität und Wirtschaftsinteressen: die "geheimen" Beziehungen der DDR zum südafrikanischen Apartheidregime* (Münster: LIT, 2005).
82. Iris Borowy, "East German Medical Aid to Nicaragua: The Politics of Solidarity between Biomedicine and Primary Health Care," *Historia, Ciencias, Saude–Manguinhos* 24, no. 2 (2017): 411–28.
83. Ulrich van der Heyden, *GDR Development Policy in Africa: Doctrine and Strategies between Illusions and Reality 1960–1990. The Example (South) Africa* (Münster: LIT, 2013), 201.

Notes

84. Marcia Schenck, *Remembering African Labor Migration to the Second World: Socialist Mobilities between Angola, Mozambique, and East Germany* (Basingstoke: Palgrave, 2023), 61.

85. Zhong Zhong Chen, "Defying Moscow, Engaging Beijing: The German Democratic Republic's Relations with the People's Republic of China, 1980–1989" (PhD dissertation, London School of Economics, 2014).

86. No New Wallpaper (April 10, 1987), *German History in Documents and Images* (online).

87. Dietrich Orlow, *Socialist Reformers and the Collapse of the GDR* (London: Palgrave, 2015).

88. Pfaff, *Exit-Voice Dynamics and the Collapse of East Germany*, 54–7.

89. Ned Richardson-Little, "The Failure of the Socialist Declaration of Human Rights: Ideology, Legitimacy, and Elite Defection at the End of State Socialism," *East Central Europe* 46, no. 2–3 (2019): 318–41.

90. James Mark, Bogdan Iacob, Ljubica Spaskovska, and Tobias Rupprecht, *1989: A Global History of Eastern Europe* (Cambridge: Cambridge University Press, 2019), chapter 2.

91. Konrad Jarausch and Volker Gransow, *Uniting Germany: Documents and Debates, 1944–1993* (New York: Berghahn, 1994), 34.

92. Quinn Slobodian, "China Is Not Far! Alternative Internationalism and the Tiananmen Square Massacre in 1989 East Germany," in *Alternative Globalizations: Eastern Europe and the Postcolonial World*, ed. James Mark, et al. (Bloomington, IN: Indiana University Press, 2020).

93. Matthew Longo, *The Picnic: An Escape to Freedom and the Collapse of the Iron Curtain* (London: Vintage, 2024).

94. William Michael Schmidli, *Freedom on the Offensive: Human Rights, Democracy Promotion, and US Interventionism in the Late Cold War* (Ithaca, NY: Cornell University Press, 2022); Gregory Domber, *Empowering Revolution: America, Poland, and the End of the Cold War* (Chapel Hill: University of North Carolina Press, 2014).

95. Catherine Epstein, *The Last Revolutionaries: German Communists and Their Century* (Cambridge, MA: Harvard University Press, 2003), 219.

96. Major, *Behind the Berlin Wall*, 246.

97. Karl-Dieter Opp, "The Production of Historical 'Facts': How the Wrong Number of Participants in the Leipzig Monday Demonstration on October 9, 1989, Became a Convention," *Journal of Economics and Statistics* 231, no. 5–6 (2011): 598–607.

98. Steven Pfaff, *Exit-Voice Dynamics and the Collapse of East Germany*, chap. 7.

Notes

99. Andreas Malycha, *Die SED in der Ära Honecker: Machtstrukturen, Entscheidungsmechanismen und Konfliktfelder in der Staatspartei 1971 bis 1989* (Berlin: De Gruyter, 2014), chapter VII.2.
100. Pfaff, *Exit-Voice Dynamics and the Collapse of East Germany*, 165–7.
101. Manfred Schmidt and Gerhard Ritter, *The Rise and Fall of a Socialist Welfare State: The German Democratic Republic (1949–1990) and German Unification (1989–1994)* (Wiesbaden: Springer, 2012), 110.
102. Mary Elise Sarotte, *The Collapse: The Accidental Opening of the Berlin Wall* (London: Hachette, 2014), chapter 5.
103. Stephen Kotkin, *Uncivil Society: 1989 and the Implosion of the Communist Establishment* (New York: Random House, 2009).
104. Ilko-Sascha Kowalczuk, *Endspiel*.
105. Hans Modrow's Reform Agenda (November 17, 1989) *German History in Documents and Images* (online).
106. "For Our Country," translation by Max Hertzberg (November 16, 2016) (online).
107. Helmut Kohl's Ten-Point Plan for German Unity (November 28, 1989) *German History in Documents and Images* (online).
108. David Patton, "Annus Mirabilis: 1989 and German Unification," in *The Oxford Handbook of Modern German History*, ed. Helmut Walser Smith (Oxford: Oxford University Press, 2011), 769.
109. Konrad Jarausch, *The Rush to German Unity* (Oxford: Oxford University Press, 1994), 29.
110. Reprinted in Harold James and Marla Stone, *When the Wall Came Down: Reactions to German Unification* (London: Routledge, 2014), 57–9.
111. Jakub Szumski, "Consentful Contention in Revolutionary Times: Debating Elite Corruption at Communist Party Congresses in Poland and East Germany," *Zeitschrift für Ostmitteleuropa-Forschung* 72, no. 3 (2023): 426–30.
112. Franz Oswald, *The Party That Came Out of the Cold War: The Party of Democratic Socialism in United Germany* (London: Bloomsbury, 2002), chapter 1.
113. Ned Richardson-Little, "Cold War Narcotics Trafficking, the Global War on Drugs, and East Germany's Illicit Transnational Entanglements," *Central European History* 56, no. 2 (2023): 214–35.
114. Jarausch, *The Rush to German Unity*, 87.

115. Alexander von Plato, *The End of the Cold War? Bush, Kohl, Gorbachev, and the Reunification of Germany* (New York: Palgrave, 2016).
116. Vladislav Zubok, *A Failed Empire: The Soviet Union in the Cold War from Stalin to Gorbachev* (Chapel Hill: University of North Carolina Press, 2009), 327.
117. Rainer Land, "Eine demokratische DDR? Das Projekt 'Moderner Sozialismus,'" (March 4, 2010) *Aus Politik und Zeitgeschichte* (bpb.de).
118. Schreiter, *Designing One Nation*, 184.
119. Peter Merkl, *German Unification in the European Context* (University Park, PA: Pennsylvania State Press, 2010), 242.
120. Interview with Jens Reich, "Politik ist nicht mein Beruf," *Focus Online* (September 2, 2013).
121. "DDR Volkskammerwahl 1990—Wahlspot des DA (Demokratischer Aufbruch)," *YouTube* (www.youtube.com/watch?v=sNTwCaKqK4Q).
122. Jens Gieseke, "After the Battles: The History of East German Society and its Sources," *German History* 36, no. 4 (2018): 612.
123. Peter Quint, *The Imperfect Union: Constitutional Structures of German Unification* (Princeton, NJ: Princeton University Press, 2012).
124. Jonathan Zatlin, "Unifying without Integrating: The East German Collapse and German Unity," *Central European History* 43, no. 3 (2010): 484–507.
125. Plato, *The End of the Cold War?*
126. Gerhard Ritter, *The Price of German Unity: Reunification and the Crisis of the Welfare State* (Oxford: Oxford University Press, 2011).

Conclusion: A Cold War Germany

1. Petra Lux, interviewed at 7:50 min–8:10 min in *Die Andersdenkenden: Was aus DDR-Bürgerrechtlern wurde* (ARD Historie), directed by Lutz Pehnert (2024).

Epilogue: The GDR after the End of the GDR

1. Hans-Ulrich Wehler, *Deutsche Gesellschaftsgeschichte, 1949–1999* (Munich: C.H. Beck, 2008), 361 and 425.

Notes

2. Kerstin Brückweh, Clemens Villinger, and Kathrin Zöller, *Die lange Geschichte der "Wende": Geschichtswissenschaft im Dialog* (Berlin: Ch. Links, 2020).
3. Christian Bangel et al., "East-West Exodus: The Millions Who Left," *Die Zeit*, May 30, 2019.
4. Marcus Böick, "In from the Socialist 'Cold,' but Burned by the Capitalist 'Heat'? The Dynamics of Political Revolution and Economic Transformation in Eastern Germany after 1990," *Sustainability: Science, Practice and Policy* 16, no. 1 (2020): 143–54.
5. Gerhard Ritter, *The Price of German Unity: Reunification and the Crisis of the Welfare State* (Oxford: Oxford University Press, 2011).
6. Clemens Villinger, *Vom ungerechten Plan zum gerechten Markt?: Konsum, soziale Ungleichheit und der Systemwechsel von 1989/90* (Berlin: Ch. Links, 2022).
7. Juan Espíndola Mata, *Transitional Justice after German Reunification* (Cambridge: Cambridge University Press, 2015).
8. Annette Weinke, *Law, History, and Justice: Debating German State Crimes in the Long Twentieth Century* (New York: Berghahn, 2018), 177.
9. Peter Quint, "Judging the Past: The Prosecution of East German Border Guards and the GDR Chain of Command," *Review of Politics* 61, no. 2 (1999): 303–29.
10. A. James McAdams, *Judging the Past in Unified Germany* (Cambridge: Cambridge University Press, 2001).
11. Die Enquete-Kommissionen zur Aufarbeitung der SED-Diktatur (https://enquete-online.de/materialien/); Jennifer Yoder, "Truth without Reconciliation: An Appraisal of the Enquete Commission on the SED Dictatorship in Germany," *German Politics* 8, no. 3 (1999): 59–80.
12. Ben Gook, *Divided Subjects, Invisible Borders: Re-Unified Germany After 1989* (Lanham, MD: Rowman & Littlefield, 2015); Anna Saunders, *Memorializing the GDR: Monuments and Memory after 1989* (New York: Berghahn, 2018); Hope Harrison, *After the Berlin Wall: Memory and the Making of the New Germany, 1989 to the Present* (Cambridge: Cambridge University Press, 2019); Stephen Brockmann, *The Freest Country in the World: East Germany's Final Year in Culture and Memory* (Rochester, NY: Camden House, 2023).
13. Samuel Merrill, *Networked Remembrance: Excavating Buried Memories in the Railways Beneath London and Berlin* (Oxford: Peter Lang, 2017); Doreen Pastor, *Tourism and Memory: Visitor Experiences of the Nazi and GDR Past* (Abingdon: Routledge, 2021).

Notes

14. Stiftung Ettersberg, "Vor dem Verschwinden: Spurensuche nach vergessener Kunst aus der DDR," (https://vor-dem-verschwinden.de), Erfurt.
15. Claudia Gatzka, "Geschichten wider den Osten," *Merkur* 893 (2023): 5–18.
16. Jens Gieseke, "After the Battles: The History of East German Society and its Sources," *German History* 36, no. 4 (2018): 598–620. See also Marcus Böick, Anja Hertel, and Franziska Kuschel, *Aus einem Land vor unserer Zeit: eine Lesereise durch die DDR-Geschichte* (Berlin: Metropol, 2012); Christopher Banditt, Nadine Jenke, und Sophie Lange, *DDR im Plural: Ostdeutsche Vergangenheiten und ihre Gegenwart* (Berlin: Metropol, 2023).
17. Ned Richardson-Little, "Was ist los in Erfurt? The East German Past and the Democratic Crisis of the Present" (February 19, 2020), *Geschichte der Gegenwart* (online).
18. Ned Richardson-Little, Samuel Merrill, and Leah Arlaud, "Far-Right Anniversary Politics and Social Media: The Alternative for Germany's Contestation of the East German Past on Twitter," *Memory Studies* 15, no. 6 (2022): 1360–77.
19. See for example the Dossier "Lange Weg der deutschen Einheit," produced by the BPB in 2022, online at www.bpb.de/themen/deutsche-einheit/lange-wege-der-deutschen-einheit/.
20. Patrice Poutrus, "Ostdeutsche Identität: Neo-Ostalgiker," *Die Zeit* (November 9, 2019).
21. "East German Material Culture and the Power of Memory," *Bulletin of the German Historical Institute,* Supplement 7 (2011); Nicolas Offenstadt, *Le pays disparu: Sur les traces de la RDA* (Paris: Stock, 2018).
22. Gundula Zoch, "Thirty Years after the Fall of the Berlin Wall—Do East and West Germans Still Differ in Their Attitudes to Female Employment and the Division of Housework?" *European Sociological Review* 37, no. 5 (2021): 731–50; Sabine Böttcher and Ronald Gebauer, "Kitas und Kindererziehung in Ost und West" (August 18, 2020), *bpb.de*.
23. Johanna Weinhold, *Die betrogene Generation: Der Kampf um die DDR-Zusatzrenten* (Berlin: Ch. Links, 2021).
24. Christina Morina, Tausend Aufbrüche: Die Deutschen und ihre Demokratie seit den 1980er-Jahren (Munich: Siedler, 2023).

FURTHER READING

For those interested in reading more, the following lists some key texts on a variety of themes. For topics not listed here, please consult the endnotes, which contain more extensive references. This is not an exhaustive list of texts, and the emphasis here is on works written in English where possible.

GDR Historiography

Andrew Port, "Introduction: The Banalities of East German Historiography," in *Becoming East German: Socialist Structures and Sensibilities after Hitler*, ed. Andrew Port and Mary Fulbrook (New York: Berghahn, 2013): 1–30.
Christopher Banditt, Nadine Jenke, und Sophie Lange, *DDR im Plural: Ostdeutsche Vergangenheiten und ihre Gegenwart* (Berlin: Metropol, 2023).
Daniel Siemens, ed., "What's Next? Historical Research on the GDR Three Decades after German Unification," *German History* 41, no. 2 (2023): 279–96.
Jens Gieseke, "After the Battles: The History of East German Society and Its Sources," *German History* 36, no. 4 (2018): 598–620.

The Soviet Occupation and Creation of the GDR

Devin Pendas, *Democracy, Nazi Trials, and Transitional Justice in Germany, 1945–1950* (Cambridge: Cambridge University Press, 2020).
Gareth Pritchard, *The Making of the GDR, 1945–53: From Antifascism to Stalinism* (Manchester: St. Martin's, 2000).
Norman Naimark, *The Russians in Germany: A History of the Soviet Zone of Occupation, 1945–1949* (Cambridge, MA: Harvard University Press, 1995).

The SED Dictatorship

Catherine Epstein, *The Last Revolutionaries: German Communists and Their Century* (Cambridge, MA: Harvard University Press, 2009).

Hedwig Richter, "Mass Obedience: Practices and Functions of Elections in the German Democratic Republic," in *Voting for Hitler and Stalin: Elections under 20th Century Dictatorships*, ed. Ralph Jessen and Hedwig Richter (Chicago, IL: University of Chicago Press, 2011): 103–24.

Konrad Jarausch, ed., "Care and Coercion: The GDR as Welfare Dictatorship," in *Dictatorship as Experience: Towards a Socio-Cultural History of the GDR* (New York: Berghahn, 1999): 47–69.

Rüdiger Bergien, *Inside Party Headquarters: Organizational Culture and Practice of Rule in the Socialist Unity Party of Germany* (New York: Berghahn, 2023).

The Stasi

Alison Lewis, *A State of Secrecy: Stasi Informers and the Culture of Surveillance* (Lincoln: University of Nebraska Press, 2021).

Jens Gieseke, *The History of the Stasi: East Germany's Secret Police, 1945–1990* (New York: Berghahn, 2014).

Molly Pucci, *Security Empire: The Secret Police in Communist Eastern Europe* (New Haven, CT: Yale University Press, 2020).

Samuel Huneke, "The Surveillance of Subcultures: Gay Spies, Everyday Life, and Cold War Intelligence in Divided Berlin," *Journal of Social History* 56, no. 3 (2023): 559–82.

Uwe Spiekerman, ed., "The Stasi at Home and Abroad: Domestic Order and Foreign Intelligence," *Bulletin of the German Historical Institute* Supplement 9 (2014): 1–192.

The Berlin Wall

Hans-Hermann Hertle and Maria Nooke, *Die Todesopfer an der Berliner Mauer 1961–1989. Ergebnisse eines Forschungsprojektes des ZZF Potsdam und der Stiftung Berliner Mauer*, Version 4.0 (online), Potsdam/Berlin (August 2017).

Hope Harrison, *Driving the Soviets up the Wall: Soviet-East German Relations, 1953–1961* (Princeton, NJ: Princeton University Press, 2011).

Further Reading

Manfred Wilke, *The Path to the Berlin Wall: Critical Stages in the History of Divided Germany* (New York: Berghahn, 2014).

Pertti Ahonen, *Death at the Berlin Wall* (Oxford: Oxford University Press, 2010).

The GDR Economy

Albrecht Ritschl and Tamás Vonyó, "The Roots of Economic Failure: What Explains East Germany's Falling Behind between 1945 and 1950?," *European Review of Economic History* 18, no. 2 (2014): 166–84.

André Steiner, *The Plans That Failed: An Economic History of the GDR* (New York: Berghahn, 2013).

Hartmut Berghoff and Uta Andrea Balbier, *The East German Economy, 1945–2010: Falling Behind or Catching Up?* (Cambridge: Cambridge University Press, 2013).

Sandrine Kott, *Communism Day-to-Day: State Enterprises in East German Society* (Ann Arbor: University of Michigan Press, 2014).

East Germany and the Cold War

M.E. Sarotte, *Dealing with the Devil: East Germany, Détente, and Ostpolitik, 1969–1973* (Chapel Hill: University of North Carolina Press, 2003).

Quinn Slobodian, ed., *Comrades of Color: East Germany in the Cold War World* (New York: Berghahn, 2015).

Sebastian Gehrig, *Legal Entanglements: Law, Rights and the Battle for Legitimacy in Divided Germany, 1945–1989* (New York: Berghahn, 2021).

William Glenn Gray, *Germany's Cold War: The Global Campaign to Isolate East Germany, 1949–1969* (Chapel Hill: University of North Carolina Press, 2003).

State Socialist Theory and Ideology

Ned Richardson-Little, *The Human Rights Dictatorship: Socialism, Global Solidarity and Revolution in East Germany* (Cambridge: Cambridge University Press, 2020).

Peter Caldwell, *Dictatorship, State Planning, and Social Theory in the German Democratic Republic* (Cambridge: Cambridge University Press, 2003).

Till Düppe, *The Closed World of East German Economists: Hopes and Defeats of a Generation* (Cambridge: Cambridge University Press, 2023).

The Global GDR

George Bodie, "'It Is a Shame We Are Not Neighbours': GDR Tourist Cruises to Cuba, 1961–89," *Journal of Contemporary History* 55, no. 2 (2020): 411–34.

Jennifer Altehenger, "Industrial and Chinese: Exhibiting Mao's China at the Leipzig Trade Fairs," *Journal of Contemporary History* 55, no. 4 (2020): 845–70.

Julia Sittmann, "Illusions of Care: Iraqi Students between the Ba'thist State and the Stasi in Socialist East Germany, 1958–89," *Cold War History* 18, no. 2 (2018): 187–202.

Marcia Schenck, *Remembering African Labor Migration to the Second World: Socialist Mobilities between Angola, Mozambique, and East Germany* (Basingstoke: Palgrave, 2023).

Ned Richardson-Little and Lauren Stokes, "Bordering the GDR: Everyday Transnationalism, Global Entanglements and Regimes of Mobility at the Edges of East Germany," *Central European History* 56, no. 2 (2023): 159–72.

Sara Lorenzini, *Global Development: A Cold War History* (Princeton: Princeton University Press, 2019).

Sara Pugach, *African Students in East Germany, 1949–1975* (Ann Arbor: University of Michigan Press, 2022).

Race and Racism in the GDR

Gideon Botsch, "From Skinhead-Subculture to Radical Right Movement: The Development of a 'National Opposition' in East Germany," *Contemporary European History* 21, no. 4 (2012): 553–73.

Jan Behrends, Thomas Lindenberger, and Patrice G. Poutrus, eds., *Fremde und Fremd-Sein in der DDR* (Berlin: Metropol, 2003).

Patrice G. Poutrus and Katharina Warda, "Die DDR als Migrationsgesellschaft und die rassistische Gewalt der 'Baseballschlägerjahre' in Ostdeutschland: Der Weg in die Berliner Republik," in *Erinnerungskämpfe: Neues deutsches Geschichtsbewusstsein*, ed. Jürgen Zimmerer (Ditzingen: Reclam, 2023): 375–98.

Peggy Piesche, "Making African Diasporic Pasts Possible: A Retrospective View of the GDR and Its Black (Step-)Children," in *Remapping Black Germany: New Perspectives on Afro-German History, Politics, and Culture*, ed. Sara Lennox (Amherst: University of Massachusetts Press, 2017): 226–42.

Further Reading

Women in the GDR

Alexandria Ruble, *Entangled Emancipation: Women's Rights in Cold War Germany* (Toronto: University of Toronto Press, 2023).

Donna Harsch, *Revenge of the Domestic: Women, the Family, and Communism in the German Democratic Republic* (Princeton, NJ: Princeton University Press, 2007),

Henrike Voigtländer, *Sexismus im Betrieb: Geschlecht und Herrschaft in der DDR-Industrie* (Berlin: Ch. Links, 2023).

Jane Freeland, *Feminist Transformations and Domestic Violence Activism in Divided Berlin, 1968–2002* (Oxford: Oxford University Press, 2022).

Consumerism and Material Culture

Andrew Kloiber, *Brewing Socialism: Coffee, East Germans, and Twentieth-Century Globalization* (New York: Berghahn, 2022).

Eli Rubin, *Synthetic Socialism: Plastics and Dictatorship in the German Democratic Republic* (Chapel Hill: University of North Carolina Press, 2012).

Katrin Schreiter, *Designing One Nation: The Politics of Economic Culture and Trade in Divided Germany* (Oxford: Oxford University Press, 2020).

Dissent and the Opposition

Andrew Port, *Conflict and Stability in the German Democratic Republic* (Cambridge: Cambridge University Press, 2007).

Ilko-Sascha Kowalczuk, *End Game: The 1989 Revolution in East Germany* (New York: Berghahn, 2022).

John Torpey, *Intellectuals, Socialism, and Dissent: The East German Opposition and Its Legacy* (Minneapolis: University of Minnesota Press, 1995).

Ned Richardson-Little, *The Human Rights Dictatorship: Socialism, Global Solidarity and Revolution in East Germany* (Cambridge: Cambridge University Press, 2020).

The Urban GDR

Andrew Demshuk, *Bowling for Communism: Urban Ingenuity at the End of East Germany* (Ithaca, NY: Cornell University Press, 2020).

Annemarie Sammartino, "The New Socialist Man in the *Plattenbau*: The East German Housing Program and the Development of the Socialist Way of Life," *Journal of Urban History* 44, no. 1 (2018): 78–94.

Eli Rubin, *Amnesiopolis: Modernity, Space, and Memory in East Germany* (Oxford: Oxford University Press, 2016).

The Rural GDR

Gregory Witkowski, *The Campaign State: Communist Mobilizations for the East German Countryside, 1945–1990* (Ithaca, NY: Cornell University Press, 2017).

Jens Schöne, *Frühling auf dem Lande?: die Kollektivierung der DDR-Landwirtschaft* (Berlin: Ch. Links, 2005).

Thomas Fleischman, *Communist Pigs: An Animal History of East Germany's Rise and Fall* (Seattle: University of Washington Press, 2020).

Christianity in the GDR

Bernd Schäfer, *The East German State and the Catholic Church, 1945–1989* (New York: Berghahn, 2010).

Robert Goeckel, *The Lutheran Church and the East German State: Political Conflict and Change under Ulbricht and Honecker* (Ithaca, NY: Cornell University Press, 1990).

Stephen Brown, "'Happy Birthday, Comrade Martin!' The 500th Anniversary of Luther's Birth and the Challenge to State Authority in the GDR," in *Ecumenical Perspectives Five Hundred Years after Luther's Reformation*, ed. Gerard Mannion, Dennis Doyle, and Theodore G. Dedon (Cham: Springer, 2021): 45–65.

Youth and Youth Culture

Alan McDougall, *Youth Politics in East Germany: The Free German Youth Movement, 1946–1968* (Oxford: Oxford University Press, 2004).

Dorothee Wierling, "Youth as Internal Enemy: Conflicts in the Education Dictatorship of the 1960s," in *Socialist Modern: East German Everyday Culture and Politics*, ed. Katherine Pence and Paul Betts (Ann Arbor: University of Michigan Press, 2008): 157–82.

Further Reading

Jeff Hayton, *Culture from the Slums: Punk Rock in East and West Germany* (Oxford: Oxford University Press, 2022).

Nikolai Okunew, *Red Metal: Die Heavy-Metal-Subkultur der DDR* (Berlin: Ch. Links, 2021).

Science and Technology

Colleen Anderson, "Youth Space Education and the Future of the GDR," *Central European History* 53, no. 1 (2020): 146–67.

Dolores Augustine, *Red Prometheus: Engineering and Dictatorship in East Germany, 1945–1990* (Boston, MA: MIT Press, 2007).

Johanna Folland, "'Not Even the Highest Wall Can Stop AIDS': Expertise and Viral Politics at the German-German Border," *Central European History* 56, no. 2 (2023): 255–69.

Sex and Sexuality

Jennifer Evans, *The Queer Art of History: Queer Kinship after Fascism* (Durham, NC: Duke University Press, 2023).

Josie McLellan, *Love in the Time of Communism: Intimacy and Sexuality in the GDR* (Cambridge: Cambridge University Press, 2011).

Samuel Huneke, *States of Liberation: Gay Men between Dictatorship and Democracy in Cold War Germany* (Toronto: University of Toronto Press, 2022).

Steffi Brüning, *Prostitution in der DDR: Eine Untersuchung am Beispiel von Rostock, Berlin und Leipzig, 1968 bis 1989* (Berlin: BeBra, 2020).

Sports

Alan McDougall, *The People's Game: Football, State and Society in East Germany* (Cambridge: Cambridge University Press, 2014).

Jutta Braun, "Sports and Society in the Rivalry between East and West," in *A History Shared and Divided: East and West Germany since the 1970s*, ed. Frank Bösch (New York: Berghahn, 2018): 501–50.

Mike Dennis and Jonathan Grix, *Sport under Communism: Behind the East German "Miracle"* (Basingstoke: Palgrave, 2012).

Further Reading

The June 1953 Uprising

Gary Bruce, *Resistance with the People Repression and Resistance in Eastern Germany, 1945-1955* (Lanham, MD: Rowman and Littlefield, 2003).

Jens Schöne, *Jenseits der Städte: der Volksaufstand vom Juni 1953 in der DDR* (Erfurt: Landeszentrale für politische Bildung, 2023).

Richard Millington, *State, Society and Memories of the Uprising of 17 June 1953 in the GDR* (Basingstoke: Palgrave, 2014).

Wayne Geerling, Gary Magee, and Russell Smyth, "Occupation, Reparations, and Rebellion: The Soviets and the East German Uprising of 1953," *The Journal of Interdisciplinary History* 52, no. 2 (2021): 225-50.

1989 and German Reunification

Jonathan Zatlin, "Unifying without Integrating: The East German Collapse and German Unity," *Central European History* 43, no. 3 (2010): 484-507.

Kyrill Kunakhovich, *Communism's Public Sphere: Culture as Politics in Cold War Poland and East Germany* (Ithaca, NY: Cornell University Press, 2022).

M.E. Sarotte, *The Collapse: The Accidental Opening of the Berlin Wall* (London: Hachette, 2014).

Ned Richardson-Little, "The Failure of the Socialist Declaration of Human Rights: Ideology, Legitimacy, and Elite Defection at the End of State Socialism," *East Central Europe* 46, nos. 2-3 (2019): 318-41.

Steven Pfaff, *Exit-Voice Dynamics and the Collapse of East Germany: The Crisis of Leninism and the Revolution of 1989* (Durham, NC: Duke University Press, 2006).

Memory of the GDR

Anna Saunders, *Memorializing the GDR: Monuments and Memory after 1989* (New York: Berghahn, 2018).

Hope Harrison, *After the Berlin Wall: Memory and the Making of the New Germany* (Cambridge: Cambridge University Press, 2019).

Jenny Wüstenberg, *Civil Society and Memory in Postwar Germany* (Cambridge: Cambridge, University Press, 2017).

Jon Berndt Olsen, *Tailoring Truth: Politicizing the Past and Negotiating Memory in East Germany, 1945-1990* (New York: Berghahn, 2017).

INDEX

ABBA 153–4
abortion
    and foreign workers 126
    in the FRG 206
    and the KPD 66, 198
    and the SED 30, 66, 83, 198
Abusch, Alexander 85
Ackermann, Anton 13, 21–2, 41, 51
Adams, Bryan 154
Adenauer, Konrad 128
Afghanistan 145, 169
African National Congress (ANC) 119–20, 148
Afro-German community 70, 81, 87, 126
agriculture in the GDR
    and bloc parties 23
    and collectivization 33, 44, 46, 145, 158
    and the DBD 23
    further reading 255
    and LPGs 44
    and meat 78, 80, 146, 161
    and pollution 146
    and sabotage 33
    and Soviet land reforms 17, 23, 30
    and standard of living 58, 200
    and the Stasi 96
    and the VdgB xvi, 23, 56
Albania 40, 150
Alexanderplatz (East Berlin) 74, 178–9, 181
Algeria 121, 125, 170–1
Allianz für Deutschland xiv, 188–91, 193
Allied Occupation Powers
    and blockade of Berlin 26, 45
    and Checkpoint Charlie 50

Four Power Agreement 131
    and free movement of soldiers 50
    and Khrushchev 45
    London Conference (1948) 25
    and occupation of Germany 11–13, 24–6
    Potsdam Conference 11, 13, 16
    and prosecution of Nazi crimes 14, 15
    and reparations 16
    and reunification of Germany 32–3, 186–7, 194
    and the Soviet Union 25–6, 45
Alternative für Deutschland (AfD) xiv, 212
Amnesty International 159
Ampelmännchen 210–11
Angola 119, 125, 204
antifascism
    cultural 69
    and the FRG 21
    and GDR mythology 17–23, 106
    and global GDR 141
    and pacifism 164–5
    and political parties 13–14
    and Yugoslavia 25
antisemitism 41, 84, 157. *See also* Judaism in the GDR
Apel, Erich 136
Arafat, Yasser 120
Armstrong, Louis 71–2
art and culture in the GDR. *See also* individual artists; individual writers; media in the GDR
    afterlives of 201, 209
    "Bitterfeld Way" 70
    dance 71, 155
    and demarcation 109, 132, 152

Index

and dialogue 156
and dissent 72
and emigration 160
exchange programs 111
festivals 72, 154
high art 69, 72
Kulturbund 56, 69, 192
music 70–2, 75, 123, 153–6, 177, 212, 256
normative bodies 87–8
and socialism 163, 173
Sorbian culture 86
and the Stasi 72, 74, 192–3
theater 70–1, 73, 86
Western influence on 152–3, 160
Austria
and the division of Europe 25, 175–6
and Honecker 171
immediate postwar 11, 19, 23
Axen, Hermann 85

Babelsberg (Potsdam) 158, 211
Bahro, Rudolf 163, 185
Bautzen (Saxony) 86, 90
Beatles, The 70
Becher, Johannes 69
Behrens, Fritz 90–1
Beil, Gerhard 16
Benjamin, Hilde 36–7, 85
Bentzien, Hans 16
Beria, Lavrentii 40
Berlin. *See* East Berlin; West Berlin
Berlin Republic
and afterlives of the GDR 1, 206–9, 211–13
economy of 204–5
and emigration 204
and prosecution of SED crimes 49, 74, 207–8
and the Russian military 194
and transfer payments 205
Beverly Hills Cop 153
Beyer, Franz 75
BFC Dynamo 156–7
Biermann, Wolf 160–1, 212
bilingualism 86
bloc parties. *See also* individual parties

after the Wall 182, 188
and democracy 189, 200
and the end of the GDR 182, 186, 188–9, 192–3
and ex-Nazis 55
origins of 23, 30
privileges of 55–6
and the SED 25, 29–30, 37, 92, 94
Bloch, Ernst 85, 91
Bohley, Bärbel 165–6, 168, 178
Böhme, Ibrahim 191–3
Bornholmer Straße (East Berlin) 180
Brandenburg 86, 104. *See also* individual cities
Brandt, Willy 127–32
Brazil 139, 145
Brecht, Bertolt 38, 70
Bretton Woods 24
Brezhnev, Leonid 113, 131–2
Britz Canal (Berlin) 173
Brüsewitz, Oskar 164
Bulgaria 40, 111–13, 181. *See also* Eastern Bloc
Bündnis xiv, 90, 166, 188, 190
Burke, Solomon 154
Bush, George H. W. 187
Bykovsky, Valery 112

Cambodia 121, 130
Canada 71
Carlos the Jackal 122
Carow, Heiner 157
Ceaușescu, Nicolae 113, 170, 181
Ceuta (Morocco) 1
Chemnitz (Saxony) 90, 107
Chernobyl nuclear accident 164
Chile 119, 121, 123, 126, 207
China, People's Republic of
founding of 32, 113
and the GDR 113, 116, 144, 171, 175, 177
and the socialist bloc 131
and Taiwan 117, 134
and Tiananmen Square 174–5, 202
Christlich Demokratische Union (CDU)
and abortion 30, 66, 83, 206
after the Wall 189–91

259

Index

and the Allianz für Deutschland 188–9
in the Berlin Republic xiv, 211
and Brandt 129, 150
and the DBD 23
and de Maizière 192–3
in the FRG xv, 127–8
and IMs 192–3
membership of 55
and reunification 183, 187–9, 193, 204
and SED show trials 56, 89
in the Soviet Zone 14, 17, 23, 25
Christlich-Soziale Union (CSU)
and the DSU xiv, xv, 188–9
and the expellee lobby 183
in the FRG xiv, xv, 129, 150
Churches in the GDR. *See* dissident movement; religion in the GDR; Sozialistische Einheitspartei Deutschland
citizenship
FRG 43
GDR 27, 108, 160
revocation of 158, 160, 163, 166–7
Cocker, Joe 154
coffee. *See also* consumer goods in the GDR
and emigration 161
further reading 254
and the GDR economy 139–40, 145–6, 170
shortages 45–6, 78, 80, 139
as trade currency 77, 170
collectivization. *See* agriculture in the GDR; *See under* Sozialistische Einheitspartei Deutschland, Sovietization
Committee for the Protection of Human Rights 108
constitution of the GDR
1949 founding 27, 30
1968 socialist 117–18
and *Boykotthetze* 96–7
Central Round Table 191
and division of Germany 27, 109
and Eastern Bloc 110

and the environment 163–4
and the Volksaussprache 92–3, 118
and work 57–8
consumer goods in the GDR. *See also* memory
and 1953 Uprising 34, 44
and the Berlin Wall 42, 46–7
condoms 149
and contract workers 126
and cross-border shopping 111
and emigration 158, 161
fashion 32, 77, 79
further reading 254
and Honecker 137–8, 152
vs industrial production 33, 44–6, 78
luxury goods 54, 77–80
and petitions 79, 92
plastics 2, 79–81, 149, 153–4
and rationing 33, 77–8
and reparations 33
and the SED 42, 45–6, 55, 76–81
and shortages 46, 55, 78–80, 135–6
and stores 58, 76–7, 79–80
and VEBs 44, 149
Vita Cola 112
and Western influence 153–4
and women's rights 62, 79
Corvalán, Luis 119
Council for Mutual Economic Assistance (CMEA) 110, 145, 187
Cuba 61, 111–12, 125–6
currency in the GDR
and arms sales 140, 147–8
and the cash economy 27, 76–7
Deutsche Mark 23–4, 26, 138, 194
and emigration 139, 151
and foreign debt 79–80, 137–8, 142, 146–7
and foreign exports 105
and foreigners 125–6
imagery 65
and Intershop 77, 148
and KoKo 147–8
and the market economy 194
Czechoslovakia. *See also* Eastern Bloc

Index

and communist militia 40
and environmental groups 164
and GDR relations 110–11
and human rights groups 94, 162–3
and John Heartfield 70–1
and mass demos 181
and political purges 41, 84–5, 94
and population transfers 12
and Prague Spring 23, 112–13

Dahlem, Franz 41, 85
Danz, Tamara 155, 183
Davis, Angela 87, 120
DEFA (GDR film studio) 75, 153
democracy in the GDR 182–95
Demokratie Jetzt (DJ) xiv, xv, 166, 188
Demokratische Bauernpartei Deutschlands (DBD) xiv, 23
Demokratischer Aufbruch (DA) xiv, 188, 192–3, 212
Deng Xiaoping 171
Dertinger, Georg 56, 89
Deutsche Soziale Union (DSU) xv, 188–9
Deutsche Welle 31
Die Linke xvi, 211
Dieckmann, Johannes 56
Dirty Dancing 153
dissident movement. *See also* East Berlin; individual dissidents; Initiative Frieden und Menschenrechte; Leipzig (Saxony); Neues Forum
and Central Round Table 166, 184–5, 187–8, 190–2
and the Church 84, 155, 157, 162, 166–8, 175, 183, 188, 192
and conscription 92
and dialogue 162, 175, 177, 186, 195
and the environment 162–4, 166, 168
and "Für unser Land" Appeal 183
further reading 254, 257
and human rights 162–3, 167
and peace 102, 164–8, 192
and pluralism 167
and socialist democracy 162
and the Stasi 160, 166–7, 175, 191–3, 206–7
Döbler, Hermann 49
Domröse, Angelica 160
Dresden (Saxony) 31, 39, 58, 142, 147, 172, 180–1
Dylan, Bob 154

East Berlin. *See also* Berlin Republic; infrastructure in the GDR; June 1953 Uprising; West Berlin
and Alexanderplatz demos 74, 178–81, 186
and the Berlin Wall 42–51, 103–5, 131, 173, 180, 251–2
and the Berliner Ensemble 70
creation of 11, 23–7, 32, 50, 58
and the dissident scene 157, 163, 165, 167–8, 175, 192
and exile to Dresden 172
and football 156
and mass events 120, 154
and neo-Nazis 157
and the PLO 122
public commemoration of 1, 21, 106, 153, 203
and queer life 67, 156
and Reagan 176
and SED institutions 29, 54, 186
standard of living 58
and tourism 50, 121, 141–2
and the TV tower 137
Eastern Bloc
and the ANC 113–14
and antisemitism 84
and "Brezhnev Doctrine" 113–14
and China 113–14, 171
collapse of 172, 181, 197
and de-Stalinization 41
economies of 105, 150–1, 201
and embargoes 105, 147
and fashion 79
and GDR as frontline 101
and global GDR 110–11, 138, 141
and its leaders 131–2
and mass unrest 199
and Ostpolitik 127–9

Index

and purges 41, 84–5, 94
and reform 113, 151, 169–70, 173–4
and Soviet Union 105, 111, 146, 169–70
and tourism 111–12
and the Warsaw Pact 40, 92, 110, 112–13, 134
economy of the GDR. *See also* agriculture in the GDR; global GDR; industry of the GDR; sabotage; technology in the GDR; *See under* social life in the GDR, class divisions
after the Wall 182, 204–5
and barter 77
and the black market 42, 139
and central planning 44–5, 59–60
and conservative modernism 153–4
and contract workers 111, 124–5, 140, 170–1, 204
and the Eastern Bloc 110–11
and Economic System of Socialism 136–7
and foreign currency 76–7, 105, 138–42
and foreign debt 79–80, 101–2, 137, 144–5, 178, 180, 187, 199, 205
and foreign students 124, 140
and the FRG 43–5, 77–8, 105–6, 142, 150–1, 187–8
further reading 252
and globalization 143
and gray market 58, 77
and high-tech sector 137, 144, 146–7
and KoKo 138–9, 147
and "modern socialism" 187
and New Economic System 136
and oil 110, 139, 144–6
and private businesses 44, 46, 55, 58, 137
and reparations 16–17, 33, 43–4, 109–10
and the social market economy 58, 106, 187, 194
and the Soviet Union 10, 16, 169–70
and Western films 153

Egypt 115–16, 130
Eisenach (Thuringia) 152–3
Eisenhüttenstadt (Brandenburg) 107
Eisler, Hanns 70
elections
after the Wall 188–9
ritualization of 30, 149, 174, 178
in the Soviet Zone (1946) 22–3, 64
emigration
after the Wall 182, 204
backlash in the FRG 188
and the Berlin Wall 43, 46, 104, 151, 157, 161, 180
and crime of 47–8
and exit visas 47, 151, 158–9, 175, 199
to the GDR 38, 43, 121–5
and the GDR economy 45–6, 88, 139, 151
and labor shortages 16, 62, 111, 158
motivations for 158
and opposition to the SED 10, 25, 30, 88
and retirement 88, 158
and Sovietization 46
spikes 159, 161, 175–6, 194, 204
and the Stasi 97, 158, 160
and Western NGOs 159
Engels, Friedrich 28–9, 106
environment. *See also* waterways
and activism 162–4, 166, 168
"chemical triangle" 146
and the GDR constitution 163–4
and pollution 105, 146, 162–4, 167
Eppelmann, Rainer 165
Erfurt (Thuringia) 131, 168, 185
Erhard, Ludwig 128
Esch, Arno 30
E.T. 153
Ethiopia 140, 170
"Eurocommunism" 163

Falcke, Heino 168
family life in the GDR. *See also* abortion; consumer goods in the GDR; leisure in the GDR; population of the GDR

Index

and the Berlin Wall 48, 97, 102
and childcare 57, 64–5, 137, 165, 212–13
and "consumer socialism" 137–8
and forced adoptions 97
and gender norms 63–4
and the law 37, 92, 97
and *Plattenbauten* 148–9
and the SED 63–8
and sexuality 64, 67
and the Stasi 97–8, 158, 160, 207
FC Union 156
Fechner, Max 35
Fechter, Peter 49
Federal Republic of Germany (FRG). *See also* Berlin Republic; reunification of Germany
and 1953 Uprising 37–8
Basic Law 26, 191
and Basic Treaty 134
and Berlin Wall deaths 49–50, 173
capital of 26
care packages from 77
creation of 26
and demarcation 108–9, 132, 152
and the division of Germany 102–9
economy of 44–5
and emigration 58, 88, 139, 151, 188, 204
and exiled KPD members 90
and ex-Nazis 21, 108, 128
and the far right 157
and foreign policy 114–15
and GDR debt 150–1
and GDR elections 189
and GDR mythology 21
and gender norms 62, 64–5, 205–6
and Hallstein Doctrine 114, 116, 130
and hard currency 77
and high-tech sector 147
and Honecker 171
and Jewish refugees 115
and the KPD 106
media 31, 37, 75, 105
and the military 40
and NATO 145
and Ostpolitik 127–35, 142
and pollution 164
and reunification 183–4
and sexuality 67–8
and solidarity drives 59
and the Ten-Point Plan 183
and tourism to the GDR 121
food. *See* agriculture in the GDR; consumer goods in the GDR
foreign policy of the GDR. *See* global GDR
Frąckowiak, Halina 71
France. *See also* Allied Occupation Powers
and culture quotas 71
and decolonization 116, 125
and the UN 117
Frankfurt an der Oder (Brandenburg) 124–5
Freie Demokratische Partei (FDP) xv, xvi, 129, 183
Freie Deutsche Jugend (FDJ) xv, 31, 33–4, 106, 118, 133, 154–5, 178
Freisler, Roland 37
Freudenberg, Winfried 173
Frieden Konkret 165–6
Friedrichshain (East Berlin) xi, 83

Gaddafi, Muammar 139
Gauck, Joachim 206
Gaudian, Christian 173
gender in the GDR. *See* men in the GDR; sexuality; women in the GDR
Genscher, Hans-Dietrich 183
Germany. *See* Berlin Republic; Federal Republic of Germany; Weimar Republic
Gesundbrunnen (West Berlin) 180
Gladow, Werner 98
global GDR
and anti-imperialism 68–9, 87, 115, 119, 121–2, 142, 201
and arms sales 139–40, 148, 170
and art 72
and China 113
and coffee 139–40, 145–6
competitiveness of 147, 151

263

Index

and contract workers 81, 87, 111, 124–5, 140, 170–1, 204
and decolonization 114–18
and embargoes 105, 138–9, 147
and foreign debt 138–9
and foreign students 119, 124, 151, 170
further reading 252
inherent contradiction of 201
and Israel 115
and mass organizations 57
and oil 110–11, 139–40
and pollution 164
and post-1989 tourism 208–9
and racial difference 81, 87, 126–7, 253
and the socialist bloc 109–14, 169–70, 173–4
and solidarity drives 57, 59, 87, 119–20, 170
tourism to the GDR 120–1, 125–6, 141–2, 201
and visa-free travel 111–12, 145, 180
Globke, Hans 108
Glöde, Wolfgang 49
Gniffke, Erich 25
Goethe, Johann Wolfgang von 69–70
Goldbroiler 80
Gomułka, Władysław 41
Gorbachev, Mikhail 169, 176, 182, 194, 202
Görlitz (Saxony) 124–5
Grass, Günther 184
Greece 23, 119, 121
Grotewohl, Otto 19–20, 29, 115
Gueffroy, Chris 173
Guinea 116
Gysi, Gregor 185
Gysi, Klaus 85

Hagen, Nina 212
Hager, Kurt 29, 153
Halle (Saxony-Anhalt) 58, 146
Harich, Wolfgang 90, 185
Havemann, Katja 165
Havemann, Robert 91, 160–1, 165
health. *See also* abortion
and disability 87–8
and healthcare 54, 57, 60, 122, 147, 149
Heartfield, John 70–1
Heisig, Bernhard 69–70
Helsinki Accords 134–5, 150, 159, 207
Hennecke, Adolf 60
Hermann, Joachim 132
Hermlin, Stephan 85
Herrnstadt, Rudolf 40
Heym, Stefan 85, 160, 203
hippopotamus, Bonn 189
Hirohito, Emperor 171
hobbies in the GDR. *See* leisure in the GDR
Hockauf, Frida 60
Honecker, Erich
after the Wall 207–8
and CIA conspiracy 176
and "consumer socialism" 137–8, 199
and demarcation 70, 75, 152
and emigration crisis 143
and the FDJ 132
and GDR identity 108–9, 176
and Helsinki Accords 135
and kitsch 2
and Kohl 171
and reform communism 169
resignation of 143, 177–8
and the Sonderzug 154
and Soviet reforms 169–72
and Ulbricht 132
and understanding of communism 176–7
Honecker, Margot 132–3, 207
housing in the GDR
and accessibility 88
and cash economy 76
further reading 254–5
and public culture 34, 106
quality 146, 148–9
and SED membership 54–5
and squatting 149
and the Stasi 96, 160
and state legitimacy 49, 103, 138, 148, 176–7, 209
types xvii, 107, 137, 148, 149

Index

Hoyer, Katja 4
Hoyerswerda (Saxony) 79, 86–7, 127
Hungary
    and the Communist Party 19, 94, 170, 173
    and contract workers 111, 124
    as holiday destination 111
    Pan-European Picnic 175–6
    and Soviet influence 25, 41

IKEA 147
India 32, 124
industry of the GDR. *See also* consumer goods in the GDR; sabotage; technology in the GDR; working life in the GDR
    after the Wall 204–5
    chemical 105, 146
    "chemistry program" 78
    coal 43, 60–1, 86–7, 146, 162, 205
    high-tech 137, 144, 146–7, 201
    housing 107, 137, 148
    plastics 78, 139
    and reparations 16, 22, 33
    and sabotage 36, 89
    and Sovietization 33, 44–6
    and standard of living 148
    textile 60, 63, 137
    and Volkseigene Betriebe (VEB) 44, 57, 78, 125, 136, 147, 149, 205
infrastructure in the GDR. *See also* economy of the GDR; housing in the GDR; technology in the GDR; transportation in the GDR
    communications 75, 96, 103, 149
    garbage 147
    media 31, 137
    and oil 111, 139, 146
    sewage 103
    stores 58, 76–7, 79–80
Initiative Frieden und Menschenrechte (IFM) xv, 167–8, 188, 189, 192
International League for Human Rights 159
Iran-Iraq war 147–8
Iraq 130, 140–1
Ireland, Northern 165

Israel 1, 32, 84, 115, 130
Italy 23–5, 124, 163

Jahn, Roland 167
Jähn, Sigmund 111–12
Janka, Walter 90
Japan 141–2, 147, 171
Jaruzelski, Wojciech 174
Judaism in the GDR. *See also* antisemitism
    community organizations 57
    and Holocaust victims 21, 84–5
    Jewish identity in the GDR 84–5
    Jewish individuals 36, 38–9, 41, 73–4, 85
    population 81, 84
June 1953 Uprising
    after-effects of 40, 44, 56, 89, 110, 132
    causes of 34
    in comparison 46–7, 62, 162, 175
    events of 32–9, 51
    further reading 257
Junker class 17
justice in the GDR 15, 35–7, 94–5, 97, 158, 207–8. *See also* citizenship; policing; Sozialistische Einheitspartei Deutschland, show trials

Kaiser, Jakob 25
Kampfgruppe gegen Unmenschlichkeit 37, 89
Katrancı, Cengaver 50
Keßler, Heinz 207
Kennedy, John F. 50
Khrushchev, Nikita 40–1, 45–6, 131
Kiesinger, Georg 128
Kissinger, Henry 135
kitsch. *See* memory
Klemperer, Victor 38–9
Kohl, Helmut 143, 150, 171, 183, 187, 189, 204
Kollwitz, Käthe 69
Kommerzielle Koordinierung (KoKo) 138–9, 147–8, 185
Kommunistische Partei Deutschlands (KPD)

Index

and abortion 66, 73, 198
and FRG ban 106, 108
and merger with the SPD 19–21, 29, 42, 89, 198
pre-1949, 13–14, 17–19, 132
in *Sputnik* 172
Köpenick (East Berlin) 1
Korea 32, 134
Krenz, Egon 143, 178–81, 208, 212
Kreuzberg (West Berlin) 50
Kroboth, Siegfried 50
Krug, Manfred 75, 160
Kukuczka, Czesław 49
Kunze, Reiner 193

Lafontaine, Oskar 188
Lamberz, Werner 178
Legende von Paul und Paula (*The Legend of Paul and Paula*) 75, 160
Leipzig (Saxony)
  bowling alley 150
  dissident movement 168–9
  FDJ rally 118
  further reading 254
  Monday demonstrations 175, 177, 179, 182, 185
  October 7 demonstrations 176
  School (of modern art) 69
  standard of living 58
  Stasi headquarters 185–6
  tourism 141
  Trade Fair 113, 120, 125, 147
leisure in the GDR. *See also* art and culture in the GDR; sports in the GDR
  bowling 107, 150
  camping 95, 111, 176
  dancing 107
  film & TV 68–70, 72, 74–5, 123, 153–4, 157
  football 60–1, 156–7
  hunting 54, 78
  knitting & sewing 32, 78–9
  and pollution 164
  reading 31–2, 79
  restaurants 107
  tourism 61, 111–12, 145

and VEBs 60–1
and the workplace 60
Lenin, Vladimir
  person of 131
  philosophy of 22, 28–9
  statue of 1–2, 203
Leuna (Saxony-Anhalt) 111
Liberal-Demokratische Partei Deutschlands (LDPD) xv, 14, 17, 23, 30, 55–6
Libya 139, 178
Liebknecht, Karl 18, 60, 168
Lietz, Bruno 16
Lindenberg, Udo 154
Linse, Walter 89
Litfin, Günter 49
lizards, sand 1
Luther, Martin 152–3
Luxemburg, Rosa 18, 168

Maetzig, Kurt 75
Maffay, Peter 154
Mahlsdorf, Charlotte von 67
Maizière, Lothar de 191–4
Mandela, Nelson 119
Mann, Heinrich 70
Mao Zedong 114, 171
Marienfelde (West Berlin) resettlement camp 43, 46
Marx, Karl
  memory of 41, 54, 63, 106–7
  philosophy of 28–9, 91
Marxism-Leninism 28–9
Marzahn (East Berlin) 149
Masur, Kurt 176
material culture. *See also* memory
  and consumer goods 80–1, 152, 154, 197, 212
  and GDR historiography 3, 212
  and identification documents 27, 180
  and kitsch 2, 210
Mattheuer, Wolfgang 69–70
Mecklenburg 11, 13, 192. *See also* Rostock
media in the GDR. *See also* leisure in the GDR
  censorship of 72, 153, 155

Index

film & TV 75, 153, 180, 210
foreign news 119
Neues Deutschland 31, 40, 174–5
print publications 31–2, 55, 159, 172
radio 31, 37, 71, 176
SED control over 31–2
Writer's Union 56
memory. *See also* Engels, Friedrich; Lenin, Vladimir; Liebknecht, Karl; Luxemburg, Rosa; Marx, Karl
and Berlin (1987) 153–4
and border guards 49
and erasure 208–11
further reading 257
and the GDR 208–12
and the Holocaust 85–6, 95, 115
and Luther 153
and Luxemburg-Liebknecht 168
and Ostalgie 210, 212
and plastics 2, 78–9, 81
and Prussia 106, 153
and the Second World War 60, 75, 106, 141
and Spanish Civil War 21
and technology 65
and the UN 203
and the Weimar Republic 172, 198
and women 65
men in the GDR
foreign 87
further reading 254, 256
gender norms 64–5, 74
homosexuality 67–8, 95, 156–7
military service 92
sexism 62–3
Merkel, Angela 75, 192, 212
Merker, Paul 41, 85
Mert, Çetin 50
Mexico 1, 70, 85, 90
Mielke, Erich 42, 132, 135, 156, 177–8, 185, 207–8. *See also* Ministry for State Security (Stasi)
military in the GDR. *See also* Allied Occupation Powers; paramilitaries in the GDR; Soviet Zone of Occupation; Volkspolizei
and allied soldiers 50, 56
and arms sales 139–40, 148, 170
and conscription 92, 164–5
and ex-Nazis 56
Kasernierte Volkspolizei (KVP) 33–4, 40
Nationale Volksarmee (NVA) 40, 54, 92–3, 113, 177, 201–2
and peace movement 164–5
and privileges 54–5
Soviet Forces 13, 16, 22, 26, 34–5, 66, 109, 194, 202
Ministry for State Security (Stasi). *See also* Mielke; sabotage
and the 1953 Uprising 35
afterlife of 185, 189, 206–7
and ban on *Sputnik* 172
and the border 103
and Carlos the Jackal 122
and the CDU/CSU 129
and collapse of 185–6, 193
and culture 72, 74, 192–3
and defectors 94, 103
and de-Stalinization 42
and the dissident movement 166–8, 174, 176
and elections 30, 174
and emigration 43, 158–60
evolution of 39, 94–5, 159–60
and football 156
and foreign visitors 125–6, 140, 201
and the FRG 102, 129, 145
further reading 251
and IMs 96, 98–9, 104–5, 123, 159–60, 191–3
and language 96–7
and loyal opposition 161
mythology of 1
and overwhelm 175–6
and paranoia 160–2, 197
and Party purges 55
and petitions 159
policing the SED 95–6
privileges 54–5
and punks 155–6
and rural GDR 96
and sexuality 67, 95

267

Index

and street protests 174
and surveillance 95–9, 125, 140, 165–6
and tourism 208
and the workplace 62
and *Zersetzung* 160
Mittag, Günter 132, 177–8, 185
Mitzenheim, Moritz 82
Mödlareuth (Thuringia/Bavaria) 103
Modrow, Hans 171, 180–2, 184–7, 194
Morocco 1
Mozambique 125, 140, 170–1, 204
Müller, Vincenz 56
Müller-Stahl, Armin 160

Nagy, Imre 41
Namibia 122, 170
Nasser, Gamal Abdel 115
National-Demokratische Partei Deutschlands (NDPD) xv, xvi, 23, 29, 55–6
nationalization. *See* economy of the GDR; industry of the GDR. *See under* Sozialistische Einheitspartei Deutschland, Sovietization
Nazi Germany
  aftermath of 5, 9, 21, 23, 85–6, 198
  and culture 69
  and ex-Nazis 10–11, 14–16, 30, 89–90
  and gender norms 64
  and the Gestapo 94
  and the KPD 18, 198
  and the NVA 40
  and V2 rocket program 17
  and Victor Klemperer 38
neo-Nazism 106, 157, 185
Neues Forum 175, 186
Neukölln (West Berlin) 173
Neustadt bei Coburg (Bavaria) 103
Nicaragua 119, 133, 154, 170
Niemen, Czesław 71
Nigeria 124
Norden, Albert 85, 108
North Korea 59, 114, 119, 124, 134

nudism 67–8
Nyerere, Julius 116

Oberländer, Theodor 108

Pakistan 32
Palast der Republik 107, 154, 208–9
Palestine
  border regimes 1, 32
  GDR solidarity 115, 119
  liberation movement 120–2
Pankey, Aubrey 70–1
Pankow (East Berlin) 54, 154
paramilitaries in the GDR. *See also* military in the GDR
  Gesellschaft für Sport und Technik 56
  Kampfgruppen der Arbeiterklasse 40, 47, 93, 177, 201
  and workplaces 59
Partei des Demokratischen Sozialismus (PDS) xvi, 185, 188, 190, 211
Peet, John 32
PEGIDA xvi, 212
Pflugbeil, Sebastian 183
Pieck, Wilhelm
  activities of 19–20, 29, 42, 61
  memory of 20, 61
Piesik, Franciszek 49
Pinochet, Augusto 119, 121
Poland. *See also* Eastern Bloc
  borders of 11–12, 110, 129, 134, 184, 194
  and Catholicism 84
  and culture 71–2
  and de-Stalinization 41
  and GDR relations 110
  and Helmut Kohl 183
  KOR 167
  Solidarność 145, 162, 174, 176
  and Wall deaths 49
policing. *See also* justice in the GDR; military in the GDR; Ministry for State Security (Stasi); paramilitaries in the GDR; Volkspolizei; West Berlin

Index

the border 48, 173, 180, 195
evolution of 94–5
and mass violence 201–2
and the SED 93–9
in TV & film 75–6, 153, 160
Poppe, Gerd 165, 192
Poppe, Ulrike 165–6, 183, 192
population of the GDR 43, 46, 48, 64, 137
Prenzlauer Berg (East Berlin) 165, 180
Presley, Elvis 70–1, 123
prostitution. *See* sex work
Puhdys (band) 75

Querdenker 212

racism. *See* global GDR; social life in the GDR
Reagan, Ronald 176
Red Army Faction (RAF) xvi, 122
Reed, Dean 122–4
refugees to the GDR 17, 43, 81, 87, 119, 121–2, 125–6, 207
religion in the GDR. *See also* dissident movement
atheism 81–3
and campaigning skills 189
Catholicism 66, 83–4, 93
and the CDU 55
Christian Science 82
and the deaf 88
further reading 255
Jehovah's Witnesses 36, 82
and Luther 152–3
Moravian Brethren 82
and political protest 66, 92, 189
Protestantism 66, 82–4, 93, 168, 189
and punks 155–6
and Sovietization 33
reunification of Germany
before 1989 32–3, 130
and Brandt 130
and Bush 187
and the dissident movement 166, 188–9
and the FRG 105, 134, 183, 191
and FRG intellectuals 183–4
and the "Für unser Land" appeal 183
further reading 257
and GDR historiography 4, 203, 213, 250
and GDR society 203–4
and Günther Grass 184
and Harich 90
and Hocker 132
and Honecker 109
and Khrushchev 45
and Kohl 183
and Merker 85
and Modrow 182
and Reagan 176
and Stalin 32–3
and Waigel 183
and the Zentraler Runder Tisch 187
Romania 113, 131, 144, 151, 169, 181. *See also* Eastern Bloc
Rostock (Mecklenburg) 58, 72, 125
Rügen, island of (Pomerania) 31, 145

sabotage 33, 36, 62, 89, 94, 96, 98
Santana, Carlos 154
Savoca, Giuseppe 50
Saxony 11, 13, 22, 30–1, 86. *See also* Bautzen; Dresden; Hoyerswerda; Leipzig
Schabowski, Günther 178, 180, 208
Schalck-Golodkowski, Alexander 138, 185
Schirdewan, Karl 42
Schmidt, Helmut 145
Schmieder, Werner 16
Schnur, Wolfgang 191–2
Schönefeld Airport (East Berlin) 121, 151
Schorlemmer, Friedrich 183
Schumacher, Kurt 22
Schürer, Gerhard 180
Schwedt (Brandenburg) 111
Seghers, Anna 70, 85
Sékou Touré, Ahmed 116
Senk, Andreas 50
sex work 58, 201, 256

269

Index

sexuality 3, 66–8, 149, 156–7, 256. *See also* abortion
Siekmann, Ida 49
Silly (band) 155
Slánský, Rudolf 41, 85
sleep, deprivation 97, 180
Sobottka, Gustav 13
social life in the GDR. *See also* bloc parties; Freie Deutsche Jugend; leisure in the GDR
    after the Wall 203–6
    and class divisions 54–5, 58, 62, 64, 70, 77, 91–2, 125–6, 148, 158, 200
    and demos 74, 174–82, 205
    and disability 87–8
    and feeling of collapse 175–6
    and manifestos 90, 163, 165–6, 175, 183
    organized 56–7, 156, 200
    and petitions 55, 79, 89, 92–3, 148–9, 151, 159, 162, 172, 199
    racism 71, 87, 126–7, 253
    and surveillance xviii, 93–9, 158–60
    and system collapse 158, 172–3, 177, 180
Sonneberg (Thuringia) 103
Sorbian minority xv, 57, 81, 86–7
South Africa 119–21, 148, 170
South West African People's Organization (SWAPO, Namibia) 122, 170
Soviet Military Administration in Germany (SMAD) 12–13, 17, 22–3, 26, 30
Soviet Union. *See also* Allied Occupation Powers; Eastern Bloc; Gorbachev, Mikhail
    and 1946 election 22
    and 1953 Uprising 40
    and antisemitism 41, 84
    and the Berlin Wall 46
    and culture 69
    and de-Stalinization 41
    and Détente 127–35
    and division of Europe 10–12
    and exiled KPD members 18–19, 90
    and the GDR 109–14, 176
    and Moscow show trials 14
    and occupation of Germany 9–10
    and oil 110–11, 139, 146
    and peaceful coexistence 109, 132, 135
    and reparations 34, 43, 109–10
    and secret police 14
    and space program 17
    and subsidies 45–6
    and Ulbricht 132
Soviet Zone of Occupation. *See also* Soviet Military Administration in Germany (SMAD)
    and abortion 66
    and culture 73–4
    and denazification 14–16
    and expropriations 17, 23, 30, 33, 158
    further reading 250–1
    and the KPD 19
    and mass rape 22, 66, 109
    and political parties 13
    and reparations 16–17, 33
    and special camps 14–15, 94
Sozialdemokratische Partei Deutschlands (SPD)
    and expulsions 193
    in the GDR 188–91
    and IMs 191–3
    and internal dissent 25
    and merger with the KPD 19–21, 29, 89
    Ost-Büro 89
    Ostpolitik 127–9
    and the SDP 192
    in the Soviet Zone 14, 22–3
    in the Weimar Republic 17–18
Sozialistische Einheitspartei Deutschland. *See also* abortion; bloc parties; Eastern Bloc; June 1953 Uprising; individual facets of the GDR; individual party members; memory
    afterlives of 211–12
    and antifascism 17–23, 164–5
    border regime 48–9, 102–9, 151, 173

Index

and the CDU 56, 89, 128
Central Committee of 16, 27–8, 31, 37, 70, 108, 181
and "Chinese Solution," 175, 177, 202
and the Churches 81–2, 85, 92, 94–5, 164–5
and collapse 197, 202
and culture 32, 68–76, 80, 152
and democratic socialism 184
and de-Stalinization 41–2, 185
and dialogue 162, 175–8, 199
and elections 21–3, 64, 174, 178
and the environment 105, 163–4
and ex-Nazis 16, 108, 198
further reading 252–3
and GDR identity 106–9, 201, 212
and gender norms 64, 74
and Helsinki Accords 135
and improvisation 150
and internal dissent 25, 28, 35, 37, 39, 41–2, 171
and the Linke 211
and mass consultations 92–3, 118, 162
as a mass organization 53–6
and one-party rule 10, 51, 84, 180–2, 184–5, 199, 201
and open dialogue 199
opposition to 88–93
origins of 9, 19–21
and paranoia 37, 47, 62, 85, 90, 98, 176, 197, 202
and the PDS xvi, 185, 188, 190
and petitions 55, 79, 89, 92–3, 148–9, 151, 159, 162, 172, 199
and policing 93–9
Politburo of 27, 29, 42, 85, 132, 136, 171, 178, 181
and Prague Spring 113
purges within 35, 39, 41–2, 55, 90–1, 94, 206
and reform 172, 174–5, 178, 181–2
and reform communism 169, 191
and reparations 9, 34, 43–4
and show trials 33, 36–7, 39, 56
and socialist democracy 162, 174
and the Soviet Union 169, 171–2, 176, 197, 199
and Sovietization 9–10, 21, 24, 33–4, 44–6
and UN human rights covenants 118
and unanimity 30, 118, 174, 178
and Western sabotage 174–5
and Willy Brandt 128
and workplaces 58–9, 62–3
space 17, 77, 82–3, 111–12
Spanish Civil War
  and GDR mythology 21
  and the KPD 13, 73, 90
  refugees in the GDR 121
  and Willy Brandt 128
sports in the GDR
  Betriebssportgemeinschaften 60
  doping 156
  football 60–1, 156–7
  further reading 256
  Olympics 143
  in the workplace 60–1
Spree River 50
Springsteen, Bruce 154–5
Staatsrat der DDR 42, 181
Stalin, Joseph
  death of 34
  and division of Germany 11, 23, 32–3
  and the KPD 13–14, 18–19
  memory of 34, 41, 60, 106–7, 120
  and the Soviet Zone 22, 24
Steinstücken (West Berlin) 104
Stoph, Willi 131, 181, 185, 207
Strauss, Franz Joseph 150
Sudan 130
Syria 130

Tangerine Dream 155
Tanzania 116
technology in the GDR. *See also* space
  and the Berlin Wall 48, 105
  and consumer goods 78–9
  and consumer socialism 136–8, 144–5
  and cybernetics 136

271

and embargoes 105, 138–9, 147
and foreign students 124, 140
further reading 256
and GDR experts 113, 115–16
and high-tech projects 144–5, 147
and Japan 141
and KoKo 138–9
and mass organizations 56
and oil crisis 146
and reparations 17
and socialist revolution 136–7
and Sovietization 44
Teltow Canal (Berlin) 49
Templin, Wolfgang 167–8
Ten-Point Plan (Kohl) 183, 187–8
Thälmann, Ernst
  activities of 18
  memory of 21, 56, 75
Thuringia 11, 34, 82, 103, 211. *See also* Erfurt; Eisenach
Tito, Josip Broz 25, 114, 169
Ti'ulpanov, Sergei 13
Tomsky, Nikolai 1
Torgau (Saxony) 98
totalitarianism 3–4, 25, 53, 99, 208
transportation in the GDR
  air travel 121, 151
  automobile 79–80, 131, 146
  and the division of Germany 42, 102–4, 131
  motorcycle 78, 126
  pedestrian 210–11
  public transit 76, 88, 103
  and reparations 16
Treptower Park (East Berlin) 154
Treuhandanstalt 204–5
Trinks, Otto 61
Trotsky, Leon 18
Tübke, Werner 69–70
Turkey 24

U61000 microchip 147
U Thant 117
Ulbricht, Walter
  before 1949, 13–14, 18–19, 23, 74
  after 1971, 131–2
  and consolidation of power 27, 37, 40, 42
  and culture 70, 75
  and the GDR economy 136–8, 146–7, 199
  and internal dissent 90–1
  and memory 2
  and Prague Spring 113
  and Sovietization of the GDR 21–2, 33–4, 43–6
  and Stalinism 41–2, 51
  and the UN 116–17
  and the Wall 46
Umwelt-Bibliothek 168
United Kingdom. *See* Allied Occupation Powers
United Nations 114, 116–18, 127, 134–5, 164
United States. *See also* Allied Occupation Powers
  blockbusters 153
  and the CIA 25, 37, 89, 176
  civil rights movement 120
  in culture 68–9
  and Détente 127–35
  and division of Berlin 50
  and high-tech sector 147
  Marshall Plan 23, 44
  and racism 71–2, 87
  and US performers 123–4, 154

Verner, Paul 178
Vietnam 59, 101, 119, 125–6, 140, 204
Volkskammer
  1990 elections 166, 182, 188, 202
  activities of 29–30, 66
  and democracy 200
  and Palast der Republik 107
  president 56
  and reunification 194
  Round Table 184–5, 191
  and the SED 184
  structure of 27
  unanimity of 30, 194
Volkspolizei
  and 1953 Uprising 34–5
  and 1989 election 174

Index

and border regime 104
in comparison 93
and demos 174, 177, 195, 201–2
and dissent 95
and exclaves 104
origins of 26
and queer life 67
Vuchetich, Yevgeny 164
Vyshinsky, Andrei 36

Waigel, Theo 183
Wander, Maxie 65
Wandlitz (East Berlin) 54
waterways
    and the Berlin Wall 48–50, 173
    and the GDR border 11, 103, 105, 110, 134, 173, 194
    and pollution 164
Wehage, Christel and Eckhard 49
Wehler, Hans-Ulrich 203
Weigel, Helene 70
Weimar Republic
    and abortion 66
    and Afro-German community 81
    and art 69–71, 73
    constitution 117
    and defensive democracy 106
    and nudism 67
    SPD & KPD during 17–18, 132, 172, 198, 208
West Berlin. *See also* Berlin Republic; infrastructure in the GDR; Marienfelde (West Berlin) resettlement camp
    and the Berlin Wall 50, 103–5, 131, 180, 251–2
    blockade of 26, 45
    and border policy 151
    and the division of Germany 102
    early years 42–3
    escape attempts 48–50, 105, 173, 185
    gasoline supply 139
    immigrant communities 50, 121
    as outpost of freedom 50–1
    and police 26, 49
    radio & TV 31
    resistance organizations 89
    shopping 42, 47
    and Stasi activities 94, 102, 105
    and Wall deaths 48–50, 173
    waterways 48–50, 173
    and Willy Brandt 128
Wittenberg (Saxony-Anhalt) 152–3
Wolf, Christa 72–4, 160, 178, 183
Wolf, Friedrich 73–4
Wolf, Konrad 72–4
Wolf, Markus 73–4, 85, 178, 207–8
Women for Peace 165
women in the GDR. *See also* abortion; leisure in the GDR; men in the GDR; sexuality
    and 1946 election 22
    after the Wall 204–6
    and consumer goods 62, 79
    and consumer socialism 137–8
    and emigration 204
    Frauenbund (DFD) xv, 56, 66
    further reading 254, 256
    and gender norms 63–8, 74, 205–6, 212–13
    and mass rape 22, 66, 109
    women's publications 32, 65–6, 79
    and the workplace 62–5, 205–6
working life in the GDR
    after the Wall 204–5
    and the Berlin Wall 48
    canteens 78
    and collapse 172
    and conscription 92
    and contract workers 82, 111, 124–6, 170–1, 204
    and dissent 62
    FDGB 56, 58–9, 61, 112, 119, 133
    hero(ine) of labor 2, 59–61, 148
    and housing 107, 200
    and labor shortages 58, 62, 148
    and memorialization 106
    military careers 54, 56
    and prison work 97
    and retirement 88, 158, 213
    as right & obligation 200–1
    and the SED 47, 54–5
    sex work 58
    and sexism 62–3

Index

and solidarity drives 59, 119
and Sovietization 33, 44
and strikes 34
and tourist industry 148
and unionizing 58–9, 198
and vacations 61
and VEBs 57
and wages 43, 58
and working conditions 58–65

Yemen 130
youth in the GDR. *See also* Freie Deutsche Jugend
    further reading 255–6
    Jugendweihe 82–3
    and media 31, 107, 119, 210
    military conscription 92, 173
    and music 71, 120, 154–6
    neo-Nazis 157
    non-conformity 95
    in popular culture 71, 74–5
    and punishment 98, 155
    and punks 95, 155, 157
    and reunification 203
    and schooling 29, 78, 98, 164, 172, 256
    and sexuality 67, 157
    Thälmann Pioneers 56, 98, 133
Yugoslavia 25, 114, 169

Zaisser, Wilhelm 40
Zanzibar 116
Zehlendorf (West Berlin) 173
Zentraler Runder Tisch 166, 185–7, 190–2
Zersetzung 160
Zetkin, Clara 106
Zimbabwe 121
Zionism 41, 84–5, 115
Zossen (Brandenburg) 147
Zweig, Arnold 85